A DECLARATION OF ENERGY INDEPENDENCE

How Freedom from Foreign Oil Can Improve National Security, Our Economy, and the Environment

JAY HAKES

WILEY

JOHN WILEY & SONS, INC.

Published by John Wiley & Sons, Inc., Hoboken, New Jersey.
Published simultaneously in Canada.

For general information on our other products and services please contact our Customer Care
Department within the United States at (800) 762-2974, outside the United States at (317) 572-3993,
or fax (317) 572-4002.

Wiley also publishes its books in a variety of electronic formats. Some content that appears in print
may not be available in electronic books. For more information about Wiley products, visit our Web
site at www.wiley.com.

Library of Congress Cataloging-in-Publication Data:

Hakes, Jay E.
    A declaration of energy independence : how freedom from foreign oil can improve
national security, our economy, and the environment / Jay E. Hakes.
      p. cm.
    Includes bibliographical references and index.
    ISBN 978-0-470-26763-9 (cloth : acid-free paper)
      1. Energy policy—United States.   2. Petroleum industry and trade—Political
aspects—United States.   3. Power resources—United States.   4. World politics—
21st century. I. Title.
HD9502.U52H336 2008
333.790973—dc22
                                                                 2008009617

Printed in the United States of America.

10 9 8 7 6 5 4 3 2 1

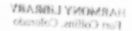

Contents

Introduction

Why Energy Independence Matters More than Iraq

The roots of many of our great national predicaments trace back to energy. American troops leave their families to fight in the Persian Gulf, not incidentally the region of the world with the greatest known reserves of oil. A falling U.S. dollar faces the risk of oil-exporting countries switching their investments from dollars to euros. A United Nations panel of scientists reports the planet is warming, due mainly to the combustion of fossil fuels.

On a more personal level, motorists passing gasoline stations are jolted by large signs listing prices going well beyond what could even be imagined just a few years ago. Soaring energy prices in recent years have weakened the overall U.S. economy and could wreck greater economic havoc in the future.

When serious energy threats loom, political candidates and officeholders have for decades advocated American energy independence to reduce or eliminate reliance on foreign oil. To add rhetorical flourish, they have gone on to demand an effort to develop alternative fuels with an intensity equal to the Manhattan Project (which beat the Germans to the development of the atomic bomb), or the Apollo project (which beat the Russians to land a man on the moon).

President George W. Bush added a new twist to the energy oratory in 2006, when he complained that America's addiction to oil was driving up gasoline prices and threatening national security.

During the presidential primaries of 2008, the four major candidates who survived Super Tuesday, regardless of party, all called for American energy independence. This is clearly an idea with great popular appeal.

What should we make of all this talk? Is there any substance behind the verbiage? Is energy independence a massive project we really want to take on? Is it even possible? Do we need to rethink what we mean by energy independence?

MAJOR RISKS TO NATIONAL SECURITY, THE ECONOMY, AND THE ENVIRONMENT

This book argues that American dependence on foreign oil at current levels (60 percent of total consumption) constitutes a grave security and economic risk with greater consequences than the war in Iraq. As much as laissez-faire economists want to deny the obvious, importing oil from the Persian Gulf and other unstable regions has much bigger strategic impacts than getting, for instance, televisions or running shoes from Asia.

For starters, the harmful effects of an interruption in the supply of petroleum (a word interchangeable with oil) are much greater. Petroleum products play many vital roles in moving people and things around. The Army and Air Force can conduct missions only when fueled by oil. (The Navy makes extensive use of nuclear power.) Trucks that carry goods to Wal–Mart and shoppers headed to their stores also rely on oil. So do critical services ranging from the delivery of food to emergency medical care provided by speeding ambulances. People in the Northeast need heating oil to get through frigid winters. In short, the sudden absence of oil would shut down any modern economy and render its armed forces powerless.

The risks of an interruption are not just hypothetical. A five-month Arab oil embargo in 1973–1974 crippled the American economy and led to long lines at service stations. In some states, half the stations ran out of fuel. Just five years later, the Iranian Revolution led to another massive loss of oil, the return of gasoline lines, and raging inflation. Then, in 1980, war between Iraq and Iran suddenly slashed world oil supplies by five million barrels of oil a day (8 percent). World oil supplies got clobbered again after Iraq invaded Kuwait in 1990.

Even if oil now represents a smaller part of the total economy than in the 1970s, and the complete loss of oil from the world's largest exporter, Saudi Arabia, is regarded as unlikely, the United States cannot remain oblivious to the possibility that some combination of factors could produce a shortage greater than ever before. Such scenarios for massive interruptions are no more improbable than the great interruptions of the past, as viewed by various White Houses *just hours before they actually occurred.* Even when we have enough oil, policymakers have to deal with the fact that oil exporters can exert pressure on America just by threatening to block supplies.

Do we also have to worry that the United States will have to commit military forces to protect its access to foreign oil? The historical record reveals that this has been U.S. policy for decades.

There has been a tendency within polite circles in Washington to treat dependence on Persian Gulf oil and the costly—in terms of lives and money—U.S. military presence in Iraq as two separate issues. In 2007, Alan Greenspan—top economic advisor to presidents Nixon and Ford and head of the Federal Reserve Board during the presidencies of Reagan, Clinton, and the two Bushes—performed a great public service by confirming the presence of the big elephant in the room. "I am saddened that it is politically inconvenient to acknowledge what everyone knows," he wrote in his memoir *The Age of Turbulence,* "the Iraq war is largely about oil."[1] The world's reliance on oil from the Persian Gulf can have a high price indeed.

Apart from abrupt interruptions in global oil deliveries and the need for U.S. armed forces to protect American access, there are other, more subtle forces at work that undermine U.S. independence. The twelve nations of the Organization of the Petroleum Exporting Countries (OPEC) maintain a policy of keeping oil supplies below what is needed for the growing world market, a strategy of making more money by producing less oil.[2] In recent years, they have succeeded beyond their fondest hopes. The world has seen a persistent seller's market in which oil prices remained well above the cost to bring on new supplies. Part of the success of oil exporters rests on the persistent growth in American demand for gasoline in the face of prices that have more than tripled. In the current tight oil market, any actual or potential interruption of supplies from wars in Iraq or Nigeria is quickly magnified, with oil traders rapidly bidding up prices.

The combination of record imports and record prices has created a trade deficit in energy greater than the much-ballyhooed one with China, and has poured vast sums of money into the oil-exporting countries. The amount of money involved is stunning: the United States is currently spending a billion dollars a day on imported fuel.

The United States cannot ignore the consequences of where the money to pay for its oil is going. The growing political clout of countries like Iran, Russia, and Venezuela rests on the explosion of world oil prices in recent years. If they take actions we disapprove of or money going to the Persian Gulf ends up in the hands of terrorists, we, as the world's greatest consumer of oil, pay (at least indirectly) for it.

The 9/11 Commission found that the government of Saudi Arabia tried to cut off funds going directly to Osama bin Laden and his al Qaeda organization and that he did not have enough of a personal fortune or use money from trade in illegal drugs to fund his terrorist activities. His attacks on the United States were financed with money raised through charities and religious groups in Saudi Arabia and, to a lesser extent, neighboring countries.[3] In the major countries supplying funds for al Qaeda, the econ-omies were based on oil exports. Without money derived ultimately from oil, the terrorists could not have struck.

Some take comfort in the amount of imports that come from neighbor-ing Canada and Mexico. Indeed, in recent years they have ranked number one and two, respectively, as oil suppliers to the United States. Still, the oil we get from them falls well below what we get from OPEC. More importantly, in a global oil market, oil prices around the world tend to rise and fall in tandem, and shipments of oil to one port can be quickly diverted to another. Our consumption can drive up the prices Persian Gulf nations get for their oil, whether their customers are in the Western or Eastern hemispheres.

American energy independence has often been equated with reducing reliance on foreign oil. Given our huge appetite for imports and the insta-bility of the region with the world's greatest known reserves, this emphasis is justified. But it is not quite that simple.

Getting oil imports to zero is not the critical factor in achieving energy independence. The United States can certainly import some oil (but not at the current level of 60 percent) and still manage the risk of those imports. In addition, even if the United States imported no oil, it would have to recognize the possibility that in the event of a major interruption, foreign consumers could buy American oil and create a shortage here.

We must also consider the growing recognition in recent years that the combustion of fossil fuels is the major factor leading to the warming of the planet, along with attendant effects like rising ocean levels, melting glaciers, and expanding areas of drought and dangerous fires. If we cannot end our addiction to fossil fuels (at least as they are currently used), we will confront a lack of independence in addressing a deterioration in our quality of life that will almost certainly accelerate for our children and grand-children. The changing locations of arable land around the world already produce armed conflicts in which the United States is asked to intervene. In some areas, warming may improve the quality of life, but for the most part climate change creates additional challenges for American military and economic security and the potential for environmental disaster.

The convergence of so many predicaments tied to energy seems to make the task of dealing with them appear daunting indeed. Some laissez-faire economists question whether, in the age when economic growth benefits from international trade, making the United States energy independent is a worthy goal. They have also suggested that the costs of slowing climate change are not justified. Others consider reducing dependence on foreign energy or the emissions of greenhouse gases a good idea, but probably unrealistic given the huge momentum pushing trend lines in the other direction. Even at a time of three dollars a gallon for gasoline, American foreign policy driven by a need for imported oil, and growing interna-tional pressure to do something about global warming, it is difficult to convince some that concerted action could actually reverse the current adverse trends in energy.

Part of the prevailing skepticism about becoming less reliant on for-eign oil comes from years of hearing speeches about energy independence with no (or few) positive results. In November of 1973, just weeks after Arab oil producers imposed an embargo on the United States, President Richard Nixon went on prime time national television to call for the country to become self-sufficient in energy by 1980, an effort he called *Project Independence.* He also invoked the Manhattan and Apollo projects in his call to action. At the time of this first presidential plea for energy independence, oil imports had risen to a then–astounding 37 percent of

Many presidents have called for energy independence.

consumption. With today's figure at 60 percent, no wonder people are skeptical that we will ever see any progress.

When the 9/11 attacks hit New York City and the Pentagon, it provided, in the words of *New York Times* columnist Tom Friedman, a "crucible moment" to unite the country behind new energy policies that might make us less dependent on Persian Gulf oil, less likely to fund the terrorists who attacked, and more likely to leave a better future for our children.[4] Again, political leaders spoke out in strong terms after 9/11, but were slow to offer substantive solutions to the energy problems connected to the attack.

We keep hearing as well about the amazing new technologies that are going to rescue us from our energy problems. Yet the most important breakthroughs in nuclear power came when Harry Truman was president and (later Admiral) Hyman Rickover led the effort to develop light water reactors for the nuclear navy. Nixon was invited during his first term to a demonstration of hydrogen fuel cells, which have been touted ever since as the big breakthrough just around the corner. The United States assumed world leadership in solar cell technology and passed generous subsidies for ethanol and other forms of renewable energy under Jimmy Carter, yet the share of renewables in the energy mix is no greater today than it was under Carter. In 1993, the Clinton administration joined with the U.S. automobile industry in a much-publicized effort to "build a car with up to 80 miles per gallon at the level of performance, utility and cost of owner-ship that today's consumers demand," after which the fuel efficiency of the national fleet declined. Should we believe more recent hype about the *new* emerging technologies?

The great theologian Reinhold Niebuhr once prayed: "God, give us grace to accept with serenity the things that cannot be changed, courage to change the things that can be changed, and the wisdom to distinguish one from the other." It would be hard to blame people who concluded that, given the recent record, our current dependence on foreign oil and global warming are things we should "accept with serenity."

FINDING SOLUTIONS

This book argues that rising dependence on foreign oil and threats from climate changes are things we should have the courage to change. My goal is to show both how we got into this mess *and* how we can get out of it. Now is the ideal time to take a fresh look at energy policy and the solutions that are available.

Traditionally, the costs of various solutions to our energy problems have been compared to the benefits for the economy, the environment, *or* national security. We should start comparing the costs against the benefits for the economy, the environment, *and* national security. We also need to calculate the impacts on our children and grandchildren of policies (good or bad) adopted today. If we accurately cumulate the advantages of moving boldly on energy, we can better envisage reasons why action is better than passivity. The substance of our recent tepid energy policies can finally begin to match the bold political rhetoric.

My favorite example of a policy ripe for immediate adoption requires that automobiles and trucks meet steadily escalating fuel-efficiency stand-ards. Dramatic increases in the efficiency of vehicles allows the United States to greatly reduce its use of oil. This, in turn, cuts reliance on foreign supplies. It also chops the U.S. balance-of-payments deficit. Less money goes to regimes like Iran. The environment will greatly benefit. It will likely lower world oil prices. At some point, a combination of measures to reduce oil imports reduces the need for an American military presence in the Middle East. If all these benefits are added up, the cost of building the improved vehicles appears rather small. (Plus, drivers save most or all of the costs of more expensive vehicles with lower fuel costs.)

The United States is only part of the world transportation system, but a very large part. We consume a quarter of the world's oil. Because of our economic dominance, we have the ability to greatly affect the global market in many ways, for good or ill. If we greatly improve the fuel economy of our cars and trucks, there will likely be beneficial spillover effects elsewhere in the world.

In all, I identify seven solutions that can help reduce dependence on foreign oil, strengthen the economy, and reduce emissions of greenhouse gases. Several of these recommendations deal with all three problems at the same time. I call these solutions *threefers*.

It would be harder to believe we can conquer our energy challenges if we had not done so once before. As surprising as it may seem, the United States cut its oil imports in half from 1977 to 1982—a sharp reversal of the growing reliance on foreign fuel up to that time. This forgotten victory soon brought an end to OPEC's domination of the world oil market, a condition it was not able to overcome until 1999. Although imports never got to zero, America was able to reclaim for a time its energy independence. Some measures employed then are available today; others are not. The major point is that when the country is determined to do so, its actions can match its rhetoric.

We can also take great encouragement from the passage of the Energy Independence and Security Act of 2007. This bill launches a new national effort to dramatically increase auto efficiency and contains many other measures that have real teeth. The adoption of tough energy measures for the first time since 1980 signals a major shift in the political landscape in Washington. It also suggests there will be additional opportunities to better align national energy policy with national security, economic, and environmental goals with even bolder action.

Readers may reasonably ask why they should accept the diagnosis of current energy problems and the solutions to them contained in this book. From 1993 to 2000, I served as the administrator of the Energy Information Administration (EIA)—the government's nonpartisan agency for the collection, dissemination, and analysis of energy data. Although EIA did not endorse specific policies, it frequently responded to requests from Congress and the administration to analyze various options proposed by others. Using economic models it had developed, EIA could chart the future impacts of potential changes in federal energy legislation. The lesson for me, as I oversaw and presented these studies, was that much is gained when assumptions are transparent and political ideology is supplanted by careful analysis and accurate data. We were able to cut through a lot of the partisan jockeying over trends in world oil markets, the reliability of the electric grid, and the costs of reducing carbon emissions.

Now that I am free to suggest energy policies that I think will benefit the nation, I try to look at the best studies available, examine the many interactions within the world of energy, and make recommendations based on the evidence.

The best-attended press conferences at EIA came when I was presenting the agency's projections of future trends. Such exercises are valuable, but given the limits of forecasting, it is important not to place all one's analytic eggs in a single basket.

As a result, when I left EIA, I determined to take a closer look at the history of energy policy as a possible lens to the future. I spent considerable time exploring the White House archives of Richard Nixon, Gerald Ford, and Jimmy Carter and utilized, as well, information from several other presidential libraries, much of it classified until recent years. I also pored through the record of the oil disruptions of the 1970s at the American Automobile Association and the archives of former energy czar William Simon at Lafayette University. Although this book deals with today's problems, exploring their roots has helped identify the arguments that have stood the test of time and those that have not.

The effort to learn more about the future by considering the historical context included a careful review of the data series maintained by EIA. This approach led to some reinterpretation of trends in oil imports, nuclear power, and other major aspects of the energy mix. Many of these trends have not been given the attention they deserve.

Looking at the world of energy from many perspectives has greatly assisted the effort in this book to offer cost-effective solutions allowing the nation to declare its energy independence by reducing reliance on foreign oil and cutting emissions of greenhouse gases to a level that provides a good start toward slowing global warming.

Having a good grasp of this history has helped me assess the likely impacts of the Energy Independence and Security Act. This book will provide an early assessment of this 800-page-plus bill. Though many focus on what was left out, there was sufficient substance remaining to rank this legislation favorably alongside the great energy packages of the 1970s that collectively helped us temporarily win back our energy independence. This new burst of congressional action contributes to my belief that we can lick the problem of energy dependence, if we keep at it.

To put both my solutions for energy independence and recent developments in energy policy in context, we must begin by understanding how we lost the energy independence we enjoyed through the 1960s.

PART ONE

The Problem of America's Energy Dependence

Chapter 1

America's Plunge into Reliance on Foreign Oil

For about a century, the United States dominated the expanding world oil market, able to dictate terms to other nations great and small. Then in the early 1970s, the country quickly plunged into dependence on imported oil. Private lives were suddenly disrupted by gasoline lines, and public officials struggled to convince the electorate they had effective solutions to America's new energy woes. The story of how this dramatic reversal of fortune happened provides a necessary foundation for figuring out how to reduce our current dependence on imported oil.

THE SPECTER OF OIL IMPORTS

In the late 1940s, America reached a major energy milestone. After nine decades of more oil going out (mainly as gasoline and other products) than coming in, the country became a net importer. By 1950, net imports were running about half a million barrels a day, or about 8 percent of U.S. consumption. The transition from oil-exporting nation to oil-importing nation was not unanticipated.[1]

Before the end of World War II, the wise men of government and industry began to ponder some emerging new realities. It appeared America could not sustain its prodigious increases in oil production much longer. Moreover, oil from the Middle East, while still minor, would clearly play a much larger role after the war. Reserves there went well beyond any discoveries the world had ever seen. Moreover, with sparse populations and low levels of industrialization, these countries had little need for the oil themselves, making their growing levels of supplies available to Europe and eventually the United States. The warnings of the period resonate even many decades later.

Sumner Pike, a member of the Securities and Exchange Commission (SEC) with experience in the oil business, raised alarms in 1942 about the threat of future reliance on imported oil. He cautioned, "I visualize with a good deal of horror our sudden necessitous entrance in some not far distant day into the foreign markets, and boy at that time will we be held up!" He recommended against restricting imports from the Middle East, advising, "We might just as well get started in those markets as early as possible and while we can do those countries some good, and effect the transition from an exporting to an importing nation gradually in the meantime not trying to find all our domestic oil at once."[2]

Two years later, Eugene Ayres, head of research and development for Gulf Oil, urged that national security be given priority over low prices. He wrote Franklin Roosevelt's energy czar Harold Ickes that cheap imports would block the development of alternatives to oil. He proposed a tax on all liquid fuels other than approved substitutes to create an incentive for private industry to contribute to national security.[3] Despite their differences on tactics, Pike and Ayres agreed on one thing—the United States had to do something to ward off future dependency on foreign oil.

Although the amounts of oil imported were initially quite modest, independent producers soon complained about the "increasing flood of oil from foreign lands" and the adverse effects on their businesses. Both domestic production and imports continued to grow, however, due in large part to a growing national appetite for gasoline.

A transportation boom required new roads to handle the traffic. In 1956, President Dwight Eisenhower launched the 40,000-mile interstate highway system (eventually expanded to over 47,000 miles), intended initially to facilitate the easy movement of military equipment during wartime. To pay for construction, the two-cents-a-gallon federal tax on gasoline was upped to four cents. One oil company executive complained gasoline was being taxed off the market, because the average motorist could not afford the rising tax bills. The new levy had the opposite effect. It financed a road system that encouraged the expansion of commercial trucking, family vacations, daily commutes, and, hence, the demand for diesel fuel and gasoline.

BUILDING A WALL

Political muscle opposing foreign oil in the late 1950s came from two influential Democrats from Texas—House Speaker Sam Rayburn and Senate Majority Leader Lyndon Johnson, both active advocates for petroleum interests in their state. Congressional leaders demanded protection for American producers and gave the president authority to block imports when in the interests of national security.

Despite his worries about adopting protectionist policies, in March of 1959 Eisenhower announced binding quotas on foreign petroleum, set at a stringent 12.2 percent of U.S. production. The caps were more generous for oil unloaded at West Coast ports and from overland sources (i.e., Canada). The rules made it particularly difficult for imports delivered to ports on the East Coast, in effect closing the door on increased deliveries from the Middle East. The quotas, though rarely remembered even by careful students of American energy policy, would prove far from temporary and would have significant impacts on later vulnerability to foreign pressure.

On the whole, quotas on foreign petroleum delivered many of the desired results through the 1960s. Domestic production continued to rise, and U.S. consumers enjoyed stable prices at the pump. Imports were constrained and came mainly from the Western hemisphere, not from the more distant and politically volatile Middle East. With added revenues due to reduced foreign competition and generous relief from federal taxes, American oil companies maintained excess productive capacity, which gave the United States great leverage in world affairs in event of a cutoff in oil supplies. Moreover, with Americans working harder to find oil than the rest of the world, they stayed on the cutting edge of oil technology. Even though importing some oil, the United States remained the world's major swing producer. It imported oil, but because of its surge capacity, was not yet dependent on that oil.

America's excess capacity demonstrated its strategic value during the 1967 Six Day War between Israel and its Arab neighbors. Strikes, sabotage, and mob disturbances shut down production entirely in some Arab countries, the result of agitation by Egypt's populist leader Gamal Abdel Nasser. Exports from the Persian Gulf were briefly reduced by 60 percent, a massive loss of about six million barrels a day to the world market. After the rebellions were quelled, the loss of oil ran about 1.5 million barrels a day—an amount still significant but more manageable.

Problems from the embargo were resolved in about a month by drawing on commercial stocks, cooperation between government and industry redirecting supplies, and surge production from the United States, Venezuela, and Iran. On the whole, the attempt to create an oil crisis as a weapon against supporters of Israel had fizzled.

As Pike warned in the 1940s, import restrictions proved to be a short-term strategy that created even bigger problems later on. They forced Americans to pay more for fuel than the prevailing world price, putting their industries at a disadvantage against foreign competitors with lower costs. The United States was also drawing down its easy-to-develop resources faster than would have been the case with free trade in oil.

Potential foreign suppliers, moreover, came to see the international oil market as more a matter of politics than economics. Import restrictions by the world's largest oil market during a period of stagnant world demand led to a sharp drop in the price Middle Eastern nations could get for their oil. As an unintended consequence of this chain of events, Saudi Arabia, Iran, Iraq, Kuwait, and Venezuela met in Baghdad to form a new alliance called the Organization of the Petroleum Exporting Countries (OPEC). Members at its founding in September of 1960 sought leverage against consuming nations blocking their access to customers and against international oil companies unilaterally reducing prices. It appeared initially that OPEC would have little impact on U.S. markets, but during the 1960s it did attract additional members—Qatar, Libya, Indonesia, the United Arab Emirates, and Algeria.

In 1968, OPEC passed a little-noticed resolution calling for government sovereignty over all its oil resources. This new policy eventually shifted control of the industry—previously exercised by the major international oil companies—into the hands of the political leaders of the OPEC countries, and made dealing with future crises more difficult.

NEW CHALLENGES

The year 1970 marked another historic turning point in the history of American energy, clearer in hindsight than at the time. United States oil production, after more than a century of steady increases, reached its peak in April. Henceforth, U.S. production would trend down rather than up. Both symbolically and substantively, this reversal, during Richard Nixon's first term as president, heralded the end of the age of American oil dominance.

The decline in production occurred during a time of explosive demand growth, the greatest ever before or since. During the 1960s, U.S. energy consumption increased a whopping 51 percent, compared to 36 percent during the previous decade. More fuel was needed for new, larger cars with features like air conditioning. Automobiles logged more miles as the increasing popularity of suburban living required longer commutes. Moreover, the fuel efficiency of passenger cars in 1970 dropped to 13.5 miles per gallon.

Americans also displayed a growing appetite for electricity, a rising share of which was generated from oil. More energy was needed for larger houses and offices. In many sections of the country, moreover, air conditioning transformed itself from a convenience to a necessity. In 1960, only 12 percent of U.S. households had installed some form of air conditioning. Fifteen years later, about half had done so.

Rising environmental concerns—reflected first in local regulations and then in the Clean Air Act of 1970—forced a switch from coal to other fuels until new technologies to clean up coal emissions could be developed. Industrial use of coal, for instance, dropped 11 percent from 1966 to 1970, due largely to concerns about air quality. As a result, oil had to help meet both the rising demand for fossil fuels in general and the gap from reduced use of coal.

Declining U.S. oil production, exploding demand, import caps, and new requirements for clean air were creating an almost perfect storm. Midlevel staffers at the Nixon White House worried the prevailing energy trends might create fuel shortages.

One obvious way to alleviate the prospective energy crunch would have been allowing more foreign oil—a course advocated by an oil import control task force established in 1969 by Nixon and chaired by Labor Secretary George Shultz. Even though the quotas had already been tweaked to allow more Canadian and Venezuelan oil, the Shultz report, released in early 1970, argued that mandatory quotas forced Americans to pay $5 billion a year more than necessary by blocking access to cheap foreign supplies. The report is worth a close look, because it included the most extensive discussion ever by the U.S. government about the issues affecting U.S. reliance on foreign oil—the same issues that continue to plague us today.

The task force minimized the threat of an oil interruption from turmoil in the Arab states, calculating "to have a problem, one must postulate something approaching a total denial to all markets of all or most Arab oil"—a situation it viewed as highly unlikely.[4] The report concluded the United States could rely during an energy disruption on its own excess capacity for surge production of almost 2 million barrels a day (a Pollyanna-ish view, since surge production was no longer possible), on extra oil from Canada (which had its own needs for imported oil), and on commercial inventories to cushion the shock.

The task force identified war with the Soviet Union as the biggest threat to oil supplies, since all imports except those from Canada would be at risk. The group concluded that no plans were needed for more than a 12-month interruption of this sort, since it would be hard to keep a war between the superpowers from going nuclear, in which case the U.S. infrastructure, which relied on oil, would be wiped out.

According to contingency plans provided to the task force by the White House, the United States could reduce oil use during an emergency with rationing, similar to measures employed in time of war. It estimated "curtailing nonessential demand" could reduce use of gasoline by 40 percent. The task force was also told of classified plans at the Defense Department for keeping indoor temperatures at 55 degrees during a winter emergency.

Without quotas, the task force estimated oil imports would grow substantially and range from 27 to 51 percent of total use by 1980 (compared to 21 percent when the report was issued). Dropping quotas would create more dependence on the Middle East, but at a level it thought could be handled. The report predicted, "New discoveries and new technology at home and abroad . . . will have a major impact on the security situation in 1985," thus providing a period during which the United States could draw down its own reserves.[5]

Shultz' view that oil imports would not be a major problem in the future because of new technologies reflected analysis being done elsewhere in the government. By the beginning of the Nixon administration, the Atomic Energy Commission estimated a quarter of electric generation would be nuclear by 1980, the share would rise to half by 2000, and virtually all electric plants built in the twenty-first century would be nuclear. Other alternative technologies like gaseous and liquid fuels produced from coal (synfuels) and oil shale were also getting attention.[6]

℮ ᷍

The recommendations of the task force fell short of winning the full endorsement of the many interests that participated in its deliberations, nor even of its own members. The National Petroleum Council testified the likelihood of an interruption was much greater than acknowledged by the economists working on the report, and invoking wartime rationing plans to counter interruptions "would be politically unacceptable to the American consumer" in peacetime.

Two federal departments represented on the task force (Commerce and Interior) also strongly resisted the report's conclusions and wanted to retain quotas. These members argued the extra cost to consumers was only $1 billion a year, a reasonable price to pay given the turbulence in the Middle East and the need to support U.S. producers.

℮ ᷍

If Nixon had had his druthers, he would have avoided involvement in the oil import question. The conflict between the northeastern states wanting inexpensive fuel and the oil-patch states wanting protection was a no-win situation politically at a time he was trying to win an ideological majority of new Republicans and conservative Democrats in the Senate.

In a letter to the White House, George H. W. Bush—son of a former United States senator from Connecticut and a rising 45-year-old Republican star in Texas—complained the abandonment of import controls would "wreak havoc on my state and its people."

A week later, Bush forwarded correspondence from his former business partner J. Hugh Liedtke. The by-then chairman of the Pennzoil Company cited the electoral impacts of Nixon's pending decision:

> I am particularly interested in the possibility that George Bush will run for the senate from Texas. . . . If, in the opinion of the administration, it becomes necessary to materially change the present import quota system, I do not think he can be elected no matter what his support may be.[7]

In his private diaries, top Nixon aide Robert Haldeman confirmed the impact of the elections on Nixon's decision, "If we do what we should, and what the task force recommends, we'd apparently end up losing at least a couple of Senate seats, including George Bush in Texas. Anticipating Nixon's eventual announcement, he penned, "Trying to figure out a way to duck the whole thing and shift it to Congress."[8]

Nixon decided not to jettison the quotas. (Bush still lost his 1970 Senate race to Democrat Lloyd Bentsen.) The president did later, however, chip away at them with a series of ad hoc decisions allowing more imports. As a result, neither producers nor consumers were given clear direction about the future of oil import policy.

ᘓ

In August of 1971, Nixon delivered a prime-time nationally televised address with a bombshell announcement that ended up distorting energy markets (and encouraging additional oil imports) for almost a decade. "I am today ordering," Nixon declared, "a freeze on all prices and wages throughout the United States for a period of 90 days."

Nixon's major goal—whether with the original freeze or later, tightly controlled increases—was to keep prices low going into his 1972 reelection campaign. As Paul Volcker—who as Under Secretary of Treasury worked on the plan—later observed, ". . . the program of August 15, 1971 . . . combined with an accommodative monetary policy to produce the strongest kind of electoral platform for Mr. Nixon: rapidly rising production and a clearly reduced rate of inflation."[9]

Low prices encouraged rapid growth in energy demand. Nonetheless, the Nixon plan did in the short term help harness inflation and was even more effective in limiting oil prices. In 1972, the retail price of gasoline remained at 36 cents a gallon for the third straight year, making this price (when controlled for inflation) the lowest in the history of oil sales. These were remarkable data. Declining domestic oil production and import restrictions were limiting the amount of fuel available, while energy consumption continued to zoom. The economists' laws of supply and demand were in suspension due to price controls.

In the weeks approaching reelection, Nixon called together his key economic advisors for a long rambling discussion about priorities for his second term. Nixon refused to talk about energy problems in public, but he confided that the growing scarcity of energy supplies was at the top of his concerns.

He told them, "It should scare the hell out of people. What are we going to do about energy and some of these other problems? I don't know."[10]

By the end of his first term, Nixon's weakening of caps on foreign oil allowed net imports to go to 4.5 million barrels a day (28 percent of consumption). Despite Nixon's crushing victory in November of 1972, it was clear to the energy experts in his administration that serious energy problems were at hand. The United States no longer reigned supreme in world oil. Production could no longer keep pace with consumption, and the nation had no clear policy on how to fill the gap.

THE UNRAVELING

Just weeks into Nixon's second term, energy analysts at the Interior Department warned White House domestic policy chief John Ehrlichman, "It is almost certain that gasoline shortages will be widespread by summer if prompt action is not taken." They said more foreign oil was needed immediately to prevent chaos.[11]

Nixon finally announced in April he was ending all quotas on foreign oil. The United States needed all the foreign oil it could get as soon as it could get it. The country no longer had the luxury of worrying about the security implications of opening its ports to oil from the Persian Gulf.

In the same message, Nixon challenged Congress to remove remaining legal barriers to building an Alaskan oil pipeline. In 1968, the Atlantic Richfield Oil (ARCO) and Humble Oil (now Exxon) announced a major discovery at Prudhoe Bay, located on the North Slope adjacent to the Arctic Ocean. Drilling to depths of more than 8,000 feet, the oil companies had found North America's largest oil field—substantially bigger than East Texas. This area, 45 miles long and 18 miles wide, contained an "elephant"—industry lingo for an oil discovery of historic proportions. Nixon asked for legislation to specifically authorize the pipeline and preempt any further legal challenges.

The energy statement included a research and development component, with a strong emphasis on Nixon's favorite technology, nuclear power. It also proposed support for energy alternatives like shale oil, geothermal energy, and solar power. Nixon claimed credit for increasing support for energy research and development by 50 percent since his first energy message in 1971, and an additional boost of 20 percent in his proposed budget for 1974.

A section on energy conservation was largely limited to appeals for voluntary action. It called for a national "conservation ethic," including practices such as "turning out lights, tuning up automobiles, reducing the use of air conditioning and heating, and purchasing products which use energy efficiently." The plea was the first peacetime call for energy conservation to come from the White House.

The April termination of quotas did not allow enough time to affect gasoline supplies for the start of the summer driving season. It took weeks and even months to reschedule oil deliveries from the Middle East and for tankers to cross the Atlantic. In addition, small independent refiners and retailers, who had received preferential treatment with import oil controls, were encountering difficulties obtaining fuel.

In May, the American Automobile Association (AAA) launched a new survey of over a thousand gasoline stations to assess the severity of the national gasoline shortage. The June 19 edition of its *Fuel Gauge* report showed the supply situation deteriorating. Forty-seven percent of stations were not operating normally. Motorists faced increased difficulty finding gasoline, particularly at night and on weekends. By the end of June, every station polled in the Northeast had curtailed hours.[12]

Disrupted service at gasoline stations increased national worries about energy. In May, *Time* magazine devoted an entire section to its cover story, "The Energy Crisis: Time for Action." A private poll for the White House later in the month revealed the gasoline shortage had risen to the nation's number two problem—second only to inflation.

Another sign attitudes were shifting, a mid-year survey found the market share of small cars had increased from 22 percent four years earlier to 40 percent. Ads in May and June for two foreign imports—the Datsun 1200 and the Volkswagen Beetle—tried something new in auto advertising. They emphasized miles per gallon (mpg) as their primary advantage, capitalizing on concerns about the scarcity of gasoline. In an ad headlined "Datsun Saves," the Japanese importer (now Nissan) touted its number one ranking in gas mileage ("30 miles per gallon or over *twice* the national average") from the Environmental Protection Agency.

Continuing shortages forced Nixon to issue a new energy message on June 29, putting more emphasis on greater fuel conservation to get through the summer. He called for a national effort to reduce energy consumption by 5 percent over the next twelve months. To achieve the goal, he suggested people raise thermostats in the summer to four degrees above normal and reduce driving speeds to 50 miles per hour. He also called for greater use of car pools and public transportation. Nixon directed the federal government to set a good example by cutting its energy use by 7 percent.

Nixon's June message also called for a vastly expanded budget of $10 billion for research and development on advanced energy technologies. On R&D funding, Nixon was, in effect, adopting the position of Senator Henry Jackson, the Senate's most influential member on energy, who earlier in the year told Bob Schieffer on CBS' *Face the Nation*, "[T]he first order of business is a 10-year program of the same urgency that we pursued the Manhattan Project in the '40s . . . and the same urgency that Kennedy pursued the space program. . ."[13]

e⁓

In August, net oil imports passed six million barrels a day for the first time and totaled 36 percent of consumption. The United States remained the world's greatest oil producer, but with raging demand for fuel, it became increasingly dependent on the prolific increases occurring in Saudi Arabia to get through the summer. As imports rose, speculation increased that Arab states might cut off oil supplies to pressure the United States to alter its policies in the Middle East. But U.S. leaders in charge of foreign policy discounted such threats, both privately and publicly.

At a press conference in early September, Nixon confidently declared the United States remained in a strong position vis-à-vis Arab producers, "Oil without a market . . . does not do a country much good." He warned that if Arab leaders did not act responsibly they would "lose their markets, and other sources will be developed."

The next week, National Security Advisor Henry Kissinger assured a congressional committee the flow of foreign oil was secure. He testified, "There appears to be no near-term alternative to increasing imports of oil from the Middle East. . . . We have excellent relationships with our principal Middle Eastern suppliers of oil, Saudi Arabia and Iran, and we do not foresee any circumstances in which they would cut our supply."[14]

It would not take long to determine whether official confidence about the reliability of foreign oil deliveries was warranted.

EMBARGO

On October 6, 1973, the Jewish holy day of Yom Kippur, 222 Egyptian supersonic jets soared across the Suez Canal into the Sinai Peninsula, controlled by Israel since the 1967 war. Syria simultaneously moved past cease-fire lines into the Golan Heights and other areas along its border with northern Israel. During the early days of the war, its potential effects on oil deliveries to the United States rated only minor consideration. Still, on the second day, Nixon told Kissinger, "[W]e don't want to be so pro-Israel that the oil states—the Arabs that are not involved in the fighting—will break ranks."[15]

Several developments confounded administration attempts to avoid inflaming Arab nations. Initial Egyptian gains persuaded Kissinger and Nixon the United States would have to provide planes and ammunition to replace Israel's early losses. At the same time, statements out of Saudi Arabia, Kuwait, Iraq, and Libya offered increasing evidence Arab countries would try to use oil to punish the United States for its support of Israel. Iraq quickly nationalized the Exxon and Mobil facilities in Basra. On October 11, U.S. oil companies informed the State Department that Saudi Arabia's King Faisal ibn Abd al-Aziz al-Saud—son of his nation's founder and the man with the world's greatest oil reserves—was angry with Kissinger's statements on the war and was threatening drastic cuts in oil production.[16]

Undeterred, on October 13 the United States launched a resupply mission to Israel that over the next few weeks became bigger than the Berlin Airlift of 1948–1949. Despite what he considered wavering on the part of Nixon, Kissinger was determined not to set any precedents by giving in to pressure from oil producers. British Ambassador Lord Cromer asked him the day the planes left for Israel, "What will be your posture . . . when the Arabs start yelling oil at you?" Kissinger replied tersely, "Defiance."[17]

Events of October 17 abruptly dashed U.S. expectations about the role of oil in the conflict. At a meeting in Kuwait, Arab producers worked out their divergent views to agree to a cut in oil production of 5 percent. A second part of the boycott included a total embargo of deliveries to the United States (and later the Netherlands) for supporting Israel. The U.S. embassy in Saudi Arabia reported the "King has never been more popular" in his country after it became clear he would join with other Arab states to use the oil weapon.[18]

With Israel gaining momentum on the battlefield but the military situation still in doubt, Nixon on October 19 sent a formal request to

Congress for $2.2 billion in aid to Israel. The radical states at the Arab oil ministers meeting responded the same day with demands for ending diplomatic relations with the United States, switching Arab financial reserves out of dollars, and cutting oil production in half—all moves successfully opposed by Saudi Arabia. The group did agree to increase the cut in production to 10 percent, after which the Iraqi representative walked out of the meeting. Within days, the Iraqi press was accusing Saudi Arabia of treason for failing to support stronger measures.

Twelve days later, Arab oil producers ramped up the pressure, announcing a massive 25 percent cut in production, with the threat of additional cuts of 5 percent each month if their demands were not met.

American options to force an end to the oil boycott were limited. The State Department determined the embargo violated a 1933 treaty with the Saudis, granting each other most favorable nation status. The diplomats concluded, however, that if such legalistic arguments led to an abrogation, "that would deprive the U.S. of usefulness of the agreement in other connections." Food provided another potential way to exert American power, particularly since floods in Pakistan and Thailand's temporary difficulties exporting grains meant the United States was furnishing over half the wheat, rice, and flour imported into Saudi Arabia at the time. Ambassador James Akins said a food boycott would "certainly cause Saudi Arabia considerable inconvenience." He observed, however, the Saudis could find other suppliers and "any counter-embargo would be ineffective in the long run and viewed as vindictive by those more friendly to U.S. interests."[19]

Both sides worked hard behind the scenes to ensure that arms sales were not affected adversely by the very public dispute over oil.

On a diplomatic mission to Saudi Arabia, Kissinger asked Faisal on November 9 to support his diplomatic efforts and told him the embargo was "a severe blow to our relations." The king replied that a decision on lifting the embargo could not be made by Saudi Arabia alone. He would need more evidence of progress on the larger issues before he could endorse such a proposal to other Arab states. Kissinger had not expected quick agreement in Saudi Arabia, noting in his memoirs, "Riyadh is not the place for scoring dramatic breakthroughs."[20]

The war was effectively ended by mid–November, though Egypt and Israel still had to work out a specific agreement on postwar lines. Even with evidence Kissinger's foray into the Arab world had achieved some positive results, American officials found it difficult to read what the Saudis required for oil sanctions to be lifted.

"PROJECT INDEPENDENCE"

Nixon delivered his first major televised address about the embargo on November 7. To help reduce the need for oil, he called for a mandatory reduction in air traffic and relaxed controls on sulfur emissions to allow greater burning of coal. Nixon also made bold proposals for reducing highway speed limits to 50 miles per hour, thermostats to 68 degrees in residences (even lower in offices), and commercial lighting at night. He commended the state of Oregon for promoting staggered work hours, mass transit, and carpooling. In addition, he advocated shifting production of electricity away from oil—at the time responsible for 17 percent of generation.

Reversing his long-time resistance to calls from Senator Jackson for mandatory federal allocation of oil, Nixon proposed the government now make the decisions about the distribution of scarce oil supplies. The president tried to put the best face on this and other unpleasant news by declaring, "We have an energy crisis but there is no crisis of the American spirit."

The program for scientific research, in particular, lent itself to rhetorical embellishment. The most radical concept in early drafts of the speech was a call for expansive research programs to "return this country to a largely self-sufficient energy supply posture." The day before the speech, Nixon aide Gen. Al Haig passed on a suggestion from chief economist Herb Stein. Haig told Nixon, "[Y]ou may wish to name the effort to achieve self-sufficiency 'Project Independence.' This fits well with the rhetoric of the Bicentennial era."[21]

Nixon adopted the language in his vision of a better future:

> Let us set as our national goal, in the spirit of Apollo and with the determination of the Manhattan Project, that by the end of this decade, we will have developed the potential to meet our own energy needs without depending on any foreign energy sources. Let us pledge that by 1980, under Project Independence, we shall be able to meet America's energy needs from America's own energy resources.

Nixon was telling the public that technology would end reliance on foreign oil within seven years, an idea several advisors found implausible.

MANAGING THE CRISIS

Ten days later, Faisal reiterated more Israeli withdrawals were needed to change oil policy. Yet the next day, Arab oil ministers announced they would hold the production cuts to 20 percent, largely as a gesture to friendly European nations.

The task of assessing the impact of the interruption on the U.S. market fell to the Interior Department. Its analysts projected a shortfall of 1.4 million barrels a day in the fourth quarter of 1973, 8 percent of expected demand. For the first quarter of 1974, when there would be sufficient time for the Arab cuts to be felt in the distant American market, Interior projected an ominous deficit of 3.5 million barrels a day—a daunting 20 percent of expected demand.

Interior assumed an airtight embargo cutting off all U.S. imports of oil from Arab producers. To get to a greater loss of 3.5 million barrels a day, it was necessary to add losses resulting from the production cuts. The world at the time was consuming roughly 60 million barrels of oil a day, 20 million coming from Arab producers. With a fifth of Arab production cut, the international market would lose about four million barrels a day (about 7 percent of the world's supply).

On the demand side, forecasters saw a gigantic 9 percent increase in the first quarter of 1974 over the equivalent period in 1973. They concluded the rampaging consumption evident in recent years would not be affected by the higher prices seen in 1973 or by various conservation policies already in place.

Though these estimates became the basis of U.S. policy throughout the embargo, they were shockingly inept. They totally ignored the likelihood oil deliveries from non-Arab sources could be shifted away from countries not under the embargo to replace some of the losses of countries that were. Equally problematic, the energy team projected that of a worldwide shortage of four million barrels a day, the United States would have to absorb 3.5 million. Government calculations that a 7 percent cut in world oil production would lead to a 20 percent shortfall in the United States were preposterous, even assuming (equally amazingly) rapidly growing demand in the face of high prices and government conservation programs. All adverse factors were being cumulated, even though they were overlapping. It was equivalent to a mortality study that counted each death from three causes as three separate deaths.

At the time, Senator Jackson and others in Congress agreed the pending shortage of petroleum in the United States would likely reach

20 percent or more. Administration projections of a smaller deficit would have made its concerns sound weak compared to those coming from an alarmist press and Congress.

❧

Public worries about energy led on November 25 to another prime time television address from the president, filled with more rhetoric about energy independence. Nixon commended Congress for recently passing legislation on both the Alaska pipeline—which Interior Secretary Rogers Morton estimated would eventually add two million barrels a day to domestic supplies—and emergency petroleum allocation. Mandatory federal controls in the Emergency Petroleum Allocation Act of 1973 were designed to promote equitable distribution of available products and to protect independent oil companies. The act also codified price controls on oil, making it difficult for any president to end them without congressional cooperation.

Nixon's address also praised the American people for responding to his last speech with "a spirit of sacrifice." He announced, nonetheless, additional conservation measures to reduce demand. He called for the closing of all gasoline stations every weekend between 9:00 P.M. Saturday and midnight Sunday to discourage weekend driving and for cooperation from state and local governments. By this time, six states had lowered their speed limits to at least 55 mph. Just five weeks into the embargo, the nation was adopting measures to deal with the anticipated shortfall of oil.

News of the embargo and pleas from the government to conserve helped further alter American views about energy. In a late November Gallup poll, 62 percent of people said they were using less electricity. To save gasoline, 62 percent reported driving slower, 41 percent using the car less, and 8 percent joining a car pool. Americans were adopting the conservation ethic. [22]

❧

To deal with the energy crisis, Nixon on December 4 announced formation of a federal energy office, to be headed by Deputy Secretary of Treasury William Simon, who said he was asked by Nixon to act as an energy czar.

Around the time of the reorganization, energy officials received encouraging news. Imports did not drop as quickly as expected. Even more positive, demand for oil fell well below anticipated levels. Warmer weather helped save heating oil in the northeastern states during November, and the National Weather Service projected favorable temperatures through February. Savings also came from sharp drops in the use of jet fuel and from electric utilities using less oil. Demand for gasoline fell 15 percent below forecast, suggesting a substantial response to the president's energy message. Europe and Japan also experienced sharp drops in fuel use.

The budget office used some of these data to challenge the Interior estimates of the shortage adopted by Simon. Taking into account large price increases since 1972, reductions in spending from an economic slowdown, and the impact of federal policies already adopted, the Office of Management and Budget (OMB) figured the shortage for the first quarter of 1974 would be in the range of one million barrels a day, less than a third of the government's official number.[23]

The ultimate test of the embargo was its impact on consumers. In the first months of the boycott, disruptions at the pump turned out to be bothersome, but no greater than those of the previous June. A new AAA survey in mid-December reported with some relief that 80 percent of gasoline stations expected to be open on holiday eves. Despite many positive signals, Simon regarded December's reprieve as only temporary and resisted adjustments to official projections.

Hopeful signs didn't keep the national mood from turning sour. The stock market fell 165 points (17 percent) in a single month, one of the steepest drops in history, and viewed as a major byproduct of the embargo. Adding to the bad news, small and formerly docile nations seemed to be dictating terms to a world power.

Zealous press coverage contributed to a national frenzy over energy. A mid-November cover of *Time* was headlined, "The Arabs' New Oil Squeeze: Dim Outs, Slowdowns, Chills." The magazine opined:

> Even if the Arabs were to reopen their taps tomorrow, the world would never again be the same. The sudden shortage of fuel has finally jolted governments into a realization that the era of cheap and ample energy is dead and that people will have to learn to live permanently with less heating, lighting, and transport and pay more for each of them.[24]

A declining quality of life seemed certain.

National concerns about energy spurred Congress to extend Daylight Saving Time and reduce speed limits. Traffic controls had traditionally been set by states, but now the Department of Transportation would cut off funds for states not complying with a 55-mph cap. Nixon continued to complain about congressional inaction, but it moved with some vigor in the last two months of the year.

Oil producers in the Middle East held crucial meetings late in December in Iran and Kuwait. At Tehran, the oil ministers again increased the price of oil, this time from $5 to $12 a barrel. With the price as late as mid-October having stood at $3, the new jump was stunning in its size. The quadrupling of prices in ten weeks for a major commodity was without precedent.

This bold action went largely uncontested by the industrialized nations. The U.S. ambassador in Riyadh cabled back to Washington, "OPEC is probably surprised at the helpless reaction from the consumers." Saudi Oil Minister Ahmed Zaki Yamani bemoaned to U.S. diplomats his lonely role at the meeting, trying to limit the increase, and asked why the United States was not doing more to restrain its close ally Mohammed Reza Pahlavi, the Shah of Iran. The irreverent oil minister mused that his best chance to get support came from Iraq "strangely enough . . . not because they don't want more money or because they have developed a love affair for Saudi Arabia, but because they hate Iran more."[25]

The meeting in Kuwait also fell well short of U.S. expectations. Arab OPEC did agree to lower its cut in production to 10 percent. Nixon and Kissinger were frustrated by what they thought of as a total lack of Arab cooperation in ending the embargo. Though Arab producers didn't give the Americans what they wanted, they did give them part of what they needed—a substantial loosening of their stranglehold on world oil supplies. Strangely, U.S. officials and media took little notice of the significant easing of the production cuts. Nixon's energy czar continued to cling to his now even more badly outdated projections on the oil shortage.

At the end of December, Nixon demonstrated his own commitment to saving energy with a symbolic change in his travel plans. He canceled his normal flight via Air Force One back to San Clemente for the holidays. Instead, the First Couple traveled on a United Airlines commercial aircraft, taking five-and-a-half hours. They returned from California on an

Air Force Jetstar. With the smaller plane having to make a stop for refueling, they arrived back at the White House at three in the morning.[26]

In the early weeks of 1974, the task of restoring oil deliveries from the Arab world assumed increasing urgency. Tankers en route before the embargo had now unloaded their oil. The time it took to deliver cargoes from the Persian Gulf to U.S. ports delayed the impact of production cuts in November and early December. It now had the reverse effect. Arab oil production rose 10 percent in January, just as promised in late December. However, total U.S. imports, after dropping 13 percent in December, fell an additional 11 percent in January.

The president's weakened political position added pressure on his Secretary of State to negotiate a quick end to the embargo. According to a skeptical Kissinger, Nixon was "in thrall to the idea that a dramatic lifting of the embargo under his personal leadership was the cure-all for his Watergate agonies."[27]

Kissinger left shortly after midnight on January 11 for his third whirlwind trip to the Middle East in three months. A disengagement of Egyptian and Israeli troops was finally agreed to, encouraging American hopes for a quick end to the embargo. Egyptian President Anwar Sadat had promised to press for such action after disengagement—a pledge he kept. Egypt, however, was not a major oil producer and could not prevail unilaterally on Saudi Arabia and other Arab exporters to resume full production. Radical states like Libya could not be ignored. Also, with negotiations to disengage Syrian and Israeli forces stalled, the Saudis were reluctant to end the embargo without Syria's consent.

On January 21, Syrian President Hafez al-Assad demanded continuation of the embargo until agreement was reached on his country's disengagement. National Security Advisor Henry Kissinger finally had to tell the President that Arab oil producers were not going to let him announce a return to normal oil deliveries by the State of the Union speech scheduled for January 30.

Back home, Simon's federal energy office used its authority over industry to stringently limit oil coming to the market. With dwindling oil imports and mandatory allocation taking hold, motorists in January faced shocks at the pumps far more stunning than any before. The AAA *Fuel Gauge* survey during the month found only half of gas stations staying open after 7:00 P.M. Seventeen percent were limiting purchases of fuel. Even more ominous, 2 percent of stations had exhausted their supplies.[28]

A confidential poll conducted by the White House showed that, by mid-January, 37 percent of the population reported difficulties obtaining motor fuel—a big jump from the 16 percent in December. At the same time, 60 percent of respondents indicated the energy shortage had affected their lifestyle.[29]

Problems at the pumps and extensive news coverage of the embargo jolted public opinion. Americans for the first time considered energy the nation's number one problem. In the first week of January, 46 percent of respondents in a Gallup poll ranked the energy crisis the most important issue facing the country. About 40 percent of the public saw the need to change lifestyles because of the energy crisis as a change for the worse, but 43 percent saw it as a change for the better.[30]

"THE FIRST PRIORITY"

In his nationally televised 1974 State of the Union address, Nixon declared it "the first in which the one priority, the first priority, is energy." Pledges to achieve energy independence and to avoid gasoline rationing earned mild applause. But he offered few ideas beyond those from the previous year.

An embattled Nixon tried to adopt the most optimistic interpretation of the chances for ending the embargo. But his cautious aides thought an immediate diplomatic breakthrough unlikely and any evidence of impatience to get one a sign of weakness. Kissinger stayed in frequent communication with the Saudis on what the president was authorized to say.[31]

Nixon described the disengagement of Egyptian and Israeli forces in terms that exaggerated the chances for restoring the flow of oil but were vague enough to satisfy his advisers. Four days later, however, Faisal officially informed the United States of an Arab consensus, which came as little surprise to the Americans: the embargo would not end without more progress on disengagement between Israel and Syria.

Despite Nixon's attempt to strike an optimistic tone, the fuel crisis at home continued to escalate. The American Automobile Association reported that by the end of January, many dealers had run out of monthly allocations. Unable to get fresh supplies, the percentage of stations without any fuel jumped to 16 percent. In the Northeast and Northwest, most open stations were imposing quotas on purchases and closing by noon or mid-afternoon. Arrival of new supplies helped in the early days of February, but about 10 percent of retailers still reported no available gas.

An unpleasant byproduct of the energy crisis in early February was a national truckers' strike. Major grievances included lower speed limits and the rising cost of diesel fuel, which with federal price controls could not be quickly passed on to customers. Stations without fuel and Sunday closings were also exacting their toll. Truckers defying the stoppage reported being shot at in Virginia, Missouri, Tennessee, Texas, and Ohio. A driver in Pennsylvania was killed when a boulder was dropped on his cab from an overpass. Attorney General William Saxbe called on governors to "use every resource at their command to see that we do not descend into anarchy."

Motorists began to see long lines of trucks protected by the National Guard and police, part of the inspiration for a new anthem for the CB radio craze, the chart-topping "Convoy" by the legendary C. W. McCall, a.k.a. "Rubber Duck."

Problems of managing lines at the pumps stimulated innovative responses from government and industry. To reduce long waits, Oregon asked motorists to limit purchases of gasoline to odd or even days, based on the number on their license tags. Seven other states and the District of Columbia followed the Oregon example and adopted voluntary plans. Maryland, Virginia, New Jersey, New York, Delaware, and Hawaii went further and mandated the odd-even system. Motorists on the Florida Turnpike had to show they had less than half a tank of gasoline before they could purchase additional fuel. Along the East Coast, many stations operated on split shifts—closing during the middle of the day to spread out the time gasoline was available.

Facing growing shortages and a barrage of complaints from state and local officials, the energy office announced on February 19 additional allotments for hard-hit states. Still, the crisis continued to worsen, reaching its peak late in the month. One of every five dealers reported no gasoline at all was available. National averages masked the greater severity of problems in some regions. The Carolinas were hit worst, with half their stations reporting they had run out of fuel. Florida (with 40 percent out) and Pennsylvania (37 percent out) ranked next in the shortage of supplies.

Unlike preembargo supply problems, the new shortages were accompanied by major increases in prices at the pump. From October to December, the cost of gasoline rose 3.5 cents a gallon. From December to April of 1974, it jumped another 10 cents. Motorists who had been paying $6 to fill a fifteen-gallon tank in October were by April paying over $8. They were also getting less service for their money. To control costs, dealers were reducing customer inducements like trading stamps, free maps, windshield washes, and oil checks.

Federal price controllers allowed retailers to pass on their costs, but a quirk allowing refiners and dealers to raise prices only on the first of the month contributed to the shortages. The energy office announced in mid-February that service stations would be allowed to add an additional two cents on retail prices, based on higher costs for crude oil, and raise their profit margins from 8 to 10 cents a gallon on March 1. This pricing policy created a significant incentive to withhold supplies at the end of February, and that is when shortages at the pump, in fact, reached their peak.[32]

There was one silver lining in the dark cloud of the gasoline shortage. In the first week of February, the National Safety Council reported that about 1,000 fewer people were killed in traffic accidents in the United States in 1973 than in 1972, the greatest reductions coming in December, when the energy shortage hit and many speed limits had been lowered. Several weeks later, the National Highway Safety Administration announced fatalities for the month of January were 853 (23 percent) below January of the previous year. The embargo was irritating motorists and dragging down the economy, but it was also saving lives.

In March, as larger allocations started arriving around the country, the number of stations without fuel suddenly plunged. Simon's release of inventories had finally made a difference. Even with the embargo still in place, the shortage had eased. Gas lines were disappearing.

END OF THE EMBARGO

Diplomats from Egypt and Saudi Arabia privately informed Kissinger and Nixon at a meeting on February 16 that the embargo would end. A U.S.

commitment to continue to work for peace in the Middle East allowed Arab officials to say they had gotten something out of the oil weapon. Since working on disengagement between Israel and Syria was something they planned to do anyway, Nixon and Kissinger felt they had made no concessions, thereby avoiding any demonstration of weakness that might invite future oil boycotts. Finally, on March 18, after Arab producers reined in the radical states, Kissinger informed Nixon the embargo was lifted. The Saudis announced they would increase production by one million barrels a day.

Temptations to celebrate the end of the embargo were tempered by a decision by OPEC to freeze oil prices. Yamani had promised lower prices, while many producers had pushed to raise them. Keeping current levels in place helped find middle ground needed to get a consensus on terminating the boycott (though Syria and Libya still refused to sign the agreement) and alerted American drivers that any expectations for lower prices at the pump when the embargo was lifted were at best premature.

Supplies had been interrupted for five months, with peak loss of imports coming in February. At that point, they fell 1.2 million barrels a day (19 percent) below September levels. Because most oil consumed in the United States still came from domestic sources, the peak total monthly loss of oil was about 8 percent of total United States supplies. The oil weapon had packed a wallop, but by itself delivered far from a knockout punch.

Availability of gasoline continued to improve through the end of March, avoiding the end-of-the-month panics in January and February. The American Automobile Association reported, "Gas Easier to Find, Harder to Pay For," as increasing supplies were accompanied by high prices. By early May, about half of the states with odd-even plans dropped them, as lines at the pump vanished. By June and July, the situation was even better. For the high-demand Fourth of July holiday, AAA reported gasoline supplies as "plentiful." In the public's view, the oil shortage was over.

After the embargo, public focus on energy fell in the absence of gas lines drawing attention to America's oil dependency. Presidential statements on energy, conspicuous in January, became increasingly rare. Energy's rank as a national problem dropped in the polls.

Yet Simon felt the worst part of the crisis remained, because OPEC price increases were a greater threat to the United States than the five months of the embargo. With Americans paying much more for foreign oil, a big chunk of U.S. financial resources would be sucked out of the national economy in the form of an energy trade deficit and transferred to the Middle East.

The aggregate numbers for higher costs were staggering. In 1972, the U.S. bill for foreign oil was about $4 billion. The next year, the price rose to about $7 billion. In 1974, the first year affected by the late 1973 actions of OPEC, the cost jumped to about $25 billion. The total tab for imported oil had soared to more than six times its level just two years earlier. This leap occurred despite a 4 percent drop in U.S. oil consumption in 1974, the first decline in history.

The increasing cost of imported oil had a dramatic impact on the U.S. balance of trade. In 1974, the net energy trade deficit ran $22 billion. By contrast, the non-energy balance for the year ran a positive $18 billion. The outflow of money from the United States was matched by inflows into the Persian Gulf. Suddenly oil producers were raking in more money than could be immediately spent. From 1972 to 1974, the gross domestic product of Saudi Arabia more than tripled. Other oil-exporting nations were also experiencing extraordinary economic expansion, even with reduced oil exports during the embargo.

The United States was paying a heavy price for its new dependency on foreign oil. Over the years, measures like import quotas, price controls, and fuel allocation were adopted to deal with the symptoms of falling domestic production and rapidly rising demand. They only made matters worse. After the embargo, many in and out of government were looking for new solutions that might reverse negative trends in energy and bring about the kind of energy independence Nixon had talked about.

SEARCHING FOR ANSWERS

The dominant coverage by journalists and historians of the Nixon pardon has obscured Gerald Ford's intense efforts to deal with energy after being sworn in as president on August 9, 1974.[33] The former congressman from Michigan was well aware the tide of oil imports continued to rise. He quickly vowed in his first address to Congress that to avoid another energy crisis he would push Project Independence. Ford stayed personally involved in energy policy in a way unmatched by Nixon, even during the embargo. He made energy a frequent topic at cabinet meetings and discussed it often in his private and public remarks.

The energy agenda in the later months of 1974 was propelled by initiatives during the embargo. October legislation creating a new Energy Research and Development Administration combined all the R&D functions for nuclear, fossil, and renewable energy spread throughout the government into a single agency. With new funds pouring into energy research, the reorganization was far from a trivial matter. The budget rose from $1.25 billion in 1973 to $2.5 billion in 1975. Controlled for the rate of inflation, these expenditures greatly eclipse the tepid energy research efforts of today.

In November and December, Congress, with strong White House support, passed additional measures. A mass transit program authorized $12 billion through 1980, which Ford called "significant in our fight against excessive use of petroleum." Congress then made permanent the temporary 55 mph speed limit adopted during the Arab boycott.

Early in the year, Congress ordered the administration to produce a national energy plan by November, called the "Project Independence" report. Within weeks of taking office, Ford decided to keep the deadline for energy independence at 1980, a challenging target just six years off. The administration also debated internally about whether to set a more immediate goal of lowering imports by one million barrels (from six million to five million barrels) a day by the end of 1975. Against the advice of most advisors, Ford decided to take the political risk of publicly advocating the stretch short-term goal whose success or failure could be assessed before the next presidential election.

The "Project Independence" report, written by the Federal Energy Administration, had some impact on the energy plan developed by Ford. But his inner circle viewed it as too tilted toward energy conservation and government mandates.

Ford unveiled his energy strategy in two major speeches during January of 1975. A live televised fireside chat on the economy and energy, broadcast in prime time, conveyed a strong commitment to robust action on energy. Ford, with characteristic candor, admitted, "Americans are no longer in full control of their own national destiny, when that destiny depends on uncertain foreign fuel at high prices fixed by others."

The president announced he would invoke emergency powers to phase in a fee on foreign oil reaching $3 a barrel over the next three months to discourage imports and force Congress to take action. He admitted, "Yes, gasoline and oil will cost even more than they do now."

Ford's energy plan included a windfall profits tax and a threat to return to oil import quotas if necessary. He also urged Congress to grant a five-year delay on new auto pollution standards to achieve a 40 percent improvement in miles per gallon, implying (incorrectly) all the savings would come from adjusting environmental mandates. He vowed to veto any new spending programs, except for energy.

By accepting higher prices, Ford took a different path than Nixon, who always favored politically popular low prices whatever the eventual consequences. Like his predecessor, however, he invoked the bicentennial and previous times of crisis when the American people "closed ranks, rolled up their sleeves, and rallied to do whatever had to be done."

Post-speech commentary illustrated at least one difficulty Ford's programs would face. Noting the large number of components in the economic and energy programs, CBS reporter George Herman said that it was good advanced texts had been handed out, but the proposals were still complicated.

At his State of the Union address on January 15, Ford continued to speak bluntly, saying, "I've got bad news, and I don't expect much, if any, applause." Going beyond the energy measures in his earlier message, he called for deregulating natural gas prices, amending the Clean Air Act to allow greater use of coal, providing tax credits for construction of electric power plants that didn't use oil or gas, producing one million barrels a day of synthetic fuels and shale oil by 1985, authorizing a floor price for oil to protect alternative energy from a price crash, and creating a new tax credit for installing additional home insulation. He also proposed "a strategic storage program of 1 billion barrels of oil for domestic needs and 300 million barrels for national defense purposes."

Reaction to the President's flurry of energy proposals was dominated by Democrats generally hostile to the tax on imports. Massachusetts Governor Michael Dukakis accused Ford of holding New England hostage. Public officials from the Northeast, joined by ten regional utilities, filed a legal challenge to Ford's authority to impose the import fee. House Speaker Carl Albert, delivering the official Democratic reply on major television networks, complained Ford's import tax would have "an astounding inflationary impact."[34] Labor unions, service station operators, and homebuilders complained about the added cost for fuel.

Ford quickly became frustrated with the slow pace of his old congressional colleagues in dealing with the country's dangerous dependence on foreign oil. In late January, he chafed to reporters, "We've diddled and dawdled long enough." Confrontations between the two branches of government over the oil import fee contributed to a sense the Republican president and Democratic Congress were far apart on energy matters.

More than Ford was willing to acknowledge, however, the House and Senate were working hard in their own messy ways to forge a new energy policy. Chairman Al Ullman managed to get a twenty-three-cent gasoline tax through his House Ways and Means Committee, but in June it suffered a crushing defeat on the floor, despite the support of Democratic powerhouses like Majority Leader Tip O'Neill (MA), Jim Wright (TX), Richard Bolling (MO), Morris Udall (AR), John Dingell (MI), and Dan Rostenkowski (IL).

O'Neill then led an effort to retain at least a three-cent tax dedicated to an energy trust fund, asking on the floor, "Have we got the guts to stand up and vote for the future of America?" Even this more modest measure failed, after road builders lobbied against using gas tax revenues for purposes other than roads.

Editorial boards pilloried the House for failing to pass a strong energy bill. The *New York Times* called the tax votes an "act of irresponsibility that greatly increases this country's vulnerability to economic coercion by the oil cartel." The *Washington Post* wrote, "Energy policy is now the most divisive regional issue to afflict this country since civil rights."[35]

The House votes on the gasoline tax were another historic fork in the road of energy history. Just three days earlier, Switzerland passed a national referendum to raise its gasoline tax by 50 percent to 45 cents a gallon, part of a post-embargo trend in Europe toward much higher taxes. By 1976, only two industrialized nations had gasoline prices below one dollar a gallon—Canada at 71 cents and the United States at 58 cents.[36]

American energy policy seemed totally adrift, but appearances were deceiving.

Chapter 2

A Forgotten Victory Gives Hope: How America Solved Its Last Energy Crisis and Cut Oil Imports in Half

According to conventional wisdom, America went to sleep at the switch after the Arab oil embargo exposed the nation's dangerous dependence on foreign oil. Though widely accepted, this view ignores the substantial progress in response to the embargo, progress we would now be well-served to understand.

The period from 1974 to 1982 provides plenty of evidence of massive policy and market failures. Big jumps in energy prices, inflation, and interest rates brought pain to many Americans. Presidents and Congresses often bickered over energy, exposing at times a lack of national resolve. The reappearance of gasoline lines and the seizing of American hostages in what had previously been the United States' strongest ally in the Persian Gulf came to symbolize our global impotence. But that is not all there is to the story.

Somehow, a successful national energy policy emerged out of the chaos. The United States slashed its reliance on foreign oil. Regrettably, few people remember that we actually cut our oil imports in half—perhaps the most dramatic turn in a major energy trend line in history. This became the forgotten victory of energy independence. But consider this—if we won the battle for energy independence once, maybe we can do it again.

To understand how we get in and out of energy messes, we need to review the dramatic energy struggles from the presidency of Gerald Ford to the first years of Ronald Reagan and assess their later impacts.

"The Most Parochial Issue that Could Ever Hit the Floor"

Even with gasoline taxes going down to ignominious defeat in the spring of 1975, Congress faced a myriad of other energy proposals intended to prevent the debacle of another oil embargo. On many, the members were able to find consensus and win explicit or tacit approval from the White House. But another item remained every bit as contentious as taxes.

President Ford called for terminating oil price controls—the ones initiated by Nixon in 1971—to avoid over consumption and under production of oil, but he ran into stiff opposition from Democrats vowing to keep prices low. According to Senator Jackson, "[A]nything we do to increase the price of gasoline or home heating oil to the American people would be selling out the people of this country." Ford had leverage on the matter with the bully pulpit of the White House, the threat of vetoes, and the support of oil patch Democrats. Oklahoma governor David Boren (D) lobbied vigorously for decontrolling the price of oil. "If the price of candy bars in this country was set at two cents a bar and the cost of producing a candy bar was eighty-nine cents," Boren told audiences, "we would have a candy bar shortage."[1]

Congress bent but did not bow to White House pressure on oil prices. It finally agreed to a bill lowering them in the short run, but permitting the president to terminate all controls in 1979. Given the frequency with which such dates were extended, the outcome was viewed more as a loss than a victory for Ford.

Intense battles over oil pricing distracted attention from other important measures included in an omnibus bill that finally cleared the Congress in December. The Energy Policy and Conservation Act of 1975 authorized, in part, a strategic petroleum reserve with a capacity of one billion barrels. The volumes contemplated for storage could provide a substantial cushion for another oil embargo and enhance national security. The legislation also expanded the federal government's authority to order major electric generators to switch to coal in place of oil or natural gas. In 1975, petroleum consumption by electric utilities was four-and-a-half times higher than 10 years earlier and stood at 15 percent of total electric production. The 1.4 million barrels of oil a day consumed by the electric industry represented a huge target of opportunity.

The bill established, as well, state energy conservation programs with federal financial and technical assistance. Within six months, each state had to submit a feasibility study for achieving a 5 percent reduction in projected energy consumption by 1980. States were encouraged to permit right turns at red lights to save fuel lost while idling. (Virtually all states legalized such turns by 1977.)

The key conservation item in the bill was mandatory (rather than voluntary, as favored by some) fuel efficiency standards for new automobiles. By doubling the efficiency of cars to 27.5 miles per gallon by 1985, Congress hoped to chop consumption of gasoline and diesel fuel, which together accounted for about half of all U.S. oil use. In effect, Congress adopted efficiency standards on vehicles as a substitute for taxes on fuels.

The Energy Policy and Conservation Act constituted a substantial response to the Arab oil embargo that took important steps toward energy independence. Yet, at the time and in later years, it was the bill that got no respect. Members who had watched the sausage being made were frustrated with the concessions needed to secure passage. "This, perhaps, has been the most parochial issue that could ever hit the floor," complained House Majority Leader Tip O'Neill (who supported the bill). Feisty Senator Lowell Weicker Jr. (R–Conn. and the only senator from New England to vote no) declared, "When we needed a national energy policy, we got a political energy cop-out." He called the final bill "worse than nothing."[2]

Republican Senator John Tower of Texas led the fight for a veto. "The bill is an absolute and total disaster," he told the president privately. He argued that extending price controls would lead to importing more Arab oil, because American rigs used to explore and drill for oil in the United States would either be placed in storage or shipped to Canada. Senator Chuck Percy (R–IL) countered that he believed deeply in the free market but tilted toward signing. He said without the bill the only conservation measure in place after two years of debate would be the 55-mph speed limit.[3]

Frank Zarb, Ford's principle negotiator on the energy bill, urged the president to consider the immediate negative impacts of the sudden decontrol that would occur with a veto. These included a six-cents-per-gallon increase in gasoline prices, disruptions for refiners and service stations receiving special preferences under the controls, windfall profits for the oil industry, and escalating costs for farmers, fishermen, airlines, petrochemical companies, and asphalt contractors. He concluded the president's options "should be evaluated largely in terms of the political posture" needed in the coming months, reminding the president he would face a Democratic Congress and the voters of New Hampshire early the following year.[4] On Monday, December 22—the day Ford announced his position—his staff was still feverishly working on drafts of statements justifying both sides of the veto decision. But Ford informed Zarb the day before that he would allow the bill to become law.

The *Washington Post* on December 26 endorsed Ford's decision but had a hard time explaining why. Its editorial complained about "bad policy" in the legislation, but acknowledged, "There comes a point at which almost any decision is better than none." Treasury Secretary Simon, in his 1978 memoirs, called the decision to sign the bill "tragic" and "the worst error of the Ford administration."[5] It is difficult to find any ringing endorsements of our first broad energy legislation or recognition of the potential impacts of the strategic petroleum reserve, auto efficiency standards, or mandatory conversion to coal on energy independence.

Reflecting the ambivalence of the White House, there was no joyous signing ceremony with the president handing out pens to bill sponsors. Ford justified his support of the bill in terse remarks lasting under two minutes. When a reporter asked whether the bill was an administration or a congressional program, the normally gregarious president walked out of the room without answering.

In 1976, Ford had to focus his attention on the presidential election, but he did not neglect energy. He pushed for an Energy Independence Authority, a $100 billion program in some versions, to finance alternative fuels, particularly synthetic fuels that would convert the country's abundant coal resources into liquid fuels for transportation. The synfuels proposal was scaled back and then eventually defeated by a coalition of conservatives fearing government intervention in energy markets and environmentalists worried about damage to air and water from producing synfuels. On the campaign trail, Ford ignored the massive energy package passed at the end of 1975.

A big problem for Ford was that his announced goal for reducing oil imports proved unattainable. From 1974 to 1976, oil imports did not go down by one million barrels a day, the goal he had announced. They jumped, in fact, from six million barrels to seven million. In 1974, the United States imported 35 percent of its oil. By 1976, it was 41 percent. The American energy balance of trade deficit grew from $24 billion a year to $30 billion.

At the first televised presidential debate in 16 years in September, Democratic nominee Jimmy Carter complained, "I think almost every other developed nation in the world has an energy policy except us." In his rebuttal, Ford mentioned some of his accomplishments, but could not deny that OPEC was even more firmly in control of the world oil market and that American energy independence seemed more elusive than ever.

"THE MORAL EQUIVALENT OF WAR"

Carter signaled in the early days of his presidency his intent to move quickly on "a comprehensive, long-range energy policy." His first fireside chat (wearing a camel-colored cardigan sweater now on display at the Carter Presidential Library in Atlanta) just two weeks after his inauguration emphasized the energy problem. Following the reasoning of the 1974 Project Independence report derided by Ford's advisors, Carter proclaimed, "Our program will emphasize conservation. The amount of energy being wasted which could be saved is greater than the total energy that we are importing from other countries."

The former governor of Georgia told people solving the energy problem would involve "some sacrifice." He noted, for example, that keeping thermostats at 65 degrees during the day and 55 degrees at night could save half the natural gas shortage brought on by that winter's frigid temperatures. When Carter ordered the new settings at the White House his wife Rosalynn pled for some relief, but after the president refused to yield, she purchased long underwear, which she wore for the rest of the winter.[6] To further demonstrate the urgency of energy policy, Carter promised he would present a comprehensive energy plan in 90 days.

Preparation of the plan was led by James Schlesinger, who under Nixon and Ford was the Chairman of the Atomic Energy Commission, Director of the Central Intelligence Agency, and Secretary of Defense before being dismissed from Ford's cabinet in 1975. By the time the plan was presented in two prime-time nationally televised addresses in April, it included 113 components, going well beyond the Ford energy proposals in complexity. Carter told Schlesinger the first draft was "extremely complicated (I can't understand it). . . . A crucial element is *simplicity*. Even perfect equity can't be sold if Americans can't understand it."[7]

The complexity problem was partially resolved with the help of Admiral Hyman Rickover, Carter's legendary boss during the development of the Navy's nuclear submarines, who sent the president a short note sketching out ideas for the speech just days before the unveiling of the energy plan. He called for sacrifices for the common good and said the energy challenge should be considered (borrowing the words of William James) "the moral equivalent of war—except that we will be uniting our efforts to build—not destroy." The day before the address, Carter wrote the new language into the draft of his speech.[8]

Carter believed a war was necessary because the world's oil reserves were being rapidly depleted, necessitating strong measures to avoid a major catastrophe. He based his view, in part, on a classified study by the Central Intelligence Agency, released by the White House. Its assessment of future oil supplies was dire. It predicted a sharp reduction in Soviet Union oil production within several years, turning it from an exporter to a major importer of oil. New supplies from Alaska and the North Sea off Britain and Norway would help for several years, but the world then had few places to turn for additional oil. The only major option was Saudi Arabia, which had the potential to double its capacity and offset growing demand through the mid-1980s. The agency doubted, however, "the Saudis will be able, or willing, do to so." "Wanting to conserve their valuable resource and having no immediate need for money," it said, "the Saudis have no economic incentives to expand production." The analysis identified "greatly increased conservation" as the only viable alternative to energy and economic disruptions.[9]

The principal objective of Carter's war was reducing oil imports to six million barrels a day by 1985, well under the nine million in 1977 and even further below consensus forecasts for the mid-1980s. The major weapon would be reducing energy use. "Conservation is the only way that we can buy a barrel of oil for about $2," he told his audience. "It costs about $13 to waste it."

Unlike previous presidents, Carter embraced gasoline taxes as a way to curtail the wasteful use of oil. In mid-February, he wrote "good" next to a recommendation for a gasoline tax, ignoring the political risk of the measure.

Despite opposition from key advisors, Carter decided to go with an increase of five cents per gallon a year up to a cumulative cap of 50 cents. If goals to reduce oil imports were met, the tax would be postponed or even rescinded. Revenues from the tax would be rebated to the American people progressively through the federal income tax system and by direct payments to people who did not pay taxes. Carter also proposed a complex tax on crude oil that was expected to raise the cost of gasoline an additional seven cents a gallon. Because such taxes were regressive, he proposed rebating this tax on a per capita basis.

Carter's other tax targeted autos failing to meet mileage efficiency standards. Proceeds from the tax on gas guzzlers would be rebated to purchasers of cars produced in the United States getting better mileage than the standards mandated.

Carter also offered carrots in the form of tax breaks to encourage alternative energy. He called for generous tax credits for installing solar equipment, ranging from traditional roof-top collectors for heating water to the newer photovoltaic cells developed by NASA for its space missions to convert solar rays into electricity. The president penned into a late draft of the speech a specific goal the public could understand—to "use solar in more than two and a half million homes."[10] He proposed tax credits for businesses that installed energy-saving equipment and homeowners who installed additional insulation (an idea proposed by Ford but not adopted by Congress).

Carter advocated tax breaks for alcohol-blended fuels to run cars and other vehicles as well—the newest idea in the speech. The state of Nebraska took the lead on researching alcohol fuels early in the decade. Making what was then called "gasohol" generally involved converting the starch in corn to sugar, which was then fermented into alcohol (a process familiar to those who made corn liquor in a still), and finally blended with gasoline. Carter proposed a four-cent tax credit for a gallon of gasohol, a mix of 90 percent gasoline and 10 percent alcohol (190 proof or higher). This formula meant each gallon of pure ethanol would yield 40 cents in tax credits after blending. Gasohol (now called ethanol) could run traditional vehicles, utilize American grains, and displace foreign oil.

The energy plan included tougher federal efficiency standards for vehicles, requiring autos to go above 27.5 mpg after 1985 and establishing new standards for light trucks weighing up to 10,000 pounds—both measures extending coverage of the 1975 energy legislation.

There were over a hundred other ideas in the "moral equivalent of war," but two areas stood out as particularly controversial. Carter consistently endorsed the use of light water reactors to generate nuclear power (while strongly opposing the more expensive and more dangerous breeder reactors), but showed his sensitivity to nuclear opponents by sometimes calling nuclear energy a "last resort." Such language infuriated the nuclear industry, but he on other occasions left it out (at the urging of Schlesinger), making environmental organizations just as mad.

The other political hotbed was the debate over ending government controls on the prices of oil and natural gas. Though Carter encouraged the oil patch states during the closing days of his presidential campaign to believe he would support easing out controls, his plan angered the forces of deregulation. Carter and Schlesinger feared deregulating oil would let the OPEC cartel set the price for domestic oil, allow oil and gas companies to garner unearned profits, and adversely impact consumers and the rate of inflation. The administration believed the problem in energy was not having a regulatory system, but rather how that system kept prices too low. Cheap prices were politically popular, but did not account for the costs of bringing new sources of oil and gas to the market. They also discouraged conservation. The energy plan called for regulated prices to rise gradually, but did not provide for the market to set prices for either oil or gas.

The scope of the Carter energy program was impressive, but would the public and Congress be able to deal with the sheer volume of proposals, the view that substantial amounts of energy were being wasted, and the venture into sensitive issues like gasoline taxes?

HOUSES DIVIDED

Two prime-time addresses within three nights and an administration media blitz produced generally favorable reactions to Carter's energy plan. Polls showed the number of people calling the energy crisis "serious" rose five points to reach 86 percent. Many elements of the plan were popular, particularly the tax credit for home insulation and the gas guzzler tax.[11]

Reactions from the political parties fell along generally predictable lines. North Carolina's Democratic Governor Jim Hunt observed, "If anyone has any doubts of a crisis, they must be blind and deaf. That was the most carefully reasoned statement of an immense problem that I've ever heard." Senator Jackson vowed, "We are going to pass a comprehensive energy program without any doubt," though he questioned whether a gasoline tax would really cut consumption. Republican reaction to the plan was mixed. GOP National Committee chair Bill Brock organized a televised response to the president's proposals that endorsed some of their principles but challenged new taxes on gasoline and grim predictions on oil reserves.

New York Times columnist James Reston reflected the view on many editorial pages that the Carter program demonstrated political courage. He wrote that Carter's "attack on reckless waste, his insistence on conserving energy, his willingness to face some of the most powerful industrial forces of the nation, and his solemn appeals for cooperation in the long-range interests of the country have impressed the capital and won the respect even of many men and women who disagree with his proposals."[12]

Automakers criticized the gas guzzler tax, but were more open to the Carter plan than expected. Thomas Murphy, chairman of General Motors, said that with a $15 billion redesign of its product line and new family-sized cars a foot shorter and 700 pounds lighter than their predecessors, "We are on a course that is certainly in great consonance with what the President and his advisers have in mind . . . I am convinced that what's best for this country will be best for General Motors."[13]

Other indicators presaged future problems for the Carter plan. Opinion polls showed clear opposition to the gasoline tax and a feeling the overall plan failed to call for "equality of sacrifice on a fair basis," because the burden fell more heavily on some people than others.

As anticipated, some affected business groups disputed parts of the energy plan. The Natural Gas Supply Committee reflected a prevailing view in the oil and gas industry when it complained that not allowing the free market to spur the search for new supplies because they were finite was "like a man who's realized . . . he's going to die someday—who decided not to take his vitamins anymore." National Coal Association president Carl Bagge called the plan "a blueprint for disaster," because environmental restrictions were "tightening the screws" on the industry at a time it was expected to produce much more.[14]

The *Times'* William Safire blistered Carter's "Malthusian energy program," as a case of "flim-flam" because Carter had violated a campaign pledge to deregulate new natural gas. An editorial cartoon in the *Worthington Daily Globe* (MN) pictured Carter as Moses with hammer in hand building an ark, as bystanders snickered while ignoring a massive dark cloud on the horizon called "Energy Disaster."[15]

Initial legislative action on the energy plan belied the common perception that Carter and Congress were always at loggerheads. On August 2, both houses of Congress passed Carter's proposal for a new Department of Energy by wide margins. Two days later, Carter signed the bill and announced (to no one's surprise) the nomination of Schlesinger as the first energy secretary. Later the same day, the Senate confirmed him by acclamation.

Even more impressive, the Carter energy plan sped through the House of Representatives after new Speaker O'Neill took the unprecedented step of forming an ad hoc Committee on Energy to oversee the work of the 17 standing committees and subcommittees that would have to report out (and could potentially stymie) the thick package of bills. One casualty in the House was the gasoline tax, which was first weakened and then voted down on the floor by a margin of better than seven to one.

The energy package, with some differences from the original Carter plan, passed the House in August by a comfortable 244-177 margin, just before the summer recess. The swift victory earned accolades in the press for O'Neill and Carter. Schlesinger called the Massachusetts politician "the greatest Speaker of the House in the modern era." According to syndicated columnist Joseph Kraft, "That praise expresses an admiration verging on reverence that is widely felt for O'Neill's performance in managing the President's energy program." With the signing of the bill creating the Energy Department on August 4 and the House completing action on energy legislation the next day, the cover story's headline in the next *Time* magazine trumpeted a "Clean Sweep for Jimmy."[16]

The Senate was a different matter. New Majority Leader Robert Byrd (D-WV) had to accept the jurisdictions of powerful standing committees. More importantly, the body was sharply divided on whether to decontrol natural gas prices. The impasse stymied progress on other parts of the package. Frustrated by legislative delays, Carter announced on November 4 the cancellation of a 25,000-mile foreign trip covering four continents so he could stay home to push for his energy package.

Four days later, the president delivered a nationally televised address on energy—his fourth of the year. He complimented Congress for coming to "grips with some of the most complex and difficult decisions that a legislative body has ever been asked to make." He warned that "excessive importing of foreign oil is a tremendous and rapidly increasing drain on our nation's economy" and making "the very security of our nation increasingly dependent on uncertain energy supplies." He called his energy plan "a good insurance policy for the future, in which relatively small premiums that we pay today will protect us in the years ahead."

Carter's strenuous effort could not break the logjam over natural gas. On December 10, Byrd announced he had given up hope of passing the energy package in 1977, and two days later Carter agreed. With almost all issues other than natural gas resolved, Carter's first year in office came close to producing banner results in energy legislation. With the energy package held up, however, the *Washington Post* reflected the general view, when it called congressional inaction "a deeply damaging defeat for Mr. Carter," because "it was the President's top priority, launched last spring . . . to address 'the greatest challenge our country will face in our lifetimes.'"[17]

Failure to pass the plan was a particularly hard blow, since U.S. oil imports in 1977 had grown by 1.5 million barrels a day—the biggest jump in history. Imports now stood at 48 percent of consumption—the tenth straight year the share rose and more than double than when Nixon took office.

When consideration of the energy package resumed early in 1978, both sides of the natural gas debate began to seek middle ground. But, with no end-of-year deadline in sight, work on the legislation had lost its sense of urgency. Through the fall, the House and the Senate inched toward a gradual plan for deregulating natural gas prices and a comprehensive energy strategy.

The natural gas compromise attracted fierce attacks in the House. O'Neill had to quell a late effort to split off the natural gas compromise and likely make the whole package impossible to pass. He suffered a setback when the Rules Committee on October 12 tied on two votes to keep the package intact. The next day, after calls from Carter and O'Neill, Representative Bernie Sisk switched his vote. The California Democrat said he became convinced the energy bill was needed to bolster the value of the dollar and that he would not be a party to killing it. The reversal in committee cleared the omnibus bill for a climactic vote later that afternoon on whether to consider a single bill, which would virtually assure passage.

On the floor, Republican moderate John Anderson, fighting for a separate vote on natural gas, cited the range of organizations opposing the compromise, from the AFL-CIO to the U.S. Chamber of Commerce. Democratic stalwart Richard Bolling countered that at stake was "the national interest, not the sum of the special interests." After the full House took its customary 15 minutes to vote, the tally stood tied 200 to 200. The next five minutes produced new votes and one switch. Once the proponents of keeping the bill intact gained a 207-206 majority, O'Neill slammed down his gavel and declared the motion had carried.

At the next day's Saturday session, the Senate took up its final part of the energy package. Beating back an attempted filibuster, the Senate easily passed its final section of the energy plan 60 to 17. The House, eager to adjourn, then quickly took up the final energy package at 2:40 A.M. Sunday morning. After four hours of debate, the bill passed by a comfortable margin just before the break of dawn. A year later than expected, substantial portions of the Carter energy plan had passed the Congress.

The final package did not contain Carter's taxes on gasoline and crude oil. Also missing were the toughening of auto efficiency after 1985. So, did this lengthy struggle produce important results?

Senator Robert Morgan (D-NC) praised the adoption of the new tax breaks for gasohol, suggesting it would allow the United States to "grow our oil" after the Arab sands went dry. Gasohol was not the only alternative energy source to get tax incentives. Homeowners could get tax credits of up to $300 for installing solar, wind, or geothermal equipment. Businesses also could get tax credits for using alternative fuels. Similarly, insulation and other conservation equipment could earn generous tax credits for homeowners and businesses.

In addition to these carrots, the final legislation contained some big sticks. The gas guzzler tax survived (though not with the rebate to more efficient cars) and remains in effect today. Less noticed, the energy package toughened restrictions on the use of gas or oil in the generation of electricity and empowered the energy secretary to order the use of other fuels in existing plants when feasible (authority the Carter administration used).

Also, the agreement to higher natural gas prices signaled that the government no longer believed that low energy prices were the only goal of national energy policy. Conservation also needed to be considered.

The *Washington Post* gave the 1978 energy package better reviews than the one passed in 1975. It called the new legislation "the great overshadowing accomplishment of the 95th Congress."[18] But it was really the combination of both massive energy bills that put U.S. energy on a new footing. It was now the policy of the federal government to wean the country off the use of oil by means of conservation and the development of alternative fuels. There were now specific policies in place to achieve what Nixon first called "Project Independence."

There was other good news on the energy front coming from Alaska. The first oil from the giant Prudhoe Bay fields finally reached the end of the pipeline at Valdez late in the evening, July 28, 1977. The first delivery was transferred several days later into an Atlantic Richfield Company (ARCO) tanker for delivery to a refinery at Cherry Point, Washington. But it was not until 1978 that the pipeline carried enough crude to have a major impact on American markets. By April, it was delivering over one million barrels a day, suddenly making Alaskan oil about one-seventh of total domestic production. The continuing decline in production in the lower 48 states was more than offset by the latest American "elephant" in Alaska. United States oil production grew by half a million barrels a day in 1978, the first increase since 1970.

With a fairly modest 2 percent growth in petroleum demand, the new production allowed the United States to cut oil imports. The share of foreign oil dropped from 46.5 percent the previous year to 42.5 percent in 1978. The price for a gallon of gasoline rose a penny to 63 cents in 1978, but, controlled for inflation, fell eight cents. With a fresh set of energy policies in place and new oil flowing from Alaska, the stage appeared set for a recovery from the blow of the Arab oil embargo. But as final passage of Carter's energy package absorbed the attention of energy experts in Washington, events across the globe raised the possibility that American fuel supplies were about to get another jolt, every bit as serious as the embargo.

AMERICA'S SECOND ENERGY CRISIS

When the second great flurry of energy legislation passed on October 15, Carter responded, "We have declared to ourselves and to the world our intent to control our use of energy and thereby to control our own destiny as a nation." Yet near the end of a joyous signing ceremony on November 9, Schlesinger inserted the celebration's only cautionary note. "At a time where a single country in the Middle East in turmoil can cause difficulties for the entire industrialized world," he observed, "we shall have to do better."

Between passage and signing, Carter and Schlesinger learned of a new problem—a strike of Iranian oil workers cutting production by 600,000 barrels a day. The disruption threatened the reign of the Shah of Iran, who had been trying to put down local revolts through most of the year and needed oil revenues to support his lavish style of rule. Though a minor share of Iran's total production, the deficit still equaled 1 percent of total world oil supplies. The White House and Congress had been working for almost two years to get new energy legislation. New troubles in Iran meant there would be no time to take an easy victory lap.

The Shah tried to restore oil production, but output by the second week of November reached a low of 900,000 barrels a day, barely enough for Iran's domestic needs. The loss to the world market of five million barrels a day from Iran constituted a twelfth of total world production before the strikes began.

The Iranian government then offered returning workers wage boosts of 40 percent and achieved some success in restoring production in the following weeks. But the Shah's major opponent, religious leader Ayatollah Khomeini, personally endorsed the strikes the first week of December, igniting a new wave of shut-downs.

At its annual December meeting, OPEC, reflecting on the new oil shortage, raised its prices yet again, this time by an unexpectedly large 14 percent. The situation in Iran became even more chaotic after the OPEC meeting. On the 23rd, an American oil executive was assassinated, prompting the exodus of foreign oil technicians. Oil production dropped so low that some domestic needs for kerosene—used for lighting and cooking—and for gasoline went unmet. With Iran's continuing inability to export oil, the loss to the world market was greater than at the peak of the 1973 embargo.

Considering the magnitude of the oil shortage, American policymakers adopted a rather languid approach to the energy implications of the problem. Turmoil in Iran broke out during an avalanche of other important developments around the world. The follow-up to the Camp David peace talks between Egypt and Israel demanded a monumental amount of effort and attention. But even issues like civil war in Namibia, steps to normalize relations with China (announced on December 15), a Libyan invasion of Chad, border clashes between Nicaragua and Costa Rica, warfare between Christians and Muslims in Lebanon, the fight for majority rule in Rhodesia, efforts to stop Pakistan from gaining the ability to produce weapons-grade uranium, and attempts to diffuse Greek/Turkish tensions on Cyprus all demanded attention from the foreign policy establishment and distracted from the disintegration in Iran.

In addition, there was an important reason not to panic over the prospects for a global oil shortage—production increases in Saudi Arabia. The Saudis took the public position that they were continuing to produce at their official OPEC ceiling of 8.5 million barrels a day, shielding them from criticism by other Arab nations. But, in fact, U.S. officials knew the world's leading exporter had raised its output to over ten million barrels a day after the strikes in Iran broke out. For the time being, the Saudis were offsetting some of the loss from across the Persian Gulf.

In the first week of 1979, Schlesinger told the president that the collapse of oil production in Iran "does not pose substantial problems in the short term." According to the Energy Secretary, the shortfall from Iran could be offset primarily by the surge production from Saudi Arabia. Extra production by the Saudis and others, he asserted (correctly), added over three million barrels to supplies—enough to cut the deficit below two million. Schlesinger discouraged Carter from issuing a strong personal plea for conservation, since such action would signal serious government concern. The Secretary believed the risk the public would top off their gasoline and heating-oil tanks outweighed the benefit of a strong conservation effort.[19]

The Shah departed Tehran for Egypt on January 16, claiming he was taking a vacation. He would never return. Khomeini arrived back in Iran on February 1, and a government under his direction took power just 11 days later.

Then, in the last week of January, the major U.S. strategy for dealing with the shortage collapsed. Secretary of State Cyrus Vance informed Carter of a confidential report that the Saudis were cutting back production below ten million barrels a day, news that soon reached the trade and general media.[20]

With the new circumstances, Carter spoke more forcefully about the need for conservation. At a February 2 news conference, the president warned, "The curtailment of Iran's energy supplies . . . underscores the vulnerability about which I spoke when I presented our proposal for a comprehensive energy plan." He briefly called for voluntary efforts to obey the speed limit, again lower thermostats to 65 degrees during the winter, and shift to carpooling and mass transit—measures he called sufficient to offset the reduction in supplies from Iran. To get ready for a major oil shortage, the Energy Department began dusting off its old plans for government allocation of oil.

The Saudis lowered production again in April. The decision to drop below nine million barrels a day became the tipping point that brought back the struggle to get fuel at American service stations. Long lines at the pump suddenly popped up across the state of California in late April—the first such disruptions since the Arab oil embargo. By May 3, the *Los Angeles Times* found lines as long as a mile. The shortages caught many by surprise, since the state had only recently faced a glut of crude oil because of rising deliveries from Alaska.

Almost immediately, Governor Jerry Brown announced an emergency gas plan for his state. To reduce lines at service stations, he proposed fines for dealers topping off tanks more than half full and authorized the odd-even plan from the days of the embargo, allowing motorists to purchase gasoline only on alternate days, based on their license numbers.

As during the Arab embargo, the federal oil allocation rules—in the words of White House policy chief Stuart Eizenstat, "filled with bureaucratic gobbledygook, comprehensible to no one but gas allocation experts"—aggravated the shortage. The base years for allocation were outdated, penalizing fast-growing states like California. In addition, the generous set-asides for the military and agriculture had a particularly severe impact on California drivers. Unlike Nixon, Carter ordered modifications to put the rules in better sync with reality, but in the middle of a new crisis it was difficult to keep up with events.

As things calmed down in California during May, angry motorists found themselves having to queue up on the East Coast. For reasons never fully explained, the scramble for fuel was most severe in the nation's capital. In its May 17 report, the AAA identified Washington as the only area of the country with no gasoline stations open on Sunday. By the second week of June, the vast majority of the District's 1,500 stations were only open two to four hours a day. Even senior White House officials found themselves trapped in frustrating lines. The governors of Maryland and Virginia and the mayor of Washington moved quickly to impose odd-even and minimum purchase requirements in their jurisdictions, hoping to shorten the lines.

Reflecting mushrooming panic at the pump, the May 21 cover of *Newsweek* showed a distraught motorist carrying a gasoline can amid a jam of immobile automobiles with the headline "A Long Dry Summer?" A May Gallup poll showed that 33 percent of the public considered energy the most important problem facing the country, compared to just 14 percent in February. In public concern, energy trailed only inflation, itself closely tied to rising oil prices.[21]

Gas lines spread along the East Coast in early June. Drivers on the Delaware Turnpike encountered caps on purchases of $3 to $4. In New York City, lines that had begun on Friday to beat weekend station closings started to form as early as Wednesday. In extreme cases, it took drivers five hours to refuel. Resort hotels and suburban movie theaters reported drops in business due to the uncertainty of oil supplies. As conditions worsened, odd-even restrictions on purchases became the norm in the Northeastern states.

With a gasoline crisis at home, Carter in June departed for a long-standing commitment to negotiate an arms limitations treaty with Soviet leader Leonid Brezhnev in Vienna and then a few days later for an economic summit in Tokyo. During the trip to Asia, the oil crisis back home worsened. In late June, fuel disruptions sparked a rebellion of commercial truck drivers, hurt by set-asides of diesel fuel for farmers and by delays in federal approval for rate hikes to reflect their higher fuel costs. Strikes by independent drivers stalled deliveries of food, fuel, and other goods, leading to job layoffs in several areas. Eighteen truckers were arrested in Massachusetts for forming a barricade around a produce center supplying 80 percent of New England's fresh fruit and produce. In Florida, blockades of fuel depots added to the gasoline shortages. One oil trucker defying the strike south of Miami attracted a caravan of 25 cars as he made his way to a service station. "I feel like the Pied Piper," he said, when the crowd cheered as he began filling the station's tanks.

The strike drew a quick response from federal and state officials. Nine governors called out state police and the National Guard to shepherd convoys of trucks carrying food and fuel. In Florida, Governor Bob Graham commandeered trucks from private companies and put troops from the Guard on board armed with M-16 rifles.

For its part, the Carter administration agreed to put truckers on a more equal basis with farmers in securing diesel fuel. The White House also continued to work with Senator Edward Kennedy and his staff (including former Harvard economist and later Supreme Court Justice Stephen Breyer) on deregulating prices for the trucking industry, which would allow greater flexibility for passing on fuel costs. Although the trucker strikes were short-lived, they presented a strong negative picture to the public. In internal correspondence on June 29, three White House speech-writers cited the independent trucker strike as "just further evidence that the social fabric is crumbling."[22]

At the end of June, gas lines were springing up in such far-flung locales as St. Louis, New Orleans, Minneapolis, and Charlotte. Even motorists in oil-rich Houston found themselves trapped in the queues. The AAA report of June 29 found the greatest disruptions in Delaware, Pennsylvania, and New Jersey, where more than half of the retail outlets could not provide customers a full selection of gasoline.

A Gallup poll at the height of the crisis found one in five drivers around the country had waited at least a half hour for their last purchase of fuel. But the national figures hid the real story. In rural areas, people refueling faced few delays. In large cities, however, half the drivers waited in line a half hour or more for gasoline, one in seven for at least two hours.[23]

A RENEWED SEARCH FOR SOLUTIONS

The second American oil crisis reinvigorated efforts to find new solutions. The timing of one major decision was dictated by the Energy Conservation and Policy Act, which ended all controls on domestic oil automatically on September 30, 1981, but also gave the president full authority to alter or abolish the pricing system effective June 1, 1979. The bitter struggle over oil price controls was back like a hydra, and Carter would have to make his decision with a big gap in the world's oil supply forcing up prices.

At a Bonn economic summit in July of 1978, Carter committed to raise U.S. oil prices to the world level by the end of 1980 by decontrolling the price of crude oil. As State Department advisors reminded him, failure to deliver on this promise would damage American credibility.[24]

Treasury Secretary Michael Blumenthal became the strongest advocate in the administration for full and unconditional decontrol of domestic oil prices effective June 1. He advised quick action "offers you an opportunity to take complete charge of a major problem, which has been locked in political stalemate for 8 years, and to resolve it in the national interest with a single, bold stroke." Blumenthal argued that, whatever the short-term effects, cutting energy imports by reducing consumption and raising domestic production would help the economy as soon as 1980 and even more so later.[25] After Carter rejected his proposal as "too much all at once," Blumenthal joined Schlesinger and Vance in advocating phased decontrol that would be rapid enough to meet the requirements of the Bonn commitment.[26]

Vice President Walter Mondale and Eizenstat believed the adverse effects of decontrol justified missing the Bonn deadline. The Vice President stated that because people would continue driving despite the higher cost of fuel, there would be little dampening effect on demand from decontrolling oil. Eizenstat said he did not want to risk losing consumer, labor, and Northeastern interests because of decontrol "at a time when significant elements of our base within the Democratic Party are disaffected because of the budget cuts."[27]

The position of Alfred Kahn epitomized the dilemma facing Carter on decontrol. As an academic and state official, he had become known as a great American apostle of the twentieth century for deregulating markets. His current jobs as Advisor on Inflation to the President and chairman of the Council on Wages and Price Stability gave him responsibility for the inflation problem that had bedeviled every administration of the 1970s. Prices were rising faster in 1979 than at any time since the 1940s. Kahn had taken a tough assignment.

Kahn argued the decontrol of oil prices would boost inflation more than indicated by the economic models used by the White House, because reversing the momentum of inflation required holding down the big wage demands of labor unions with large contracts that were up for renegotiation in 1979. Allowing oil prices to rise might be a "last straw" for labor leaders and cost the White House the credibility it needed to restrain wage escalation. As a result, Kahn wanted to stretch out oil decontrol as much as possible, even to the point of amending the law to eliminate the decontrol deadline.

After wrestling with conflicting advice, Carter finally announced in a nationally televised April 5 address drafted by Hendrik Hertzberg that "a phased decontrol of oil prices will begin on June 1 and continue at a fairly uniform rate over the next 28 months." He warned in a line alluding to Napoleon's march into Russia, "Our nation is dangerously dependent on a thin line of tankers stretching half-way around the Earth, originating in the Middle East and around the Persian Gulf, one of the most unstable regions in the world." To cut the risk, the United States would have to stop holding oil prices below its replacement value. Carter didn't try to disguise his position—"This is a painful step, and I'll give it to you straight: Each of us will have to use less oil and pay more for it."

In his April 5 address, Carter also made the case for a windfall profits tax that would buffer the public's complaints it was paying more for oil so producers would gain profits they had not earned. "As Government controls end," he asserted, "prices will go up on oil which has already been discovered, and unless we tax the oil companies, they will reap huge and undeserved windfall profits." He argued that producers would still get substantial new income that would "provide plenty of incentive for increased domestic production."

Carter wanted to put the revenues from the tax in an "energy security fund." The fund would be used "to protect low-income families from energy price increases, to build a more efficient mass transportation system, and to put American genius to work solving our long-range energy problems." He warned that special interest groups would squabble over the proceeds from the tax and urged viewers to make their voice heard so his plan would not be blocked by "the selfishness of a few."

Carter's energy policies of 1979 put more emphasis on increasing energy supplies than did his energy plan two years earlier, a position that was popular in Congress. He proposed supplementing what had become a $3.5 billion annual budget for energy research with part of the windfall profits tax. Gone was his previous hesitancy to spend vast sums on what in the Ford years were called the exotic fuels—solar energy, gasohol, oil shale, and gaseous and liquid fuels made from coal.

At the time of Carter's April 5 energy address, a bold new initiative on solar energy was not quite ready. The dedication of the White House solar system and the announcement of the new solar policy were finally scheduled for June 20. Thirty-two thermal collectors totaling 611 square feet were placed on the roof of the West Wing facing due south at a 33-degree tilt to capture the maximum effects of the sun. Glycol (which would not freeze during the winter) would be run through the system at a rate of 10 gallons a minute to transfer the heat to a 600-gallon water tank in the building. The kitchen of the White House mess would be the primary user of the solar-heated water and would have access to steam heat as a back-up when weather conditions reduced the capacity of the solar system. The solar panels were visible from Pennsylvania Avenue, helping the system, in the words of the staff, "provide a highly visible demonstration of solar energy and the Carter Administration's commitment to alternate energy resources."[28]

In substance, Carter called for the bold goal of generating 20 percent of the nation's energy from renewable energy (a term pretty much interchangeable with solar energy at the time) by the end of the century. He also proposed a variety of tax credits and the creation of a Solar Bank, initially funded at $100 million a year, enough to finance an estimated 100,000 new and retrofitted solar units the first year. Carter's desire to promote solar energy had previously been inhibited by his reluctance to inject more money into a program that had already seen massive increases during the Ford years. Now, the Solar Bank could be funded from the proceeds of the windfall profits tax when approved by Congress.

The president made a stirring case for his new program, saying, "No one can ever embargo the Sun or interrupt its delivery to us." He predicted the solar collectors would still be on the White House, supplying cheap, efficient energy at the end of the century. "A generation from now," he cautioned, "this solar heater can either be a curiosity, a museum piece, an example of a road not taken, or it can be just a small part of one of the greatest and most exciting adventures ever undertaken by the American people: harnessing the power of the Sun to enrich our lives as we move away from crippling dependence on foreign oil." (The collectors were removed from the White House roof in 1986, and one of them now sits on display in the museum of the Carter Library.)

The gas lines forced the president to give yet another talk to the nation on energy. A speech scheduled for July 4 was abruptly cancelled. After intense pleas from his pollster, Pat Caddell, that the nation's problems transcended energy, Carter decided he could not deliver the speech as drafted, in part because it was too similar to his previous major addresses on energy. He stayed at Camp David meeting with a wide variety of

Americans about the state of the nation until July 14, just before his speech the next night.

The first 20 minutes of the eagerly awaited speech focused on a "crisis of confidence" in the United States. Carter lamented that people were losing faith that "the days of our children would be better than our own." He evoked the memories of the United States overcoming the Great Depression, winning two world wars, and putting a man on the moon. He urged Americans to reject the path of "constant conflict between narrow interests ending in chaos and immobility" for a better one of a "common purpose and the restoration of American values."

When he turned to energy, Carter continued to look directly into the camera and declared, with a voice almost shouting, "Beginning this moment, this Nation will never use more foreign oil than we did in 1977—never." He added, "The generation-long growth in our dependence on foreign oil will be stopped dead in its tracks right now and then reversed as we move through the 1980's."

The rest of the speech concentrated on how the United States would meet its objectives for oil. Carter promised to use his presidential authority to set quotas on imports. He also proposed "the most massive peace-time commitment of funds and resources in our Nation's history to develop America's own alternative sources of fuel—from coal, from oil shale, from plant products for gasohol, from unconventional gas, from the Sun." The push for alternative fuels would include an energy security corporation that would lead the effort to replace two-and-a-half million barrels a day of imported oil by 1990. The corporation would issue up to $5 billion in energy bonds to finance its projects.

After Carter finished, several television pundits compared his oratory to a sermon, and ABC's Sam Donaldson called it "an extraordinary performance." Roger Peterson, also of ABC, told viewers the Carter energy plan was "extremely ambitious," committing three times as much to the synthetic fuels as the Apollo project cost. CBS White House correspondent Leslie Stahl said she heard a "new voice" from Carter, "louder" and "firmer" than before. She said the pledge not to import one additional drop of oil was "still echoing in my ears."

With gas lines ebbing during the month, the address helped get the president a modest bump in the polls. But Carter's critics soon branded it the "malaise" speech (a term used by Cadell, but never by Carter). They charged he was blaming the American people for the problems he had created.

MORE WORK TO DO

Carter's 1980 State of the Union address, delivered on January 23—the seventh by an American president since the launching of the Arab oil embargo—stressed the need for a strong American energy policy. No one in the chamber doubted the danger of world reliance on oil from the Persian Gulf. In November, Iranian students had captured American personnel in Tehran, leading to severe U.S. sanctions until the hostages were released. In December, the Soviet Union invaded Afghanistan, which seemed to confirm long-held fears that the Soviets harbored designs on the Persian Gulf.

Though Afghanistan itself did not export oil, it lay dangerously close to the world's great petroleum exporters and abutted the country still holding American hostages. Afghanistan posed, declared Carter, "the most serious threat to the peace since the Second World War." The president welcomed the worldwide condemnation of the "Soviet attempt to extend its colonial domination" and the outrage of the Muslim world over "this aggression against an Islamic people." He also called the Soviet invasion "a grave threat to the free movement of Middle East oil."

Carter said the United States was imposing economic sanctions on the Soviets, cutting its access to advanced technology and agricultural products. He urged as well a U.S. boycott of the 1980 Olympic Games in Moscow. On the diplomatic side, Carter reported that to prevent conflict in the Middle East, the United States was "now engaged in further negotiations to provide full autonomy for the people of the West Bank and Gaza, to resolve the Palestinian issue in all its aspects, and to preserve the peace and security of Israel."

The president also threatened the use of military pressure. He declared, with particular fervor, "An attempt by any outside force to gain control of the Persian Gulf region will be regarded as an assault on the vital interests of the United States of America, and such an assault will be repelled by any means necessary, including military force." He announced, "We are improving our capability to deploy U.S. military forces rapidly to distant areas."

Carter insisted the need for "a clear, comprehensive energy policy" had never been more urgent. "The crises in Iran and Afghanistan have dramatized a very important lesson: Our excessive dependence on foreign oil is a clear and present danger to our Nation's security." Reliance on foreign oil was also damaging the national economy. He said, "The single biggest factor in . . the increase in inflation last year was from one cause: the skyrocketing prices of

OPEC oil." The president said he and Congress had worked together for three years on energy policy and now needed "to complete final action."

❧

Turmoil in the Persian Gulf provided the final impetus to passage of most of Carter's second wave of energy proposals. Congress finally completed action on the windfall profits tax on March 27. The wide margin of passage in both the House and the Senate belied the bill's tough journey through the process. A smiling Carter exulted at an April 2 signing ceremony; "We have faced political attacks, we have faced special interests' pressures, and we have triumphed." At the event, both Senate Leader Byrd and House Ways and Means Chairman Ullman praised Senate Finance Chairman Russell Long (who, along with junior senator from Louisiana Bennett Johnston, voted for the bill) for his "statesmanship" during the lengthy conference proceedings.

The $227 billion bill imposed the largest tax ever on a single U.S. industry. The impacts of the bill went far beyond the tax itself. As Carter suggested at the signing, the tax on the growing profits of the oil industry helped create a climate in which the phase-out of price controls on crude oil could proceed. Each facilitated the success of the other.

The revenues from the taxes also made possible generous incentives to homeowners and businesses who switched to renewable energy. The flagship program increased the tax credit for residential solar, wind, and geothermal equipment to 40 percent. Because the incentive was a credit rather than a deduction, purchasers of solar panels would now have to pay only 60 percent of the cost. The bill also provided a tax credit of $3 a barrel for synthetic fuels if the price of oil fell below $29.50 a barrel, to protect investors from a downturn in prices, and extended the tax break for gasohol from 1984 to 1992.

The windfall profits bill also extended aid to poor families affected by higher energy prices. The initial annual authorization of $3.1 billion was slated for delivery through state governments. Low-income assistance was another part of a package to buffer the impacts of higher prices under decontrol.

In June, Congress passed by overwhelming margins another priority Carter energy proposal—a $20 billion program to spur development of synthetic fuels. Under its provisions, a Synthetic Fuels Corporation would use generous price and loan guarantees to encourage private industries to make substitutes for natural gas and oil from coal, oil shale, tar sands, and water (hydrogen). The act set the goal for 1987 at a hefty 500,000 barrels a day. The act failed to reach the spending levels proposed by Carter, but still constituted a significant reversal of the congressional rejection of similar proposals from President Ford. As it turned out, the synfuels bill marked the end of the last substantial package of energy legislation in the twentieth century.

Iraq versus Iran

Saddam Hussein, having recently formally assumed the presidency of Iraq after years as its de facto leader, on September 7 delivered an address to the Iraqi parliament carried on Baghdad radio. He announced cancellation of a 1975 agreement conceding to Iran's claim that their mutual border laid on the Iraq side of the Shatt-el-Arab estuary (an extension of the confluence of the Tigris and Euphrates rivers) rather than the mid-point, as the Iraqis had long claimed. Iraq was forced to accept the humiliating concession as part of a bargain that Iran under the Shah (and indirectly the United States and Israel) would terminate support for the Kurdish insurrection in Iraq. The location of the boundary was vital to both countries, since the waterway was the vital pathway to the Persian Gulf for oil produced in both countries. With Iran's army weakened after the fall of the Shah, Saddam saw an opportunity to get revenge.

The conflict was stoked by memories of conflicts over thousands of years. Saddam evoked ancient battles between Mesopotamia and Elam to rouse his troops. Personal hostility between Saddam and Khomeini, who had been forced out of exile in Iraq in 1978, further fueled the combat. Hussein accused the Ayatollah of using Islam to advance "Persian expansionist ambitions." Radio broadcasts from Iran referred to Iraq's leaders as "a bunch of atheist charlatans" and to Saddam as a "Zionist American stooge."

On the 22nd, nine Iraqi divisions crossed Shatt-el-Arab into Iran's western province of Khuzestan. The area was an attractive target due to its abundant oil, large Arab population, and location on the Iraqi side of the Zagros Mountains, which made it less accessible to Iran's army. The attack quickly expanded toward the Persian Gulf, setting the giant refinery at Abadan ablaze and bombing oil storage tanks on Kharg Island.

The invasion caught Iran by surprise. Moreover, its army had recently purged much of its leadership and considerable equipment purchased by the Shah was being held by the Americans. Still, Iran responded more quickly and forcefully than Saddam or most outside observers expected. Its air force was able to bomb targets deep into Iraq and the government was able to mobilize zealous volunteers to repel the enemy. The Iranians, like the Iraqis, took particular aim at oil facilities. Its jets quickly began inflicting damage across Iraq, including the wells at Basra just across the border and the oil refinery in northern Kirkuk. Moreover, Syria, in support of Iran, cut off one of Iraq's two major oil pipelines to the West, and the other, through Turkey, was impeded by the Kurds.[29]

Within weeks, the war cut off the export of almost all of the world's oil from Iran and Iraq. In the months before the attack from Iraq, oil production in revolutionary Iran had fallen to only a quarter of the peak under the Shah, but Iraq had been producing in excess of three million barrels a day. The combined losses from the two antagonists due to the attacks stood in October at about four million barrels a day, eerily similar to those during the Arab embargo and the Iranian revolution. It appeared the United States might face its third energy crisis in just seven years.

The president attempted to allay fears about the Iran–Iraq war at a September 23 news conference in Tacoma, Washington. He vowed the United States was "staying neutral completely" and called on the Soviet Union to "stay out of any involvement in this area." On the matter of most immediate concern, he reported, "As far as I know, there is no direct effect on the life or safety of the hostages."

He painted an optimistic picture of the likely impacts of the interruption in oil deliveries, largely because the United States was importing two million barrels a day less than the year before. "This new energy policy that we've put through for conservation and producing more American energy," he bragged, "is paying off." The time lags between new policies, new investments, and actual production made it unlikely they were having much impact on production, but policies on Alaska during Nixon's first term were also helping.

Carter was right. The United States was better prepared than before to weather disruptions in international oil deliveries. The drop in U.S. imports (along with additional cuts in Europe and Japan) made the country less vulnerable to oil crises. Good diplomatic relations leading to production increases in Saudi Arabia, Kuwait, the United Arab Emirates, and

Nigeria also helped. The first elements of a new era of American energy independence, though dimly seen at the time, were beginning to emerge.

The good news was overwhelmed in the public mind by the bad news. The hostages were not released until January 20, 1981. Spurred by raging oil prices, inflation in 1980 ran even higher than in 1979. The two years marked the highest growth in U.S. inflation in recorded history. Both issues could hardly have been more visible to the American people.

Many commentators view the hostage issue as Carter's major liability in the 1980 presidential election. I take a different view. It was the inflation (along with its side effects, like record-high interest rates) that loomed largest with voters. Most careful observers would conclude that it would be impossible for any president to win reelection with the inflation rates of 1979–1980. And Carter didn't.

THE END OF CONTROLS

Ronald Reagan completed the chapter of post-embargo energy policy, shortly after replacing Carter as chief executive. In his first 10 days in office, the new president announced immediate decontrol of crude oil and gasoline. "For more than 9 years," he said, "restrictive price controls have held U.S. oil production below its potential, artificially boosted energy consumption, aggravated our balance of payments problems, and stifled technological breakthroughs." He predicted that ending controls would "promote prudent conservation and vigorous domestic production."

Reagan's rapid decontrol of oil was hardly surprising, after a season of campaign rhetoric devoted to the evils of overregulation by government. Yet many officials of the 1970s wanted to bring an end to the price controls and backed off due to fears of a sudden run-up in prices. With world oil supplies still limited by the war between Iraq and Iran, the lifting of controls remained politically controversial. New Jersey's energy commissioner quickly charged that Reagan's order would "fan the fires of inflation."[30]

People in the oil industry generally supported decontrol. The president of the Texas Independent Producers Association, for one, said the nearly 10 years of federal regulation reminded him "of a fellow in a fight with one hand tied completely behind him and the other hand partially crippled." By contrast, some small refiners and independent station owners had sought government controls to protect them from the major oil companies. They predicted chaos from abrupt decontrol and the likelihood major oil companies would skew supplies to their own stations, now able to earn greater profits.[31]

In the first week after decontrol, Exxon increased the prices of gasoline and heating oil twice, first by three cents and then by another five cents a gallon. Other companies took similar action, arguing they needed to compensate for their inability to fully pass on the cost of crude oil in 1980. Indeed, soaring energy costs, attributed to Reagan's sudden decontrol in press coverage, helped push up the Consumer Price Index by a full percentage point in February.

The tide turned with April reports of declining gasoline prices. Prices at the pump peaked in March at $1.39 a gallon (equivalent to $3.30 in 2007 prices and at the end of 2007 still considered the record high by the Energy Information Administration). They then began a gradual descent through 1981. By December, a gallon was fetching $1.35. It was far from a market revolution, but after years of painful increases, any decrease was welcome.

"Results"

"What concerns me [about the energy problem is] lots of people with ideas but no action. *I want results,*" President Ford told his energy advisors (according to notes of the meeting) just a few weeks after taking office.[32] The sentiment is refreshing in an era when political rhetoric often overshadows substantive action.

Ford and Carter chose to make reductions in oil imports the central goal of their energy policies, even when political prudence might have suggested they speak with less specificity. It is a commonly held perception that the United States continued merrily on its way into further energy dependence despite the warnings of the 1970s. It is time to reexamine the results. Whether the goals of the 1970s were successful or not affects how we try to solve today's energy problems.

Well, the key numbers are pretty astounding. In 1977, the United States imported 8.6 million barrels a day of oil (net). In 1982, the number had shrunk to 4.3 million barrels a day—half as much. Looking at it another way, net imports made up 47 percent of consumption in 1977. By 1982, the share had fallen to 28 percent.

Some of the internal numbers are even more impressive. The OPEC share of American oil consumption dropped from 34 percent to 17 percent.

The Arab OPEC share (the oil embargoed in 1973) fell from 17 percent to 6 percent.

These results will strike many as counterintuitive. In 1977, the share of imported oil had been rising for 10 straight years, and the trend appeared inexorable. In addition, the cuts in imports exceeded the goals set by presidents and congressional leaders. This was a case of politicians delivering *more* than they promised.

Americans paid a massive price to achieve these results, but the benefits of reducing oil imports were also immense. With reduced oil demand from the United States, Europe, and Japan, world oil trade switched from a seller's market to a buyer's market. Motorists started to see drops in prices at the pump. Lower energy prices contributed to defusing inflationary pressures in the economy.

The benefits also had a national security component. The United States was in a stronger position to deal with wars in the Persian Gulf, such as the battle between Iraq and Iran. Less money was shipped to unstable regimes. If states like Libya sponsored terrorism, the industrialized nations could impose sanctions with less harm to themselves.

If Rip Van Winkle had awakened from a five-year slumber in 1982, he might have asked, "Where did the energy problem go?"

_e_⁀

How do we explain the dramatic decline in oil imports? The surge in Alaskan production played a big role. Oil production in the United States in 1982 ran about half a million barrels a day higher than five years earlier, since Alaska more than offset the continuing decline in the lower 48 states. New production in the North Sea and Mexico, while not reducing American imports, did weaken the power of OPEC in world markets. These increases were not brought on by decontrol of domestic prices. As noted MIT economist M. A. Adelman has carefully documented, the lead times for these wells were too long to have been affected by the actions of Reagan or even Carter.[33] The major breakthrough in the building of the Alaska pipeline came with congressional approval in 1973.

About a quarter of the drop in oil imports can be attributed to declining use of oil to generate electricity. Consumption of electricity was somewhat higher in 1982, but its rapid growth had slowed substantially due to factors like better insulation of buildings (encouraged by federal tax credits) and higher prices. The biggest story was the displacement of oil (ordered in many cases by federal mandates) by other fuels, most notably coal and nuclear power. Though little noticed, backing oil out of electric generation played the largest role in reducing oil imports.

Reduced use of oil to heat buildings (particularly homes) was almost as big. With higher prices and federal incentives for insulation and other conservation equipment, use of heating oil plunged by about 900,000 barrels (42 percent) a day.

Motor vehicles furnish most of the remaining explanation for the big drops in imported oil. Consumption of gasoline dropped 600,000 barrels a day (9 percent) from 1977 to 1982, despite expectations it would grow. Again, price played a part, encouraging people to drive less and buy high-mileage cars, but by 1982, distances were again on the upswing. It was during the early 1980s that the federal efficiency standards (passed under Ford and expedited by rules adopted by the Carter administration) had their greatest impact. Alaskan production, backing oil out of electric generation, reduced use of oil to heat buildings, and more efficient vehicles—all made major contributions to energy independence.

Ending the price controls helped cut reliance on foreign oil, but so did enlightened government action. Laissez-faire economists will take umbrage at the idea that government mandates could play any useful role in promoting energy independence. They will argue that a weak economy better explains the drops in oil use. The slow growth of the economy (about 1 percent a year in inflation-adjusted dollars) did dampen energy demand. But it is hard to attribute a 50 percent *cut* in oil imports to slow economic *growth*.

There are several valuable lessons from this forgotten story of regaining energy independence. First, there are no quick fixes, but there are fixes. It generally takes at least two to six years for positive effects of federal legislation to have much impact (and longer for investments in research and development). Any politician who promises immediate results is probably going to make things worse.

Second, there are no silver bullets for winning energy independence, but there is plenty of silver buckshot. Some trumpeted solutions to the energy crisis, such as making liquid transportation fuels from coal, played no role at all. Even the largest contributors could not turn around a major trend by themselves. Those who want to wage "the moral equivalent of war" must attack on many fronts.

There is one problem with winning a war. People soon want to settle back to life as usual, and complacency sets in. After losing energy independence in 1970, it took America a dozen years to regain it. It would take 17 years to lose it.

Chapter 3

Lapsing Back into Oil Addiction: Retreating from Battle under Presidents Reagan, Bush, Clinton, and Bush

America's return to energy independence in 1982 was difficult to achieve. Once won, however, the momentum of victory carried on for many years. With energy no longer a problem, presidents no longer went on prime-time television to call for strong action on energy. Also missing were great debates in Congress over the nation's energy future. As the United States entered the twenty-first century, though, energy became a major problem again. A hard-earned energy independence slipped away for a second time. How did it happen? Could things have turned out differently?

"DISMANTLE IT, ALL OF IT"

Ronald Reagan made clear during the 1980 presidential elections that he wanted to chart a different course on energy. Campaigning in Florida in

March, he complained, "They say, 'Turn down the thermostat, drive less, or don't drive at all.'" What was really needed, he said, was to return to the days before 1971 price controls and "set the oil industry loose." He expressed great optimism about American oil production: "The U.S. Geological Survey says that the potential for Alaska alone is greater than the proven reserves of Saudi Arabia."[1] Reagan's comments ranged from analysis supported by most economists (the utility of market forces in setting prices) to the preposterous (the size of Alaskan reserves).

The Republican Party platform of 1980 challenged energy orthodoxies with broad support in both political parties. The author of the energy plank, Michigan Congressman David Stockman, acknowledged that many senior GOP legislators had voted for the programs under attack—the windfall profits tax, the synfuels corporation, deep tax credits for alternative energy, mandatory efficiency standards for cars and refrigerators, and fuel allocation. "While much of the Republican herd had gone for this nonsense," he remembered of the exercise, "they were now about to get new marching orders: *Dismantle it, all of it.*"[2]

After Reagan was inaugurated, Stockman became his budget director and the principle theorist of a major reversal in energy strategy. Though the Reagan revolution fell short of what Stockman wanted, the government increasingly relied more on free markets and less on government programs to deal with energy.

While in Congress, Stockman attacked the goals of Nixon, Ford, and Carter to make the country more self-sufficient in energy. "One of the most pernicious forces loose in Washington," he wrote in a 1979 column in the *Washington Post,* "is the widely shared belief in the need for national energy independence." Despite the "deceptive allure" of energy independence, he valued the virtues of free trade and "unfettered production of capitalist wealth" with "the expansion of private welfare that automatically attends it" over reducing the risk of depending on foreign oil.[3] His dissent, which sounded so out of place in the 1970s, came to dominate thinking in Washington over the next two decades.

After failing to abolish the Department of Energy, Reagan still brought dramatic changes to the agency through the appropriations process. His 1985 budget for the department was slightly higher than the one Carter had proposed for 1982, but reflected sharply different priorities. Reagan halved the energy part of the budget including conservation, alternative fuels, and energy information, while doubling expenditures for the nuclear weapons program. The budget, staffing, and culture of DOE increasingly reflected its origins in the Atomic Energy Commission rather than the vision of Jackson, Nixon, Ford, and Carter for a comprehensive agency focusing on civilian energy.

Few energy innovations of the Carter years escaped the onslaught of the Reagan forces. During his first month in office, Reagan ordered an end to restrictions on federal buildings mandating a maximum temperature of 65 degrees in the winter and 78 in the summer.

The Solar Bank was a signature issue of the Carter presidency and one of its major legislative victories. Shortly after taking office, Reagan fired the bank's staff and proposed its budget be zeroed out. He further recommended deep cuts in the research and development budget for solar. He argued that market pricing of oil and tax breaks should provide adequate incentives for the growth of solar energy. Congress finally provided three years of appropriations for the Solar Bank, and a federal district court ordered Reagan to begin operations.

Despite Stockman's view that special interests were successfully protecting programs like solar, the Reagan administration won a major share of its battles to cut financing for solar and other forms of alternative energy. By his second term, programs to finance specific projects had virtually disappeared. Residential solar tax credits expired at the end of 1985 and were not renewed. The next summer, the solar panels at the White House, dedicated with great fanfare by Carter, were removed during roof repairs and not reinstalled, after the White House concluded they were not cost-effective.

Appropriations for energy research and development continued their slide from the heady days of post-embargo budgets. From 1976 to 1980, Congress devoted over 10 percent of all R&D spending to energy. In Reagan's second term—with attention shifting to defense, space, and health—the energy share fell below 4 percent.[4] The budget for solar research and development was less than a quarter of its peak under Carter.

The Republican platform called for an end to the 55-mph speed limit—the first major policy response to the Arab oil embargo. But the federal limit, viewed as having additional value as a safety measure, retained enough political support to survive Reagan's first term. Reagan was successful, however, slashing funding for states to enforce the law and compliance levels required for states to avoid sanctions. With lax enforcement and drivers less concerned about conserving fuel, the impact of the speed limit on driving behavior steadily diminished. In two measures passed during

Reagan dramatically reversed most of the energy initiatives of his predecessors.

Source: Reagan Presidential Library

the second term, Congress eased the speed limits to 65 mph for rural Interstates and other rural road built to Interstate standards.

For Reagan, it was new energy domestic production rather than conservation that would turn the tide against energy imports. Nowhere was the Reagan approach more clear than his efforts to open up drilling on the Outer Continental Shelf. The push to drill offshore was led by Interior Secretary James Watt. Nixon, Ford, and Carter had all pushed for more offshore drilling outside the traditional areas of the Gulf of Mexico, consistent with the assessment of most petroleum geologists that the potential there was great. The presidents of the 1970s emphasized a balance between new production and environmental protection, but Watt wanted to move the fulcrum of that balance.

Watt announced ambitious goals for an accelerated leasing program in April of 1981. By the fall, the Sierra Club had gathered 1 million signatures on a petition calling for Watt's ouster. The final version of his program, released in July of 1982, called for the sale over a five-year period of nearly 1 billion acres to the oil industry—20 times the total area offered since offshore leasing began in 1954. The secretary justified the aggressive program by noting, "It is much easier to explain to the American people why we have oil rigs off our coast than it would be to explain to mothers and fathers of this land why their sons are fighting on the sands of the Middle East as might be required if the policies of our critics were to be pursued."[5] Many coastal states and local governments threatened legal suits against the Watt plan. Members of Congress opposed to Watt began attaching riders to appropriations bills banning oil and gas leasing off the coasts of California, Florida, and Massachusetts. Watt resigned in 1983, with his beleaguered leasing plan in shambles.

MORE PROBLEMS IN THE PERSIAN GULF

Oil supplies seemed more than adequate during Reagan's first term, but it was not because conflict in the Persian Gulf had gone away. He inherited a war between Iraq and Iran that continued through most of his second term. The two protagonists continued attacking each other's oil facilities. During the worst years of the war, the two OPEC members were producing 4.5 million barrels a day below their levels before the Iranian revolution.

This turned out to be the oil shortage that was not a shortage. During the time of the conflict, oil consumption in the major industrialized nations dropped by about 15 percent, saving more barrels than lost in Iraq and Iran. The high prices and government actions of the previous years were finally having their impacts. The United States and other importing nations were (at least for the time being) not vulnerable to the interruptions in oil deliveries seen during the Arab boycott and the Iranian revolution. With the oil industry less shackled by government controls, available supplies were delivered where they were most needed.

The Persian Gulf remained, nonetheless, high on the president's agenda. Few subjects took as much presidential time in the Reagan years as the mess in Lebanon.[6] The country was not a Persian Gulf oil producer, but Shiites financed by Iran's oil money and supported by the presence of Iran's Revolutionary Guards were a major source of instability in this

Middle Eastern powder keg. Iran-sponsored terrorists captured U.S. hostages, some of whom were eventually exchanged for missiles sold to Iran, and in October of 1983 their explosives killed 241 U.S. Marines housed at the Beirut Airport. With congressional support for the mission evaporating, Reagan pulled U.S. troops out of Lebanon in February of 1984.

Later moves by Iran in the Persian Gulf led to the biggest buildup of U.S. forces in the region up to that time. In January of 1987, Iran launched a new, major attack on Iraq and continued to lay mines in the Gulf to disrupt shipping. Seven U.S. surface ships were deployed to the Persian Gulf, in the words of Reagan, "to protect U.S. interests and to maintain freedom of access and navigation to the area's oil supplies." United States forces found operations there riskier than anticipated. In May, an Iraqi F-1 fighter plane fired two missiles at the frigate *U.S.S. Stark,* killing 37 sailors aboard. Reagan accepted Saddam Hussein's immediate apology, and the Iraqis eventually paid $27 million in compensation.

Two days after the attack, in what the *New York Times* called "a deadly corridor," the Reagan administration announced that Kuwait was reregistering 11 of its oil tankers as the property of a dummy U.S. corporation. The reflagging would entitle the tankers to U.S. military protection. Major allies and the Congress quickly attacked the move. On May 21, the Senate, with bipartisan leadership, voted 91-5 to block reflagging until the Pentagon furnished a report on the risks involved, the rules of engagement, and the extent of assistance expected from oil-producing states in the region and from European allies.

Reagan responded to the criticism on May 29 with his clearest statement as president of national energy policy:

> It may be easy for some . . . to forget just how critical the Persian Gulf is to our national security. But I think everyone . . . can remember the woeful impact of the Middle East oil crisis of a few years ago: the endless, demoralizing gas lines; the shortages; the rationing; the escalating energy prices; the double-digit inflation; and the enormous dislocation that shook our economy to its foundations.

He pledged:

> But this will not happen again, not while this President serves. I'm determined our national economy will never again be held captive, that we will

not return to the days of gas lines, shortages, inflation, economic dislocation, and international humiliation. Mark this point well: The use of the vital sea lanes of the Persian Gulf will not be dictated by the Iranians. These lanes will not be allowed to come under the control of the Soviet Union. The Persian Gulf will remain open to navigation by the nations of the world.

Since the sea lanes of the Persian Gulf had never been an issue in the oil crises of the 1970s, the commitment to maintain the flow of oil from the Middle East implied that the potential use of American military forces in the region would not be limited to naval operations.

Secretary of State George Shultz remembered that critics of the president's use of force emphasized that the United States no longer received much oil directly from the Persian Gulf. They were missing the point, he said, "that oil is a fungible commodity in world trade: whatever happened in the Persian Gulf would affect the United States as the world's largest user and importer of oil." Former Nixon Secretary of Defense Elliot Richardson and Carter Secretary of State Cyrus Vance argued that protection of reflagged ships should be done under the auspices of the United Nations.[7]

On June 27, Iranian suicide patrol boats attacked two tankers in the Gulf, one Norwegian and the other Liberian. More trouble came in July when three U.S. Navy ships escorted two reflagged tankers in the Gulf. The president was awakened at 2:00 A.M. on July 24 with the news that one of the tankers—the 1,200 foot long *Bridgeton*—had struck a mine only 18 miles from the Iranian island of Farsi. As it turned out, there were no casualties and the damage to the tanker was minimal. The United States then assembled in the Persian Gulf the largest international flotilla since the Korean War, but skirmishes between the Americans and Iranians continued.[8]

In September, U.S. naval forces boarded an Iranian amphibious landing craft and seized mines found on board. In October, the State Department condemned Iranian attacks on the major port of Kuwait. In one, a Chinese-made Silkworm missile damaged a Kuwaiti tanker under U.S. registry. Though Iran's missiles were not considered very accurate, U.S. officials worried that future launches might strike liquefied natural gas facilities, which had much greater explosive potential than oil tankers. A few days later, Secretary of Defense Caspar Weinberger announced "a measured and an appropriate response" in which U.S. naval gunfire had destroyed an Iranian platform used for radar surveillance. To avoid escalation of the conflict, personnel on the platform were given 20 minutes advance notice, allowing them to abandon the site.[9]

In 1988, the United Nations continued working toward a cease-fire between Iran and Iraq. On July 3, however, the U.S. cruiser *Vincennes* shot down a civilian Iran Air jetliner flying outside its designated corridor in the Straits of Hormuz. The next week, President Reagan announced that compensation would be paid to the families of the 290 passengers killed in the incident. Finally, on August 8, both Iran and Iraq accepted the U.N. proposal for an end to their military confrontation and returned to their previous borders.

In his memoirs, Shultz praised Reagan's resolve in sticking with his controversial plan to maintain oil shipments in the Persian Gulf. After the setback wrought by the Iran-Contra affair, he proclaimed, "Ronald Reagan was back in business." Reagan himself saw his action as consistent with a 38-year-old policy to base ships and planes in the Gulf and the Arabian Sea to protect the national interest.[10]

A shift in Persian Gulf oil production brought about another major turning point in U.S. energy history, like other such junctures insufficiently recognized at the time. In 1985, Saudi Arabia concluded that the OPEC strategy of cutting production to prop up prices was collapsing. Despite aggressive production cuts and the Iraq-Iran war, world oil prices continued to fall. With revenues plummeting and exports to the United States dropping as low as 26,000 barrels a day, the Saudis risked losing their ability to influence world affairs.

In the summer of 1986, Saudi Arabia sharply reversed course and began selling as much oil as possible at market prices. The move to gain revenues from market share rather than higher prices was a stark break with Saudi practice after the Arab oil embargo. Lower prices, the Saudis now figured, would force high-cost producers benefiting from high prices out of business, allowing the Saudis to gradually reassert their influence. Later in the year, other members of OPEC, most notably Kuwait and Nigeria, followed suit and began raising their production.

Saudi Arabia was soon adding as much as four million barrels a day of production over the low point the year before (a jump of 165 percent). The rest of OPEC was supplying an additional two million barrels. Although OPEC production remained below 1981 levels, the new supplies sent a jolt through the world oil market. The price of OPEC oil, which stood at $25 a barrel in the summer of 1985, tumbled to $10 a barrel just a year later.

American drivers who paid $1.40 a gallon for unleaded regular in early 1981 enjoyed less than 80 cents a gallon in the fall of 1986. The good news at the pumps provided more evidence that supply disruptions and galloping prices were things of the past. But there were many losers from the collapse in world oil prices.

In the United States, cheap oil dealt another blow to alternative fuels, already on the ropes. The fall in prices also slammed the domestic oil industry. The 1981 drilling boom had ebbed the next year when prices eased and some big, expensive projects came up dry. But U.S. production continued to increase gradually through 1985. With the Saudi move to gain market share, however, U.S. output in 1988 sunk to its lowest level since 1977. The economies of Texas and Louisiana took a nosedive. During previous oil gluts, the government had intervened to protect the domestic industry, often under the banner of national security. Now, U.S. producers would be left to the twists and turns of the market. Reagan had promised that decontrol of oil prices would unleash domestic production, but when uncontrolled prices fell, so did production.

During 1986, another major trend line affecting energy independence switched course. In 1985, oil imports stood at their lowest point since 1971, when import quotas were lifted. But in 1986, imports jumped by over one million barrels a day. In just one year, the country went from getting 27 percent of its oil from abroad to 33 percent. The trend line in imports was going back up, but with low prices, there seemed little reason to worry.

SURPRISE FROM IRAQ

The 1973 oil embargo, the Iranian revolution, and the Iraq-Iran war all caught U.S. policymakers by surprise. Likewise, Iraq launched a brutal invasion of Kuwait on August 2, 1990, at a time when the United States believed that the countries with the second- and third-highest oil reserves in the world were working out their differences.

Six days later, President George H. W. Bush, who replaced Reagan the year before, told the nation that to counter the Iraqi occupation of Kuwait, key units of the U.S. Air Force were arriving in neighboring Saudi Arabia (which, due to Iraqi troops on its border, appeared vulnerable to attack) to take up defensive positions. He announced he had ordered an embargo of all trade with Iraq and that he had amassed support ranging from other Arab nations to the Soviet Union and China in resisting aggression.

He warned that because the United States relied so much on imported oil (which in July bounced up close to 50 percent of consumption), the invasion could become "a major threat to its economic independence." He called on major oil-producing nations to increase output to protect the world economy and on oil companies to "show restraint and not abuse today's uncertainties to raise prices."

The call for price restraints fell on deaf ears. After the invasion, the world quickly lost three million barrels of oil a day from Iraq and almost two million from Kuwait. The disappearance of 8 percent of the world's oil was the equal of the three previous interruptions in the Persian Gulf. In just three months, the price of crude oil more than doubled, from $16 to $33 a barrel. Effects at the gas pump were somewhat muted, but the price of unleaded regular still jumped from $1.08 to $1.38—a sizable leap at the time. The cost of home heating oil went up 25 cents a gallon

Saddam had no friends among Persian Gulf oil producers, and Bush's call for higher output to fill the gap got a positive response. By December Saudi Arabia was pumping almost three million extra barrels a day, replacing over 60 percent of missing oil. The oil available from other members of Arab OPEC also grew. By the end of the year, despite the massive losses from Iraq and Kuwait, there was only a net drop of one million barrels a day from Arab producers.

America's Arab allies did more than raise oil production. Saudi Arabia and Kuwait each provided $15 billion to cover American costs of military operations. The Saudis likely provided another $15 billion in support of the war, providing generous subsidies to others who joined the coalition against Iraq.

Order was quickly restored. On January 16, 1991, Bush ordered military attacks on Iraqi targets. Immediately after the president's speech, the Department of Energy announced it would release oil from the Strategic Petroleum Reserve, which resulted in the eventual sale of 17 million barrels. On February 27, Bush was able to announce the liberation of Kuwait and a cease-fire. The administration decided not to march on to Baghdad, in part because of fears (shared by its Arab allies) that the disintegration of Iraq would strengthen Iran. In March, the price of gasoline returned to its pre-war level. On the whole, the American response won a military, diplomatic, and energy supply victory.

Did the Persian Gulf War show the United States to be energy independent or energy dependent? It is a close call, but I lean toward a judgment of energy independence. It is a close call because there were many aspects of dependence. With import levels so high, the country had reverted to higher reliance on foreign oil. The price spike in late 1990 helped fuel inflation and contributed to a mild recession, both of which weakened Bush's reelection prospects in 1992. Saudi Arabia's status as an energy superpower was amply demonstrated by the impact of its surge oil production and the strategic distribution of its oil–generated revenues.

On the other side, the lack of government price controls and allocation led to a more flexible energy market and an absence of gasoline lines or other major shortages. With overall oil consumption still constrained by auto efficiency standards and the virtual elimination of oil in electric generation, the impacts of high oil prices on the general economy were dampened. The masterful diplomacy of the Bush administration produced international cooperation that further blunted adverse impacts. Perhaps most importantly, oil did not revert to the days of a seller's market. The industrial nations were able to put severe post-war sanctions on Saddam Hussein's regime without fear the world would run short of oil. Whatever the verdict on energy independence, this contradictory evidence should not have encouraged complacency about America's energy future.

Like previous energy crises, the Persian Gulf War stimulated congressional action to find new energy policies. Environmentalists pushed a bill by Senator Richard Bryan (D-NV) to raise auto efficiency standards 40 percent by 2001. Pro-production forces wanted to open the coastal plain of Alaska's Arctic National Wildlife Refuge to oil and gas drilling. The Energy Policy Act of 1992 that eventually passed contained neither of these high-impact provisions. The bill included reforms of the electric industry and some mild tax incentives, but failed to contribute any measures that had much effect on U.S. energy independence.

THE CLINTON YEARS

Bill Clinton quickly jumped into the energy fray during his first year as president. Facing tough choices on how to balance the federal budget, he reluctantly accepted an idea from Vice President Al Gore for a broad-based energy tax to generate the needed revenue. Gore told Clinton the tax would "promote energy conservation and independence."[11] Though

Clinton worried about the impact of the tax on low-income families, he was reassured that these adverse effects would be more than offset by his earned-income tax credit.

The wonkily named BTU tax (British Thermal Units measure the heat content of energy) applied to the wholesale price of all fuels. Estimates suggested the proposal would add eight to twelve cents to the cost of a gallon of gasoline, with other fuels affected similarly. Reluctant to be associated with new taxes, the administration did not actively try to sell the energy levy, and it was strongly attacked by business groups worried about their ability to pass their costs on to consumers. It was also difficult to determine how much the tax would actually reduce energy use.

During the budget reconciliation, the Senate scrapped the BTU tax and substituted a much narrower 4.3-cents-a-gallon increase in the gasoline tax. Given the history of energy tax proposals in the United States, the Clinton proposal was a gallant try to move a bit toward the kind of energy taxes adopted in Europe and Japan. The modest gasoline tax adopted did not, however, have a discernible impact on oil imports.

Having been bruised over the tax fight and confronting a conservative Republican House of Representatives after the 1994 elections, the Clinton administration retreated from the energy battle field. It seldom discussed the problem of oil imports. When it did, it stressed the need to develop foreign sources outside the Persian Gulf, like the Caspian Sea region.

In 1995, the Congress passed (and President Clinton signed) the termination of all federal control over speed limits on American highways. With the 1973 Arab oil embargo a distant memory and safety concerns being trumped by a commitment to the freedom of drivers, all decisions on speed limits were ceded to the states, who moved quickly to raise the caps to much higher levels.

The energy rhetoric of the 1990s emphasized the need for strong energy science programs to solve problems like oil security and climate change without resorting to regulation. Clinton's first Energy Secretary, Hazel Rollins O'Leary, said after leaving the agency, that in fact, it should be renamed the "Department of Science and Technology."[12] But after a modest buildup in expenditures on energy research and development, the energy portion of total R&D by 1997 fell even below the nadir of the Reagan years. In 1978 and 1979, energy R&D spending had exceeded that for either health or space. In Clinton's second term, spending on space was triple that for energy; health was five times as much.[13]

Presidential and congressional inactivity on energy reflected a national ambivalence about whether there really was a serious problem. Until 1997, oil imports remained below their 1977 levels (on both a volumetric and percentage basis). Using 1977 as a base year provided comfort that things really were not as bad as they used to be. Perhaps new technologies and voluntary actions would preserve American energy independence (see Figure 3.1).

Even more relevant, oil imports had bottomed out in the mid-1980s and risen steadily thereafter. In 1985, the United States imported 27 percent of its oil. In 1998, the percentage stood at 52 percent. In addition, projections from the Energy Information Administration showed imports rising to 60 percent within several years. Confronted with such daunting prospects in the 1970s, Congress passed mileage efficiency standards and other mandates to reduce oil use. In the 1990s, Congress put a ban on

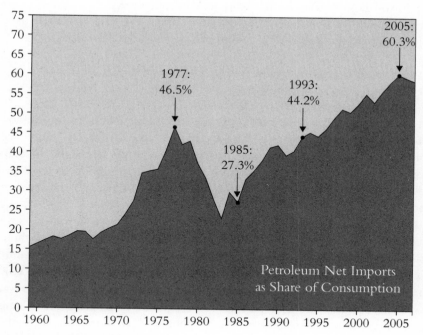

Figure 3.1 Net Imports

The threat of oil imports during the Clinton years could be interpreted in different ways depending on what it was compared to

the Transportation Department's even considering any rules that might toughen auto standards, and the Clinton administration relied solely on voluntary cooperation from U.S. automakers to improve auto efficiency. While Clinton was in office, the average mileage of new vehicles continued to drop as more drivers moved to heavier and less fuel-efficient trucks, vans, and SUVs.

As its strongest actions on energy, the Clinton administration used its rule-making authority to mandate much more efficient refrigerators and air conditioners and signed the Kyoto Protocol, which required the major industrialized nations to cut their emissions of greenhouse gases. However, Clinton never submitted the treaty for ratification by the Senate (where it had no chance of passing) and offered no plan for how the United States would meet its commitments if it was ratified.

Low oil prices during the 1990s took the sting out of the growing level of imports. An oil glut in 1998 helped drop average gasoline prices to $1.06 a gallon for the year (and even less in the closing months). This was the lowest posted price since 1989 and, controlled for inflation, the lowest in the history of the automobile. For consumers, the price collapse made energy a good news story. For energy policy, it was the "lost decade."

THE MARKET TURNS

In December of 1999, the staff of the Energy Information Administration tried to figure out what was going on in the world oil market. Commercial oil inventories took their biggest monthly plunge since the Iranian Revolution in 1979, and we were poring through the numbers to determine the reason. If the trend continued, it would be hard to get through the winter.

We considered that private customers (who were not measured in our weekly surveys) might have purchased extra supplies and set them aside temporarily in preparation for the coming of the new millennium. The government and the press were abuzz with dire possibilities of a Y2K breakdown of computers that could not handle the new dates. If there was a chance of energy outages during the traditional singing of "Auld Lang Syne," it was not totally unreasonable for people to hoard oil, just to be safe.

We learned in January, of course, that there must be another reason for the shortage, after commercial inventories continued to drop. We concluded that OPEC production cuts, announced the previous March in reaction to a world oil glut and record low prices, were proving more effective than we had anticipated.

We customarily discounted OPEC claims of production cuts due to a history of poor compliance among its members. But this time, exporting nations were adjusting their outputs to the new quotas. Long-time rivals Iran and Saudi Arabia agreed that the global collapse of oil prices meant they needed to cooperate more on oil matters. After Hugo Chavez came to power in Venezuela, this founding member of OPEC went from an unrepentant cheater on OPEC quotas to an aggressive supporter of them. OPEC was back. Its aggressive production cuts were creating a tighter oil market and a sharp increase in oil prices.

Soon, Secretary of Energy Bill Richardson and I were off to the Northeastern states to explain why the cost of heating oil and diesel fuel had doubled in just eight months. Then, we departed for Kuwait and Saudi Arabia to show that the OPEC cuts had overshot their mark. Both countries did increase their production after our trip, and prices eased somewhat the next year. But they would never return to the levels seen in the summer of 1999. With booming imports combined with sharply escalating prices, more and more money was going abroad to pay America's energy bills. When George W. Bush took his oath as president on January 20, 2001, there was little doubt that America had again lost its energy independence.

THE MISSING RESPONSE

At the end of 2001, it appeared that OPEC might be losing control of the world oil market again. Even with new cuts in production, the price for crude oil fell back below $17. The organization responded with another cut in production and announced it was setting a target price band of $22 to $28 a barrel. OPEC output fell in both 2001 and 2002, with Saudi Arabia and Venezuela absorbing the biggest cuts. Within a few years, oil prices remained steadily above the price band, moving past the $50 mark by 2005.[14]

The world oil market was getting much tighter, and OPEC production cuts were only part of the story. Little noticed at the time, Saudi Arabia's excess capacity was falling, diminishing an important tool of surge production for dealing with major interruptions in world supplies. More in the headlines, Chavez was squeezing out foreign oil companies, whose capital and expertise had helped Venezuela increase production during the 1990s.

On top of this, U.S. military operations in Iraq were followed by a drop-off in production there. Output reached its nadir during a four-month period in 2003, when Iraq pumped two million barrels (85 percent) a day less than before the war. Although Iraq's production eventually rose (but not to prewar levels), there seemed to be more scenarios around the world that indicated things could get worse before they got better. Iran and Nigeria were gradually upping their production, but neither source of supply seemed very reliable.

Market watchers also had to take into account emerging economies placing new claims on world oil supplies. Chinese oil consumption, as an extreme example, jumped 40 percent from 2000 to 2005, adding two million barrels a day to world demand. Even when OPEC began to increase output in 2003, the cost of oil continued a sharp trajectory upward. In early 2008, the spot price for crude topped $100 a barrel, an amount that would have been considered astronomical just a few years earlier. Many motorists were paying over $3 a gallon for gasoline, well over triple the cost during the price collapse of the late 1990s.

The dangers of combining high oil imports and high oil prices can be found in the U.S. balance of trade numbers. In 2001, the first year of the George W. Bush presidency, the U.S. trade deficit for energy alone ran about $110 billion. In 2006, the negative balance for energy approximated $300 billion. With transfers of wealth of this magnitude, major decisions about the value of prime U.S. real estate, the financial prospects of major U.S. companies, and even the future strength of the dollar were increasingly made in the Persian Gulf.

Previous oil crises had a clear impetus—a politically motivated embargo or a war in the Persian Gulf. The reasons for the new energy crisis of the twenty-first century are more varied. Added to the physical balance between oil supply and demand are perpetual fears that the international situation might deteriorate even further. Myself and others, when unable to explain the surge in oil prices with traditional analytic tools, now ascribe the difference to the panic factor among oil traders. Although nervous traders often overreact to any rumor of a possible cut in oil supplies, there are legitimate reasons to fear that expanded turmoil in the Persian Gulf or elsewhere could spark an interruption in oil supplies bigger than anything we have seen to date.

President Bush decried American "addiction" to foreign oil, tweaked mileage standards to require slightly more efficient light trucks, and signed a rather inconsequential Energy Policy Act of 2005. Still, through 2006, the White House and Congress continued to avoid any tough energy choices that might help regain American energy independence.

THE END OF COMPLACENCY

The climate of opinion in Washington suddenly changed in 2007. Significant energy measures began moving through both houses of Congress. After 26 years of inaction, the burst of activity across a broad range of issues came almost as a shock. Several measures, given no chance just a year earlier, appeared to have bipartisan support. The new (now Democratic) Congress seemed determined to address the issues of dependence on foreign oil and emissions of greenhouse gases.

Attitudes were also changing up Pennsylvania Avenue. President Bush, in his January State of the Union address, endorsed very robust new requirements for displacing oil products with ethanol and modest but still mandatory increases in auto efficiency standards.

The messy back and forth between the House and the Senate over the legislation, veto threats from the White House on provisions it did not like, and the failure of several key provisions to survive obscured what was really going on. December saw the passage of the Energy Independence and Security Act of 2007—an energy package with real teeth. The margins of victory were huge. The Senate passed the bill 86 to 8, with few in either party in opposition. Republicans split narrowly against the bill by a single vote in the House, where it still won 314 to 100. The votes reflected the quickest shift in congressional opinion on energy in history.

At the signing ceremony, Bush praised the new law for taking "a major step toward reducing our dependence on oil, confronting global climate change, expanding the production of renewable fuels and giving future generations of our country a nation that is stronger, cleaner, and more secure." At a hearing several weeks later, chairman of the Senate Energy and Natural Resources Committee, Jeff Bingaman (D-NM), predicted, "This groundbreaking legislation will save more energy than all previous energy bills we have passed."

What does the new energy law do? For the first time since 1975, Congress mandated higher averages for auto efficiency. From 2010 to 2020 the standard for all new vehicles (cars, vans, SUVs, and light trucks) must increase from 25 to 35 miles per gallon (the "ten-in-ten" provision). Over the same period, the Act phases in tough new minimum shares for ethanol in the transportation fuel mix. Together, these actions make substantial moves toward reducing American dependence on oil.

The legislation also includes a wide array of requirements for more efficient buildings, equipment, and lighting. The Act even phases out inefficient incandescent lights, which will greatly reduce demand for electricity and virtually eliminate the workhorse of indoor illumination since the days of Thomas Edison.

It will take several years for the impacts of the new legislation to be seen in energy markets. Currently, we import over 12 million barrels of oil a day, with about half of that coming from OPEC. It will take time for more ethanol and more efficient vehicles to penetrate the market and have much impact on these imports.

As the president stated, the Act does take a major step toward energy independence. If its provisions had been included in the Energy Policy Act of 1992, we would already be celebrating our return to energy independence. During our long delay in addressing energy issues, however, we have dug ourselves into a deep hole. As a result, we will need to take additional major steps.

When we have sufficient historical hindsight on the matter, passage of the Energy Independence and Security Act of 2007 will likely be seen as an important turning point and the end of a 26-year era of energy complacency. This will certainly be the case if it sets the stage for new waves of energy legislation with significant impacts.

The current commitment of U.S. ground troops to Iraq will likely affect prospects for further tough action on energy. The urgency with which we tackle our reliance on foreign oil in particular and on fossil fuels in general will depend, in part, on the linkages we see between our dependence on oil from the Persian Gulf region and our need to send troops there.

Chapter 4

Blood and Treasure: The Heavy Cost of Dependence on Middle East Oil

During America's two wars in the Persian Gulf, official government statements have played down the role of oil in the decision to commit U.S. forces. In George W. Bush's nationally televised justification for American military action against Saddam Hussein, oil was not mentioned as a reason to go to war.[1] Does this mean that access to oil does not dominate the thinking behind military planning and operations in the Middle East? Well, not exactly.

FIFTY YEARS OF PLANNING

As early as the Truman administration, Cold War worries about the proximity of the Persian Gulf to the Soviet Union spurred U.S. contingency planning for military intervention in the event the region's oil was threatened. With the United States continuing to get hardly any oil from the Middle East, the strategy focused on denying the oil to the Soviet Union if it ever invaded Saudi Arabia. (The British were expected to handle other trouble spots in the region.)

To prevent use of the oil, the plans called for U.S. personnel to insert concrete plugs in all Saudi wells within days of a Soviet invasion. In later stages of the discussions, the Chairman of the Joint Chiefs of Staff, General Omar Bradley, warned civilian officials that military forces in the area might be insufficient to actually support the mission. This would not be the last military plan to deal with strategically important oil supplies in the Gulf, nor the last time American generals questioned whether sufficient resources were being committed to rely on a military option.[2]

After the elected government of Iran nationalized British oil interests in the country, President Eisenhower in 1953 authorized the Central Intelligence Agency to cooperate with British covert operations to overthrow the government and restore the autocratic Shah Mohammed Reza Pahlavi to power. The grateful Shah negotiated new agreements that kept Iran's oil business in the hands of American and British companies. The American-financed coup successfully protected Western oil interests in the region but aborted the best chance in the Persian Gulf to develop a democratic form of government.

Later in his presidency, Eisenhower tried to avoid future U.S. dependence on Middle East oil in order to avoid the necessity of sending troops to the region. His decision to place quotas on oil imports, he said privately, was based on the need to avoid "the unacceptable alternatives of (a) resort to force to hold the source, or (b) suffer the crippling effect of its loss." He told a key advisor on oil "should a crisis arise threatening to cut the western world off from the Mid East oil, we would *have* to use force."[3] Military contingency plans to protect oil supplies in the Middle East were updated in 1958 and 1960.

President John Kennedy gave greater priority to protecting access to Saudi oil than to maintaining an alliance with Egypt's Gamal Abdel Nasser. When the mercurial Egyptian leader launched attacks on Saudi Arabian border posts over a political dispute in Yemen in 1962, the United States sent eight jets and 500 troops to the region (in a mission code-named Operation Hard Surface) to protect the Saudis.[4]

U.S. military planning for protecting oil assets in the Middle East was rarely discussed in public, but now released records over many presidencies demonstrate a sustained interest in the subject. Even a president like Eisenhower, who was reluctant to commit troops abroad, knew he might have to if America became overly dependent on foreign oil.

During his first term, President Nixon had to adjust military planning for the Persian Gulf after Britain in 1971 terminated its long-time role of providing armed forces to protect Western interests in the region. Because of the war in Vietnam, the United States was unable to deploy ships or troops to fill the vacuum. As a result, Nixon opted to build up the military strength of the Shah of Iran and depend on him to police the Gulf. The alliance with Iran would protect America's interests in the area without requiring its own military presence. Iran would even use its own oil revenues to finance the military buildup.

Nixon had been impressed by the Shah for a long time, saying, "I sensed an inner strength in him" after he first met him in the 1950s. In a foreign policy address given as a private citizen in 1967, Nixon cited Iran as an important example of a country that deserved U.S. support despite its authoritarian government. Praising Iran's "dramatic economic success," Nixon argued, "It is time for us to recognize that much as we like our own political system, American style democracy is not necessarily the best form of government for people in Asia, Africa and Latin America with entirely different backgrounds."[5]

Iran's strategic importance included borders with the Soviet Union and with Iraq. American policymakers feared Iraq could threaten both Israel and the oil fields of Kuwait and Saudi Arabia. A strong military in neighboring Iran would help curb tendencies for Iraqi adventurism. Iran's forces could also stall any Soviet attempts to reach the Persian Gulf. Nixon secretly instructed the Defense Department to place no constraints on Iran's acquisition of weapons. With vast oil wealth and Nixon's approval, the Shah built a navy and an air force with personnel about two-and-a-half times as large as Iraq, Saudi Arabia, and Kuwait combined. Its lead in advanced weaponry was even more impressive.[6]

Nixon's dependence on Iran for Persian Gulf security rested, in the final analysis, on the absence of viable alternatives. In April of 1971, Nixon held a discussion in the Oval Office with U.S. Ambassador to Tehran Douglas MacArthur II and General Alexander Haig concerning the need for a strong ally in the region. Resigned to the limited options available to the United States for countering Soviet influence, he asked plaintively, "Who else do we have?" According to Nixon, "Our Israel tie makes us unpalatable to everybody in the Arab world."[7] Non-Arab Iran would not join the opposition to Israel, was becoming a strong military force, and possessed vast reserves of oil.

American contingency plans for military intervention in the Persian Gulf were classified top secret and not meant for open discussion. So it caught many by surprise when Secretary of State Kissinger, frustrated by statements from Saudi Arabia during the Arab oil embargo, announced at a press conference, "It is clear that if pressures continue unreasonably and indefinitely, then the United States will have to consider what countermeasures it may have to take." Consistent with an understanding that this was a not very subtle threat to use military force, Kissinger ordered studies of potential countermeasures from relevant departments of the government, leading to the completion of several contingency plans, including potential military operations, by the end of the month.

Saudi Oil Minister Yamani reacted strongly by publicly threatening oil production would be cut by 80 percent if the United States, Europe, or Japan retaliated against the boycotters. He warned any use of force by the United States would be suicide because Arabs would blow up oil fields before their countries could be occupied.[8]

Relations between the United States and Saudi Arabia remained remarkably harmonious during the embargo, and the brouhaha over Kissinger's threat quickly ebbed. The Saudis notified U.S. Ambassador James Akins that King Faisal was angered and disturbed with Yamani's statements. Lest the softening in Saudi rhetoric provide too much comfort to officials in Washington, Akins later confirmed part of Yamani's warning in a cable to Kissinger: "The Saudis would seek to destroy the oil installations and fire the oil fields if an invasion is launched. The Aramco parent companies can tell the Department how credible this threat really is."[9] It was evident in the field there were more constraints on United States military force than many planners in Washington recognized.

The tight military alliance between the United States and Iran lasted a mere nine years. After the Shah fled the country in January of 1979, one of the world's greatest collections of U.S. weaponry fell under the control of the Grand Ayatollah Ruhollah Musavi Khomeini, whose rise in popular esteem had ridden a wave of bitter verbal attacks on the United States and Western culture. As the influence of Khomeini's moderate advisors waned, it became more likely that Iran's weapons would be launched to oppose rather than support U.S. objectives in the region.

The Russian invasion of Afghanistan in December of 1979 further dramatized the new military realities in the Gulf. The "Carter Doctrine," announced in January, provided the clearest statement by a U.S. president that the United States would use military force to repel Soviet attacks on the Gulf and protect vital oil supplies there. Carter acknowledged there was work to do to have the military capabilities needed to implement his commitments.

Given the political fallout from long gas lines in the spring, the taking of American hostages in Tehran in November, and the Soviet move into Afghanistan in December, the Carter administration concluded the armed services needed to be better prepared for conflict in the region. Members of the National Security Council (and the president himself) noted that the United States lacked adequate bases from which it could conduct operations. Moreover, joint military command for the Persian Gulf was split between the European and Pacific commands. The great fear at the time was a move into the Gulf by the Soviets, who could use control over the massive oil reserves there to gain influence in Europe and Japan, who depended even more than the United States on imports from the Middle East. The Carter administration concluded that the United States was not adequately prepared for further Soviet incursions.

Carter authorized steps to quietly find locations in the Gulf region from which the U.S. military could operate, but that were small enough not to arouse local antagonism. He also tried, over some resistance from the individual branches of the military, to create better interservice cooperation to handle any threats there. These efforts led to the creation of the Rapid Deployment Joint Task Force, which became the precursor of the United States Central Command (USCENTCOM), formally established by President Reagan in 1983.[10]

Both the Joint Task Force and CENTCOM began acquiring equipment and reorienting training to make them more suitable to desert conditions. How to move equipment into the region on short notice and deal with the unique climate, health, and water issues found there moved up on the military agenda.

CENTCOM conducted its first major mission, "Earnest Will," in 1987—the Reagan initiative to prevent Iranian attacks on Kuwaiti ships operating in the Gulf. By 1990, Central Command had made progress on many issues critical to effective operations in the region.

The creation of CENTCOM was prescient in hindsight. The two largest military operations after Vietnam were later conducted in its theater. We confronted, as it turned out, not the Soviet Union (the original threat) or Iran (a growing concern in the 1980s). Instead, we would twice deploy American might to deal with Iraq.

WHY IRAQ?

Attempts to soft pedal the role oil has played in U.S. military actions against Saddam Hussein make it necessary to demonstrate what is on close inspection obvious. Oil is not the only reason we went to war twice in Iraq. But it was reason enough on its own and, to a large extent, pervaded the other factors involved. If we want to accurately calculate the price of reliance on Persian Gulf oil, we must include the costs of conducting wars in Iraq.

The U.S. liberation of Kuwait in 1991 has been well chronicled. Many official statements at the time did not mention the oil factor, but there is no doubt of its primacy. The top secret directive (issued on January 15, 1991, and declassified in 1997) authorizing the war is blunt. The first sentence reads, "Access to Persian Gulf oil and the security of key friendly states in the area are vital to U.S. national security." The second sentence continues, ". . . the United States remains committed to defending its vital interests in the region, if necessary through the use of military force, against any power with interests inimical to our own."[11]

Either Saddam's naked aggression or the need for oil could have justified the U.S. decision to defend Kuwait and Saudi Arabia; in fact, world opinion rallied behind it. But Iraq's attack would likely not have occurred absent its bitter disagreement with Kuwait over OPEC production policy. The oil factor dominated both Iraq's rash attack and the American response.

Coming in the very different post-9/11 world, the second confrontation with Saddam in 2003 is more difficult to unravel and will likely remain so, even when the relevant documents are declassified.

President Bush's explanation for going to war on March 17 gave several justifications for his decision. "Intelligence gathered by this and other countries," he asserted, "leaves no doubt that the Iraqi regime continues to possess and conceal some of the most lethal weapons ever devised." He reported that Iraq had "aided, trained, and harbored terrorists, including operatives of Al Qaida." He warned of a clear danger that Iraq would furnish its "chemical, biological or, one day, nuclear weapons" to these terrorists, who could then "fulfill their stated ambitions and kill thousands or hundreds of thousands of innocent people in our country or any other." Thus, the use of force was authorized to assure national security.

None of the reasons given in the speech were true. Moreover, it is hard to find much evidence of serious due diligence to determine whether the information was true or false. Clearly, the rationale for the war was something not revealed to the public. As Alan Greenspan—a frequent advisor to presidents Nixon and Ford on energy issues and long-term chair of the Federal Reserve Board—confirmed last year, the unstated reason was oil.

The United States and Iraq have long tangled over oil issues. During the Arab oil embargo, the United States maintained positive relations with many boycotting nations behind the scenes. Not so with Iraq. Just before the embargo began, Iraq nationalized Exxon and Mobil oil facilities in Basra to protest U.S. support for Israel and took the lead in arguing the embargo was not severe enough.

The eviction of the U.S. companies was particularly frustrating because of the immense potential of oil resources in Iraq. According to published rankings, Iraq stood second in the world in conventional oil reserves. Among the world's major oil domains, Iraq has been the least explored. As a result, it is widely believed among oil experts that the published numbers may well underestimate the amount of oil there.

When Iraq's oil industry needed foreign technical assistance, Saddam Hussein turned to the French and the Russians. This decision frustrated American companies, as world oil reserves came increasingly under the control of state-owned oil companies, thus shrinking the areas open for private exploration. The oil alliance with the French and the Russians also bumped up against American foreign policy goals. As the United States attempted to maintain sanctions on Iraq during the 1990s, the French and Russians sometimes sided with Iraq. The idea that the United States could get back into the Iraq oil business was very tempting on many levels.

Iraq was kept in check during most of the 1990s due to United Nations sanctions on oil sales. The United States wanted to keep severe restrictions on Iraq's exports. With Russia and France reluctant to adopt the American position, however, it appeared international sanctions would be loosened and Saddam would eventually regain his access to massive revenues from oil sales.

In January of 1998, an organization called the Project for the New American Century (containing many senior officials from previous Republican administrations) wrote President Clinton, urging that the United States take unilateral action to remove Saddam from power. The letter said that if Iraq gained revenues from oil exports and the capacity to deliver weapons of mass destruction, "the safety of American troops in the region, of our friends and allies like Israel and the moderate Arab states, and a significant portion of the world's supply of oil will all be put at hazard."

In September, an influential signer of the letter, former Under Secretary of Defense for Policy Paul Wolfowitz, testified before a House committee that the United States should support the "enormous latent opposition to Saddam" politically, economically, and militarily. The key component of the strategy was creating a liberated zone in the southern region that would "control the largest oil field in Iraq."

Of the 18 signers of the letter to Clinton, 13 (including Wolfowitz, Donald Rumsfeld, and John Bolton) assumed foreign policy and national defense positions in the George W. Bush administration. When Bush took office, his State and Defense departments were permeated with alumni of the Project for the New American Century, publicly committed to overthrowing Saddam Hussein and putting pro-American officials in charge of the country's major oil wells.[12]

Bush's first Treasury Secretary, Paul O'Neill, records that in its early days the new administration discussed how to occupy Iraq, with specific plans on the disposition of its oil fields.[13] The planning at the highest levels for allocating Iraq's oil fields before the 9/11 attacks makes it difficult to credibly deny the connection between oil and the price subsequently paid to fight the war there.

Then there is the issue of where to put U.S. military bases in the region. American global strategy has long identified a strong need for bases in or near the Persian Gulf from which missions could be launched quickly to protect access to the region's oil. The importance of such bases became increasingly apparent after the collapse of the Shah's government. Because of popular opposition to such outposts, obtaining enough bases of the right size remained a major diplomatic challenge.

As they forged their alliance to fight the first Gulf War, the Americans asked for and received a pledge of massive financial support and a surge in oil production from the Saudis. A less-publicized but even more sensitive issue was the request to station approximately 250,000 U.S. military personnel in the kingdom. According to eyewitnesses at the meeting where this was discussed, just as King Fahd began to grant permission, some advisors began to demur. Most notably, Crown Prince Abdullah protested that more time was needed to consult with tribal and religious leaders, lest the very visible presence of Americans within the kingdom inflame public opinion. The king's welcome to the Americans prevailed, but the enlarging of the U.S. base (which grew to over half a million troops at the peak of the war) did stoke controversy and was used by Osama bin Laden to rally support against the royal family and the Americans.[14]

The U.S. kept its word to Fahd after the war and quickly slashed the number of troops on Saudi territory. From 1992 to 1997, forces remained below 2,000. Reduced troop levels did not stop terrorist attacks on American locations, however. Twenty-four Americans were killed and over 500 wounded in two separate attacks in 1994 and 1995. Subsequently, the Clinton administration, fearful of new Iraqi attacks against the kingdom, tripled the number of U.S. troops, which exceeded 7,000 during the year 2000. During the Iraq War, the Bush administration raised the number to over 10,000.

In April of 2003, Bush declared that the Iraq War had been won, and Secretary of Defense Donald Rumsfeld announced that the United States would finally move all of its combat troops out of Saudi Arabia and transfer vital CENTCOM functions to Qatar (where there would be fewer restrictions on operations). The issue of United States bases on Saudi territory near the holy cities of Islam, despite the effort to limit public knowledge of them, had been a tough issue for both sides. Even with the friendly reception in Qatar, the Americans knew that finding enough bases in the Gulf region would continue to pose a difficult challenge. With the government and the press trumpeting the victory in Iraq, its territory offered new opportunities for bases.

President Bush could have fought the war in Iraq in a way to show that it was not about oil, but he chose to take the opposite tack. Exhibit number one was the Coalition Provisional Authority that ruled Iraq from April of 2003 to June of 2004. Sanctioned by the United Nations to control all Iraq's assets but run by Americans, the Authority acted quickly to remove from power those associated with the ruling Ba'athist party, restructure the Iraqi economy, and manage the rebuilding of the country's infrastructure.

Without any say-so by the Iraqi people, the Authority dismantled the country's system of state-owned enterprises. It abolished laws and discriminatory tariffs that effectively banned foreign investment. In addition, it issued orders giving foreign investors all the rights of domestic investors and the ability to transfer all profits and dividends out of the country unfettered. Since the oil industry was 95 percent of the national economy, the major impact of the restructuring was to replace the state-run oil regime with one run by foreign investors, a situation not seen in any Arab exporting country in decades.

The United States made clear late in 2003 that its protections for foreign investors were not meant to be all-encompassing. In December, a directive from Deputy Secretary of Defense Wolfowitz barred French and Russian companies—the major investors in Iraqi oil under Saddam—from competing on contracts for Iraqi reconstruction. (They were eligible for subcontracts.) The action eased the way for American and British firms to take over the coveted Iraqi fields from their rivals. The quickness with which U.S. authorities moved to revolutionize the oil business in Iraq was not surprising in light of U.S. planning for the war.

The other test of American strategy was whether the plan was to liberate Iraq and then depart, or to stay and occupy permanent bases. Massive U.S. spending on buildings and bases cannot be justified absent an intent to stay. The new $600 million U.S. embassy—at 104 acres the largest in the world—portrays a sense of permanency and long-term mission beyond any goal so far articulated for the war. Massive investments in the Balad Air Base north of Baghdad—one of five locales supporting air operations in the country—also evidence goals that are long rather than short term.

In September of 2007, Secretary of Defense Robert Gates, responding to questions before the Senate Appropriations Committee, foresaw keeping five combat brigades (about a quarter of the current deployment) in Iraq as a long-term presence after the war. In addition, eight U.S. warships patrol the waters off southern Iraq, mainly to protect the two oil terminals through which most of the country's exports flow. In October 2007, one petty officer on the U.S.S. Whirlwind said he did not see the Iraqis taking over from the Americans anytime soon, since they had no ships of their own.[15] Beyond any military or political resolution of the Iraq quagmire, the United States has taken on expensive land and naval military commitments for which American officials can see no end in sight, to protect the flow of Gulf oil.

A Lack of Understanding

The creation of CENTCOM produced a military force capable of fighting effectively in the Gulf region. But civilian agencies have made little progress in their understanding of the region in which CENTCOM has been called to fight. Lack of knowledge can lead to miscalculations in how CENTCOM is utilized. One of the major errors in Iraq involved the role of oil in the politics of the OPEC countries.

Wolfowitz—a U.S. official whose experience in planning for American involvement in the Persian Gulf spanned four different decades—in 2003 made one of the most remembered and misleading assessments of the conflict that had begun just three days earlier. He told the House Appropriations Committee that Iraq's oil revenues would be large enough to largely finance the costs of reconstruction there.

The estimate was wrong on many counts. You have to spend money to produce oil, so revenues do not equate to what is available to spend on other things. Moreover, Saddam had not just devoted funds to his own luxuries. He had created many subsidies to win political favor. He underwrote, for instance, some of the lowest gasoline prices in the world, selling fuel to consumers for well under actual cost. The Coalition Provisional Authority chose not to terminate this expensive subsidy to avoid adverse public reaction. Then, the war brought lower oil production and much higher reconstruction costs than expected. The optimistic projections fell far short of the eventual reality, forcing outside nations to finance the reconstruction.

There was another largely overlooked failure in the analysis that bedevils the current politics of Iraq and blocks a political solution to the war, no matter how effective military operations. The Wolfowitz view was based on the idea that oil companies from the United States (and its allies) would be able to raise Iraqi production. This would take private investment that would be repaid from future revenues with profits high enough to justify the risk. Although this sounds reasonable to us, to Iraqis, or most oil-exporting nations, it does not.

The Wolfowitz formula runs counter to everything we know about the oil politics of the Middle East. In each of these nations, the initial exploration and development was conducted by companies from the United States and Europe. With very few exceptions, the foreign oil companies were eventually expelled, generally to the glee of native populations. This expression of oil nationalism denied these countries the outside investment and technical expertise needed to expand production. Still, they preferred to assert their national sovereignty over oil resources. Though this trend is widely associated with OPEC, nonmembers like Mexico, Norway, and China also opted to have public ownership of oil. The economic argument over public versus private ownership is politically irrelevant in most oil-exporting countries. Government ownership of oil is part of *their* energy independence.

Nowhere can I find any evidence that the Iraqi people want to buck the worldwide trend among exporting nations and go back to foreign ownership of their oil, or withdraw from OPEC. If companies cannot operate according to market principles, they have little incentive to make massive investments. The Bush rationale rested on an extreme improbability—that a democratic Iraq would turn its back on policies popular throughout most exporting countries, who favor national ownership of oil over access to foreign investment.

This takes us to the crux of the current impasse in Iraq. One key benchmark for the current Iraqi government has been parliamentary approval for an oil-sharing agreement. Despite the acknowledged priority of settling this issue, talks to finalize an agreement have repeatedly collapsed.

Most outside attention has focused on the difficulty of distributing oil revenues in a manner that will satisfy the Sunnis, Shiites, and Kurds. Regional competition is indeed a thorny issue. Similar debates over national versus local control of oil revenue have plagued countries like Nigeria for years and, at times, even the United States. Yet, there is an even bigger barrier to getting an oil-sharing agreement.

If the Iraqi parliament passes laws that open Iraq's oil to foreign companies, there will be a major political backlash both short and long term. Unlike regional conflict, this aspect of the rough road to an acceptable plan for oil has been largely ignored. *Time* magazine in September of 2007, however, cut to the critical issue at stake. Its article pointed to the protests by oil workers' unions about any law that privatizes the oil industry and "gives Big Oil huge profits." Whatever their economic merits, the views of the workers are widely shared throughout Iraq (and in many other places around the world). As senior lecturer in Middle East Economics at Exeter University, Kamil Mahdi, observed, "Politicians who sign [an Iraqi law to suit Western oil interests] will be consigning their careers to the dustbin."[16] Based on the history of Iraq and neighboring countries, it is hard to imagine that the tension between democratic opinion and laws favoring foreign oil companies will go away.

At What Price?

The cost of the U.S. military presence in the Persian Gulf can be calculated in many ways. The heaviest toll comes, of course, from the loss of life. Early in 2008, U.S. military fatalities in the Iraq War surpassed 4,000. To this must be added the deaths of other coalition forces, contractors, journalists, and innocent Iraqis. There is also an immense burden placed on many survivors of the war, ranging from life-altering injuries to immense pressures on young families.

The cost can also be measured in dollars. Through the end of the 2007 budget year, Congress appropriated $602 billion for military operations in Iraq and Afghanistan, and other activities associated with the war on terrorism. There was also $2 billion additional Veterans Administration funding for the war. Including the future costs of the war is more difficult than totaling past costs. However, even assuming the withdrawal of most American troops, mainline estimates for total expenditures through 2017 range from $1 trillion to $2 trillion.[17]

Even more elusive are accurate numbers on other effects on the general economy. There is certainly some loss, though, from the drop in Iraqi oil production after the war began, the panic factor in the oil markets due to hostilities in the middle of the world's great oil reserves, and the portion of the interest on the national debt that can reasonably be ascribed to the war.

Not all of these expenditures are related to American reliance on the region's oil. Afghanistan, for instance, does not export oil and did harbor terrorists (including many from Saudi Arabia) who attacked the United States. But Iraq has the second-greatest oil reserves in the world and did not harbor terrorists when the war began, and that is where the heaviest costs have accrued.

The amount spent to protect U.S. access to oil in the Middle East dwarfs all other government spending on energy. If we spent more to reduce our dependence on Persian Gulf oil, we would not have to spend as much to continue that reliance.

Chapter 5

Fossil Fuels and Global Warming: A Dangerous Experiment with the Planet

Energy production and use often clash with environmental protection. Witness the contentious debates between green advocates and energy companies over offshore drilling for oil and gas or over energy development in other sensitive areas, like the Alaska National Wildlife Refuge. The country still battles, as well, over the extent to which gains from cleaner air and water justify higher costs for fuel. As sensitive as these issues have been and still are, they are comparatively easy to resolve compared to the newest environmental issue in the headlines.

Burning fossil fuels (coal, oil, and natural gas) to create energy emits massive amounts of carbon dioxide (28 billion metric tons worldwide in 2005). These human-generated emissions add significantly to the natural levels of carbon concentrations in the atmosphere (up 35 percent from preindustrial levels).

The layer of carbon and other gases has little effect on short-wave solar radiation passing through the atmosphere to the earth, but it does partially absorb longer-wave infrared (heat) radiation reflected off the earth. The differential leads to the greenhouse effect and higher temperatures in the lower atmosphere (a good thing to a point). As carbon concentrations grow, the warming effect is magnified.

Higher global temperatures have already led to observations of secondary impacts such as rising sea levels, lower moisture levels in soils, melting ice caps, and more violent storms. Global energy use is rapidly increasing. If this trend of mounting energy use continues, the temperature effects will become increasingly disruptive of human life as we now know it, likely in ways that will be very hard to reverse once they are deemed unacceptable. These adverse impacts require us to incorporate the slowing of climate change as part of an overall strategy for energy independence.

CONTROVERSY OVER THE SCIENCE DELAYS ACTION

The first attempt by American scientists to speak with one voice on what was then known about global climate change came in studies by the National Science Foundation in 1977 and 1979. The findings of these and other investigations at the time were reflected in a report issued by Jimmy Carter's White House in January of 1981—after he had failed to win reelection and just one week before vacating the world's most powerful office.

The 92-page *Global Energy Futures and the Carbon Dioxide Problem*, written by the Council on Environmental Quality (CEQ), asserted:

> Many scientists now believe that, if global fossil fuel use grows rapidly in the decades ahead, the accompanying CO_2 increases will lead to profound and long-term alteration of the earth's climate [that] could have far-reaching adverse consequences, affecting our ability to feed a hungry and increasingly crowded world, the habitability of coastal areas and cities, and the preservation of natural areas as we know them today.

The Council said this "sobering perspective" meant the carbon problem "should become a factor in making energy policy and not simply be the subject of scientific investigation."[1]

According to the report, the clearest part of the science was the atmospheric accumulation of carbon. The growth in the greenhouse gas layer had been empirically observed for about two decades, giving confidence to model results that, by 1979, accumulations were well above natural levels.

The ties between rising accumulations of carbon, warming of the planet, and the deleterious effects from that warming were consistent with the theoretical understandings of atmospheric sciences, but not as well grounded in actual data. Because temperatures vary so greatly around the globe, it would take thousands of far-flung measurement points to determine whether the earth was, as the models suggested, actually warming, and at what rate. It would require years to get data that would provide greater certainty. In addition, the report said that physical damage from global warming would not be very visible until the end of the century.

The expectation of future effects not yet seen was based on the unusually long time lags associated with the phenomenon of climate change. With most pollution, a rise or decline in emissions is followed fairly quickly by observable changes in the quality of air or water. Carbon emissions, by contrast, stay in the atmosphere for decades. Thus, the emissions of today will still be part of concentrations and therefore impact the climate many years into the future. Moreover, "because of the oceans' thermal inertia and other compensatory factors," the report projected, "the onset of changes is delayed 2–3 decades. Once detected, however, the world's climate begins to change at a rate which is totally unprecedented in recorded history."[2] This fundamental characteristic of climate change remains largely underrated, even in the post-*An Inconvenient Truth* (Al Gore's 2006 documentary) era.

By 2007, the basic understanding of climate change among most scientists remained largely intact. The sophistication of the analysis and breadth of data, however, had grown enormously. During that year, the Intergovernmental Panel on Climate Change (IPCC), formed by the World Meteorological Organization and other United Nations environmental agencies in 1988, issued its Fourth Assessment report. With access to data from long-buried ice cores, thousands of buoys spread in water bodies around the world, and extensive observations from satellites, the scientists spoke with greater confidence than ever before about the science and the impacts of global warming.[3]

Conscious that the cautious language of science often masked an actual consensus among experts, the Fourth Assessment used the mounting evidence on climate change to more precisely define its levels of certainty. Based on observations of increases in air and ocean temperatures, widespread melting of snow and ice, and rising global sea levels, it declared that "warming of the climate system is unequivocal." It called the link between most of the increase in global temperatures since the mid-twentieth century and human activity "very likely," going beyond its previous finding of "likely." To avoid misunderstanding, the report defined "likely" as greater than a 66 percent probability of occurrence and "very likely" as a 90 percent probability.

The clarity of the language in the 2007 assessment has, within scientific circles, basically ended the debate about the connection between carbon emissions and the warming of the planet. President George W. Bush's chief science advisor, John Marburger, adopted the confidence levels of the IPCC, calling the link "unequivocal" and "90 percent likely."[4] The president also embraced the link between carbon emissions from fossil fuels and global warming in his statements on energy legislation during 2007.

Advocates on both sides of the debate can cherry pick the data that align with their views, but the globe clearly faces warmer temperatures as a result of human activities. What remain open to discussion are the impacts of the warming and the pace of the change.

On the impacts of warming, the Fourth Assessment also upped its certainty from previous statements. At expected levels of emissions, for instance, it projected:

- Larger areas affected by droughts
- Increases in the intensity of hurricanes and typhoons, flooding, and wildfires
- Ocean acidification from carbon not remaining in the atmosphere
- Additional incidence of extremely high sea levels

These projections were determined to be "likely." Failure to go even further was based less on the existence of countervailing information than the lack of the long datasets preferred by scientists. As long anticipated, the report saw the earliest and greatest effects of climate change coming in and near Arctic regions.

For those who thought the impacts would come slowly enough to allow human societies time to adapt, the assessment warned of a new danger that might arrive in about four decades if emission rates were not reduced. "Over the next century," it projected, "net carbon uptake by terrestrial ecosystems is likely to peak before mid-century and then weaken or even reverse, thus amplifying climate change." Nature has muted the impacts of human emissions so far, but its ability to do so is limited. If current trends in emissions continue, we should expect to see future changes from global warming coming more quickly and more intensely.

The Fourth Assessment employed very vigorous standards of evidence. For policymakers, it is important to take into account many studies conducted according to accepted scientific standards that are not early or powerful enough to be included in the IPCC consensus. Some studies see less-negative impacts on the environment than in the Fourth Assessment; a greater number see more extensive impacts.

Some critics of strong action to avert climate change have embraced the new IPCC report and chastised anyone who cites a scientific study not included in its 2007 assessment. The assessments, however, are issued every four years and have a difficult time keeping up with more recent studies. But even the time-lagged findings of the IPCC create a strong case for adopting policies to slow what has become a giant experiment with the planet.

THE ENERGY CONNECTION

About 80 percent of greenhouse gas emissions come from carbon dioxide, largely a result of the combustion of fossil fuels for energy. The remaining share comes from other greenhouse gases, some of which also have energy implications. In many areas of the world, for instance, oil production brings to the surface natural gas, which, lacking local infrastructure for use, is simply flared into the air as methane, releasing a very potent greenhouse gas. The organic matter in landfills also releases methane into the atmosphere, which can be captured as a fuel rather than wasted. The battle over climate change is largely a conflict over how we use energy.

Dealing with climate change is impossible without some combination of the following human responses:

- Reducing energy services (such as limiting driving distances, heating less in the winter, and cooling less in the summer)
- Providing more efficient energy services (i.e., better vehicles, buildings, appliances, and manufacturing processes)
- Displacing carbon fuels with other sources of power (such as nuclear, solar, and wind)
- Shifting among the fossil fuels from the most carbon intensive (coal) to the least (natural gas)

- Protecting and expanding forests and other biosystems that can absorb (sequester) carbon
- Capturing the carbon during the combustion process and reinjecting it belowground (an approach still largely untested)
- Adapting as individuals and societies to the impacts of climate change[5]

Given the magnitude of the climate change problem, the solution will not be one of the above. A successful strategy will probably need to include all or most of them.

Though rarely discussed, imported oil contributes more to global warming than domestic oil. Oil from tar sands in Canada—which are contributing an increasing share of North American production—are very energy-intensive to bring to the surface, meaning that, all other things being equal, a mile driven with oil from tar sands contributes considerably more carbon emissions than oil from U.S. (or many other foreign) wells. Similarly, oil produced in areas that do not control the flaring of natural gas is more dangerous than oil from countries that do. This differential provides added motivation to better manage our dependence on foreign oil.

THE POLITICS OF CLIMATE CHANGE

The first major international agreement on climate change occurred in Rio de Janeiro in 1992, after 143 nations worked out their differences. The United Nations Framework Convention on Climate Change eventually adopted gave official sanction to the consensus of scientists "that human activities have been substantially increasing the atmospheric concentrations of greenhouse gases, that these increases enhance the greenhouse effect, and that this will result on average in an additional warming of the Earth's surface and atmosphere and may adversely affect natural ecosystems and humankind."

The proceedings sparked serious disagreements about whether the industrialized countries should take the lead in mitigating climate change by adopting firm goals to reduce emissions. The suggested target at this stage of international cooperation was the developed nations "returning individually or jointly to their 1990 levels" of anthropogenic emissions of carbon dioxide and other greenhouse gases. The United States (with President George H. W. Bush in attendance) led the fight to avoid any commitments that were binding on the parties. The Earth Summit did endorse the general science behind climate change, set up new mechanisms for more scientific and technical cooperation on the subject, and establish goals for reducing emissions in industrialized nations. Because of U.S. pressure, however, it did not *require* any actions to reduce emissions. Ratification of the treaty breezed through the U.S. Senate on a voice vote.

The debate in the United States over climate change intensified after the Earth Summit in Rio. Several organizations financed by major energy companies launched strong and successful campaigns against mandatory measures to deal with carbon emissions in the United States. In an effort that included television advertising, the groups argued the science on climate change was still "uncertain," that the developed nations should not act in advance of commitments by the developing nations, and economic growth should not be sacrificed to reduce emissions.

The political effectiveness of these attacks became evident in 1997, when the Senate passed a resolution sponsored by senators Robert Byrd (D-WV) and Chuck Hagel (R-NE) by a vote of 95-0. The measure expressed the sense of the Senate that the United States should not sign any treaty that "would result in serious harm to the economy of the United States" or that would impose new greenhouse gas emissions reductions on the economically developed countries unless it "also mandates new specific scheduled commitments to limit or reduce greenhouse gas emissions for Developing Country Parties within the same compliance period." Though some voting for Byrd-Hagel denied it, the resolution was crafted to tie the hands of the Clinton administration, then preparing to enter into a new round of negotiations on climate change in Kyoto, Japan.

At Kyoto in December, the United States joined with other nations to negotiate a protocol requiring the developed nations, from 2008 to 2012, to cut their emissions, on average, 5 percent below 1990 levels. Participants realized that the now-mandatory steps outlined at Kyoto fell well short of what would eventually be necessary to substantially slow global warming.

Complaining about the lack of mandates on China and other developing countries, and about potential damage to the economy, Frank Murkowski (R), chair of the Senate Energy and Natural Resources Committee, quickly called a news conference to declare, "The Kyoto deal is dead on arrival."[6] The Senator from Alaska was right. Finding little support in the Senate for the treaty, the Clinton administration never submitted it for ratification.

The presidential campaigns in 2000 gave voters reason to believe that whoever won might support action to combat global warming. Before becoming vice president, Al Gore had been an early leader in drawing attention to the issue, and his 1992 book *Earth in the Balance* called for action at a time when few people were paying much attention. Texas Governor George W. Bush, agreed to quotas for the use of renewable fuels for electric generation and, as presidential candidate, supported legislation to cap emissions of carbon dioxide. After his election, Bush, much to the surprise of his chief of the Environmental Protection Agency, reversed his position on carbon caps.[7]

For most of his presidency, Bush accepted one metric for reducing greenhouse gases—emissions per unit of the gross domestic product (GDP). This goal was guaranteed to be met. With no special effort, every developed nation in which manufacturing as a share of the economy is dropping and service industries are rising experiences a decline in emissions per unit of GDP. Thus, the country could celebrate its "success" on climate change, with actual emissions rising as long as the economy continued to grow even more. The idea sent the world a message—it was appropriate for a country with a quarter of the world's economy to emit a quarter of the world's carbon dioxide. The failure to even give lip service to reducing U.S. carbon emissions moved the American position even further away from predominant world opinion and from the warnings of scientists.

In the absence of federal leadership, many state and local governments instituted programs addressing climate change. Notable in this regard, in 2004 California completed rulemaking, calling for a 30 percent reduction in carbon emissions from vehicles (equivalent to a 30 percent improvement in fuel economy), after which New York and several other states adopted the same standard. In addition, nine northeastern states joined together to cap and eventually cut emissions in the region. By 2007, other large states like Florida had announced bold plans to limit carbon emissions, and California greatly expanded its commitments to steep reductions.

Such efforts by state and local governments face stiff legal opposition from affected industries and the Bush administration. If some of them are implemented, however, they can begin to affect national trends. Even the threat of state actions improves the chances of getting legislative action at the federal level.

The Kyoto protocol took effect in February of 2005, having been ratified by 141 nations. Among the major industrialized countries, only the United States and Australia failed to join the agreement. (A change of government in Australia led to its agreement to the Kyoto treaty in 2007.) The actual trends in emissions, however, showed the Kyoto agreement falling far short of its goals. Emissions of a few countries (United Kingdom, Germany, Denmark, Finland, Bulgaria, Romania, Hungary, and the former Soviet Union states) fell below 1990 levels. But many more countries covered by the pact showed steep increases. Emissions in Canada, which ratified Kyoto, jumped 35 percent over the 15 years. For the two industrial nations still out of the agreement, the United States grew by 19 percent and Australia by 54 percent. Among the developing nations without any targets, India's emissions rose 22 percent, China's 137 percent.

The world's nations gathered again in December of 2007 to discuss how they could move beyond the Kyoto protocol and achieve greater reductions in emissions. Talks at the new conference in Bali became strained, as the United States (and China) held out against considering any mandatory reductions. By the end, however, there was a slight thaw. With Bush claiming credit back home for new legislation taking steps to reduce American emissions, the U.S. delegation reluctantly agreed that all options remained on the table, leaving the language sufficiently vague on whether future action might include mandatory cuts. Former Vice President Gore urged delegates from other countries to anticipate new opportunities for agreement. To loud applause, he predicted, "Over the next two years, the United States is going to be somewhere it is not now."[8]

Beyond the narrow issues of whether the United States has ratified Kyoto or whether China accepts limits lies the larger question of whether any nations outside of Europe have the political will to reduce carbon emissions. The United States and China loom particularly large, however. As the emissions of these two giants approach half of the world total, what happens in these countries will have profound impacts on the entire world. How the United States handles its own legislation to reduce or cap greenhouse gases will carry at least as much weight as its posture at international conferences.

FOUR CONTENTIOUS ISSUES

No one can deny that the issue of climate change has provoked sharp disagreements in the United States. Until 2007, the reasons for not acting prevailed over those for beginning to reduce emissions as a step toward eventually stabilizing or even reducing concentrations. Four issues in this debate stand out.

Is the Science Solid?

Those arguing against steps to reduce carbon emissions have maintained that the science of climate change is uncertain. The choice of words is tactically brilliant. A scientist who thinks something is very likely is reluctant to say that he or she is certain of the matter. Therefore, clever questioners at congressional hearings have no trouble getting expert witnesses concerned about global warming to agree the science is uncertain.

As recently as the summer of 2005, the editorialists at the *Wall Street Journal* opined, "[T]he earth is slightly warmer than it used to be a century ago, but no one knows why." They complained the U.S. Senate was "hurtling toward passage of limits on greenhouse gases, even as the scientific case for such a mini-Kyoto Protocol looks weaker all the time."[9] This position was taken in the face of a series of studies by the National Science Foundation, international scientific collaborations that consistently said confidence in the science was growing, and the absence of any evidence that Congress was about to take immediate action.

Individuals and societies act to prevent all sorts of mishaps that are far from certain to occur. Given the time lags between today's emissions and tomorrow's impacts, climate change planning faces an especially tough challenge. When a specific harm becomes visible to the human eye, it is likely the product of actions taken decades earlier. If we are unwilling to use models to suggest what is likely in the future, we will be faced with a series of increasingly serious impacts, each of which, when observed, will be for decades (or longer) irreversible. As a result, determination by scientists that significant damage is likely should be a sufficient spur to action.

The announcement by the Intergovernmental Panel in 2007 that the science of climate change has a 90 percent probability has, for the most part, quelled talk that the science is still questionable. Although the time may have come to move on to other issues, it should not be forgotten that there was a period when scientists agreed on the basics of climate change, but due to various influential groups, many public officials remained unconvinced. The brouhaha over the science has delayed action for two decades. This lost time is very difficult to make up. What might have been a more gradual path toward reducing emissions will now have to take on greater urgency.

Who Should Go First?

When the Rio summit met in 1992, it was clear the greatest increases in carbon emissions would come from the developing nations, particularly China. If anything, the growth in China has come even faster than anticipated. Some have seized on this indisputable trend to argue the United States should not undertake any binding commitments until China does likewise.

This argument is not easily dismissed. It is inconceivable that any response to global warming lacking cooperation from China could be successful in the long run. Moreover, if sufficient capital is available, the economics of limiting emissions in developing nations may be better than in the wealthier countries. In countries with advanced economies, the energy infrastructure is largely in place, whereas rapidly developing nations are creating that infrastructure. It is much more cost effective to purchase more efficient equipment initially (get it right the first time) than retrofit or swap out old equipment. Thus, the economics of investing in carbon reduction in the countries where energy use is growing most rapidly has great appeal.

Still, the more affluent nations have always gone first on major environmental issues, even when recognizing the eventual need for cooperation around the globe to achieve success. In the case of greenhouse gases, where previous contributions to concentrations weigh heavily, the United States bears special responsibility to the world to play a leading role in solving the problem. Wealthier countries have the capital and the ability to invent new technologies to address environmental problems. It is also reasonable to assume that evidence that the United States, Europe, and Japan can combine carbon reductions with economic growth will be needed to convince developing areas to follow the same path. America has to break the current impasse and prove it can successfully reduce carbon emissions. At that point, the top international priority must become getting China to better address its contributions to the problem.

China cannot do so alone. Industrialized nations may need to help subsidize some of the high-technology options. One of the best low-tech scenarios would be an extensive natural gas pipeline system that would allow Russia—which has the world's greatest reserves—to provide massive volumes to China to displace the use of coal. Such international commerce would help address the world's climate problem, greatly enhance the quality of life in China, and provide substantial revenues for the Russians.

What About the Economy?

As disputes about the science of climate change have subsided, the question of how much it would cost to reduce carbon emissions has taken on greater prominence. Advocates for strong action on climate change tend to minimize the costs, while those arguing for delay tend to exaggerate them.

The two sides reach starkly different conclusions, for instance, about the impact of carbon reduction on job gains or losses. Reducing carbon emissions will likely create jobs in industries like wind, solar, and nuclear power. It will likely reduce employment in the coal and railroad industries. Whatever the results of detailed analyses, the gains and losses to some extent cancel each other out. The effect on *net* jobs will be more muted than either side acknowledges. This view may not be very comforting, though, to workers who lose jobs in one industry and have limited ability to move into new ones.

This perspective is hardly a reason to delay action. Starting early allows transitions to take place more gradually and with less shock to employment and other aspects of the economy. Waiting will necessitate more rapid transitions and prove to have more jarring impacts.

Much discussion about economic impacts has centered on the relationship between measures to reduce carbon emissions and economic growth. In 1998, the Energy Information Administration (EIA) prepared a study (which I supervised) on the subject for the House Science Committee, called *What Does the Kyoto Protocol Mean to U.S. Energy Markets and the U.S. Economy?* The report earned kudos from conservatives because it projected (correctly in my view) higher fuel costs from adopting the Kyoto goals than shown by a White House study. On economic impacts, EIA estimated that the loss could get as high as $72 billion dollars in 2010. But taking into account the GDP was over $7 trillion at the time of the study, the overall results did not sound too bad. In all cases, the economy continued to grow. In EIA's midrange scenario, the rate of growth fell about four-tenths of a percent a year during a transition period. Then, the impacts on economic growth faded and eventually became undetectable. The biggest gap in the EIA study resulted from its inability to calculate the loss to economic growth from global warming in order to put the price of reducing emissions in perspective.

The costs of global warming were incorporated into a massive study presented in 2006 and led by Nicholas Stern, head of the United Kingdom's Government Economic Service and former chief economist of the World Bank. *The Economics of Climate Change: The Stern Review* emphasized its extensive peer review and was called by Nobel Prize–winning economist Joseph Stiglitz, "the most thorough and rigorous analysis to date of the costs and risks of climate change, and the costs and risks of reducing emissions."[10] Receiving commercial distribution in 2007, the report estimated "that if we don't act, the overall costs and risks of climate change will be equivalent to losing at least 5 percent of global GDP each year, now and forever." By contrast, it found "the costs of action—reducing greenhouse gas emissions to avoid the worst impacts of climate change—can be limited to around 1 % of global GDP each year." According to the Stern projections, there is no doubt the economy benefits from strong action on slow global warming.

Several prominent economists who work on climate change issues took Stern to task for not discounting costs based on uncertainties of outcomes and the future nature of the impacts, as would have been done in many leading economic models. Adjusting Stern's numbers to more conventional discount rates lessens some of the economic advantages of strong action to slow global warming.

It is important to note that the leading academic economists who criticized the Stern review were not arguing against taking immediate steps to lower greenhouse gas emissions. After taking into account the limitations of the Stern review and recalculating the results using widely accepted discount rates, Kenneth Arrow, winner of the 1972 Nobel Prize for economics, found the Stern estimates implied that slowing climate change passed a benefit-cost test and concluded, "there can be little serious argument over the importance of a policy of avoiding major further increases in combustion [of fossil fuel] by-products." William Nordhaus, a prominent

Yale economist involved in many university efforts around the country to model climate change, called the review "political in nature" and lacking "an appraisal of methods and assumptions by independent outside experts." Nordhaus also made clear that he found the position of President Bush against binding reductions in emissions lacking economic analysis and said, "One of the major findings in the economics of climate change has been that efficient or 'optimal' economic policies to slow climate change involve modest rates of emissions reductions in the near term, followed by sharp reductions in the medium and long term."[11]

Many laymen are uncomfortable with such complex economic models and the technical debates they engender. These models are like democracies, often flawed but better than the alternatives. Models, particularly when their inner workings are transparent to outside observers, are credible ways of accommodating vast amounts of data, weighing the importance of countervailing evidence and recognizing feedback effects that might be ignored in simpler analyses. The bottom line is that the leading economic models suggest a need to reduce emissions immediately, whether gradually at first (Arrow and Nordhaus) or more urgently (Stern).

The major contributions of the Stern and other studies are the careful introduction of the costs of climate change into the equation and the expansion of the time horizons considered. Because of the time lags in replacing the energy infrastructure and the physical momentum of climate change, the costs of dealing with it are front-loaded and the benefits very much back loaded. Any economic analysis that takes the longer view is likely to give a fairer account of costs and benefits.

Considering the many economic variables associated with both climate change and expanding the time horizon to a century strains the capabilities of much traditional economic analysis. In some cases, we may need to fall back on simple ethics. It is hard to calculate the relative costs when carbon emissions in the United States are contributing to desertification in Africa or when actions and their impacts span several generations. Yet most of us were taught at an early age to clean up our own messes and to leave the world a better place for those who come later. These may not be economic principles per se, but they undergird all successful economies.

We should be grateful to all who raise the hard economic questions. They will encourage us to seek the most cost-effective solutions. Both those who want to take quick action and those who want to go slow should agree that we want to adopt the solutions that have the lowest costs and the greatest benefits.

Slow Down Global Warming or Adapt to It?

Some opponents of bold actions to reduce greenhouse gas emissions are now giving great emphasis to a different argument. They assert it would be better to adapt to rising temperatures than to take measures to slow them. As eminent an economist as Alan Greenspan, after despairing of prospects for reducing the emissions of greenhouse gases, concludes, "Remediation is far more likely than prevention to garner adequate political and popular support."[12]

Several examples have been given to show the advantages of adaptation over emission reductions. Greenspan cites the success of the Dutch in building dikes that can counter rising sea levels and floods. Bjorn Lomborg, author of *Cool It: The Skeptical Environmentalist's Guide to Global Warming* (2007), discusses the best ways to deal with health threats arising from climate change. He asserts it is more cost effective, for instance, to buy bed nets and medicines for malaria-prone areas of Africa than to try to reduce the disease by stabilizing climate change.[13] Few would argue that adaptation is not already an important component of climate change strategy. Coastal residents are already adjusting to global warming by building farther away from the shore and absorbing higher insurance costs. Some communities devote additional resources to suppressing fires, the dangers of which are "likely" to grow because of climate change, according to the Fourth Assessment. But how much adaptation will be needed, and should it be our primary response to global warming?

There are several problems associated with relying primarily on adaptation to deal with global climate change. Justification of this position cannot rely just on analysis showing that the cost of *some* adaptations are cheaper than the *total* cost of reducing emissions. They will have to aggregate all the adaptations that might be required in order to compare apples with apples. When identifying the impacts that require adaptation, it is important to note that the rigorous methodology of the IPCC creates a greater likelihood that the impacts will be understated rather than overstated.

The adaptationists also fail to acknowledge that the impacts will become more rapid and intense. At some point, the point of remediation is passed, absent escape to another planet. As Bush advisor Marburger told the BBC in September of 2007, "The CO_2 accumulates in the atmosphere and there's no end point, it just gets hotter and hotter, and so at some point it becomes unlivable."

Recognizing that a considerable amount of climate change in the coming decades is already locked in, the adaptationists take the position that *the train has already left the station*. But there is a very strong counterpoint, namely, *there will be many more trains leaving the station*.[14]

The Greenspan tilt toward remediation contains an argument that could have profound implications for future international relations. When we rely on remediation, he says, "It has the advantage that the costs are borne by the same populace that achieves the benefits." In other words, those damaged by the emissions should be held more accountable than the sources of the damage. This "advantage" flips traditional ethics and environmental economics on their head. Now it is the victim who should pay. This new line of thought on environmental policy will have a hard time winning global support, particularly in coastal areas of Bangladesh, where poor residents will have a very difficult time adjusting to the rising sea levels that are expected.

We have some time to fine-tune our thinking as we act to prevent and remediate the effects of carbon emissions. For now, the emphasis should be on the industrialized nations quickly moving to *begin* significant reductions. The Stern report is the strongest analysis we have at present, and it presents an economically viable case for prevention.

NEW THINKING ABOUT ENERGY INDEPENDENCE

Talk of energy independence has traditionally focused on avoiding reliance on insecure foreign fuels. The damage from hurricanes Katrina and Rita has led to greater sensitivity that our economy is also vulnerable to interruptions from natural disasters. The threat of climate change opens up a third major area of concern.

Reliance on fuels—whether domestic or foreign—that bring great harm to the environment is another issue of dependence versus independence. A strong nation addresses such problems and finds cost-effective solutions. At present, the United States stands as both the greatest contributor to the existing concentrations of greenhouse gases and the only major industrial nation refusing to join international agreements to cut emissions. This stance threatens to weaken American influence on other matters. If we want to influence other nations on issues like democratization, open markets, and human rights (to name just a few), we will have to show leadership on climate change.

The early steps of leadership come easier than is generally thought. A more expansive view of energy independence, which includes the need to slow global warming, opens up the possibility of energy policy *threefers*. These are approaches that help national security, the economy, and the environment by simultaneously cutting reliance on foreign oil and carbon emissions. Many policies that encourage greater energy efficiency or expanded use of energy that does not produce carbon emissions fall into this category. They help solve a multitude of problems.

Until now, cost-benefit analyses of potential energy policies have confined the benefits to those resulting from reduced reliance on oil imports *or* carbon emissions. What if we combine the benefits? The costs do not go up. The benefits are multiplied. We get it all for the price of one.

This argument is based on more than theory. Remember the good news of oil imports dropping by half from 1977 to 1982? The story that somehow got lost in history? Well, guess what happened to carbon emissions during that period?

Carbon emissions in the United States dropped from 4,794 million metric tons in 1977 to 4,367 million in 1982—a decrease of 9 percent. This happened when we had no policy to reduce such emissions. But we did have other energy policies in place. The reductions in carbon emissions were a side benefit from these other policies, primarily implemented to cut dependence on foreign oil. The carbon reductions were, in a sense, free, because nothing special was done to produce them.

Energy policies that help national security, the economy, and the environment (the *threefers*) cannot carry us all the way to where we need to get on slowing climate change, but they can provide the foundation for a very good start. That is where the focus should be for the next several years, as we prepare for the bolder actions that will soon be needed.

Chapter 6

The Magic and Limits of Market-Based Solutions

President Ronald Reagan revolutionized thinking in Washington about the role of government in energy matters. He spoke out against federal intervention in energy markets, and his thinking dominated the 1980s. His influence on energy policy continued well after he left office. "Let the market handle it," remained the prevailing energy mantra under his successors. "Don't interfere with the laws of supply and demand."

In the 1970s, economists like Stephen Breyer, Alfred Kahn, Richard Vietor, Edward Mitchell, and Paul MacAvoy challenged the over-involvement of government in energy. The pendulum had swung too far toward government regulation, and their critiques helped revamp policy and bring about a better understanding of energy markets.

But now, with the pendulum having swung so far in the other direction, it's time to challenge the current laissez-faire approach that derides any role for government in energy policy. We have to make accurate assessments about what the government and the market can do best. We need to base these judgments on current realities, not on tired ideologies. Not surprisingly, both sides of the argument have a point.

WHEN MARKETS WORK

As market forces react to deftly balance supply and demand, they are a marvel to watch. The weekly data reports of the Energy Information Administration are closely watched by the media and energy investors. Everyone tries to get ahead of their competitors in detecting new trends. A careful reading of these reports often reveals the beneficial effects of market forces.

My favorite (remember, I am a policy wonk at heart) is trans-Atlantic trade in oil. Sometimes, tight supplies in the United States force up prices at the same time supplies are comparatively ample in Europe. If the price differential reaches a certain point (maybe $1 to $3 a barrel, depending on freight rates and other factors careful traders take into account), tankers from Europe sail westward to fetch a better price in the American market. If oil supplies are scarcer in Europe, the same effect is seen in reverse and oil shipments move east. Within a couple of weeks, the supply imbalances are worked out. It is the market at work.

We can further highlight the benefits of the trans-Atlantic commerce in oil (and other forms of energy trading) by imagining how government regulation would handle the matter. It would take a while for the problem to get on the agenda of busy public officials. Then special interests would weigh in. Lawyers would have to evaluate the options. Bureaucrats would worry that any sign of government concern might cause people to panic. It would take weeks to do the research. It would take even longer to implement whatever was decided. By the time the decision took effect, conditions could well have changed, and the tankers might be moving in the wrong direction.

When I was at the Energy Information Administration, I favored releasing data to the public as quickly as possible. This tended to squeeze out the slack in the system that allowed a customary review of them by government officials. In my view, an accurate response by energy markets was more likely to produce good results than any particular short-term action by the government.

The esteem in which markets are held has risen due to some notorious examples of government interference making matters worse. The price controls announced by Richard Nixon in 1971 helped him win reelection by keeping gasoline (and other) prices low. But as time went on, the price controls made it increasingly difficult to balance supply and demand, contributing to America's great energy crises.

In 1973, Nixon, working again with a Democratic Congress, started government allocation of oil supplies. This idea never worked very well. The officials in charge proved inept at assessing market conditions. It took too long to make decisions. The system was overly rigid and could not deal with nuances in the market. Often, fuel was in the wrong place at the wrong time.

Presidents Ford and Carter started the process of deregulation, and Reagan finished the job during his first months in office. Soon after Reagan's action, prices started a steady decline and supplies became more abundant. The evidence seemed clear that free markets were better for energy consumers than government regulation.

The good reputation of markets was enhanced by the experience of the first Persian Gulf War under President George H. W. Bush. The loss of oil exports from Iraq and Kuwait constituted a major interruption in the world market equivalent to those during the oil crises of the 1970s. Prices did shoot up near record levels, but normalcy returned much quicker than before. The negative impacts of massive chaos in world oil markets were much less in a deregulated market.

There was an even larger matter that solidified the national preference for market-based solutions to all sorts of problems. A capitalistic United States won the Cold War over a socialistic Soviet Union. The victory demonstrated the weakness of countries in which government controls curtailed freedom.

We must be careful, however, to give markets credit only when credit is due. Let us take a closer look at these major market victories. As it turns out, markets have, on several occasions, achieved great successes with the help of nonmarket forces.

When Reagan finally terminated oil price caps and allocation in 1981, government efforts to lower the demand for oil were having great effect. Auto fuel efficiency standards contributed to a big drop in the consumption of gasoline. Tax credits for better insulation of buildings were cutting demand for heating oil. Tough government rules led to the displacement of most oil used for generation of electricity. The transition away from oil was assisted by the continued addition of new nuclear power plants, a technology developed for navy submarines and ultimately for the private sector by the government. High fuel prices also played an important part in limiting demand, but the contributions of successful government programs cannot be denied.

Similarly, the role of the market in resolving oil shortages during the first Persian Gulf War has been exaggerated. The most important factor in correcting the shortage of oil was the decision by Saudi Arabia to increase its production by 3 million barrels a day—a sudden injection equivalent to 5 percent of total world demand. The United States only released a small amount of oil from its strategic reserves, but the knowledge that it had more helped calm world markets. Saudi Arabia's excess productive capacity and its willingness to use it were hardly the result of market forces. They were political decisions taken to enhance its world position and ally itself with the Americans in the fight against Saddam Hussein. Price signals and market forces worked better than the controls of yore. But credit must also be given to the diplomatic efforts of the first Bush administration, Saudi strategic judgments, and years of building American oil reserves—all examples of prudent government intervention.

We must be careful that belief in an omnipotent and benevolent market does not inspire a new religion. If we become convinced of the advantages of markets more as a matter of faith than analysis, we will find it more difficult to assess their strengths and weaknesses—an exercise essential to figuring out how to achieve energy independence.

REMEMBERING BASIC PRINCIPLES

The fiercest defenders of free markets have often acknowledged their limits. Markets work better, in their view, when they are tweaked (hopefully in limited ways) to offset these imperfections.

A critical limitation of totally free markets is their failure to account for external costs—a concept particularly relevant when constructing energy policies. The idea is important because the purchasers of fuel often do not pay the full costs of items they obtain. This happens in cases when the producer can deflect his or her costs into "the commons" and not have to pass them on to customers. A classic example of an external cost would be if any garbage generated in manufacturing is simply dumped in a neighbor's yard or a public park. In such situations, the neighbor or the general populace, rather than the company or the buyer of the product, picks up the tab for making sure the garbage is not an eyesore and does not endanger public health. Market economists want prices to send the right signals to consumers. When purchase prices do not incorporate significant external costs they do not provide the right incentives.

Over the years, the idea of external costs has not been terribly partisan or controversial. Academic economists who have come to Washington to serve in administrations both Democratic and Republican have generally accepted the concept that consumers should pay the full (external costs incorporated) price for goods, and there is an important role for government when they do not.

Still, in the 1980s and 1990s, the idea that markets might not be perfect was neglected, and the need to calculate external costs received less emphasis. This situation had led to an era of sloppy thinking, when economists applied textbook theories to current problems and paid scant attention to data that might challenge their theories or the need to think about imperfections in the market. (Beware of economists whose research is funded by business groups that hate all forms of government regulation.)

It is impossible to do serious analysis of energy economics without careful consideration of external costs. The environmental impacts of energy are immense, even without considering the role of greenhouse gases in producing global warming. The risks of costly interruption in the delivery of energy services are not included in the price paid by consumers. Neither are the military costs, whether in dollars or lives, of conflicts in the Persian Gulf incorporated into the price paid at the pump for gasoline. Market-based solutions make sense, but only when they acknowledge the significance of external costs.

THE INCONVENIENT REALITIES OF THE MARKET

As much as we may want a world oil market that operates according to the principles of a pure market, such a market simply does not exist. Moreover, the idea that this scenario could come to pass in our lifetimes is virtually unthinkable. Let us look at how energy markets really work.

Virtually all the largest oil and gas companies (measured by reserves under their control) are government owned. These government behemoths share some characteristics with investor-owned companies, but they are very different animals. National political goals often trump decision-making based on traditional economics. Most notably, government oil companies are under political pressure to maximize distribution of the proceeds of oil sales and minimize investment in future production. With low emphasis on investment, most state-owned oil companies have trouble maintaining production at levels expected from the size of their reserves.

Twelve countries with large state-owned oil companies operate as a giant cartel. The Organization of Petroleum Exporting Countries was in its early years an ineffective cartel. Its influence zoomed in the 1970s, however, as America became more dependent on foreign oil, the exporting countries nationalized their private oil companies, and the Arab oil embargo exposed the weaknesses of the major industrialized nations. The goals of the embargo were political, but during the boycott OPEC found it could limit production, raise prices, and take in much greater proceeds than when it allowed private companies to increase production. This discovery changed forever the basic nature of the world oil market.

The Organization of Petroleum Exporting Countries eventually overplayed its hand, pushing prices higher and higher by limiting production. Finally, the industrialized nations lowered their oil consumption, setting off a drop in prices and fighting among OPEC members over who should bear the brunt of further cuts in production. For almost two decades, OPEC floundered, not able to coordinate its efforts to reverse a protracted buyers' market.

The resurrection of OPEC's influence began in 1999, when key members Saudi Arabia, Iran, and Venezuela began to work more cooperatively and the organization regained its discipline in controlling production.

The success of OPEC in reasserting its control of the world oil market rested to a large extent on a change in government in Venezuela. This South American country had, during the 1990s, welcomed investments by Western oil companies and pretty much ignored OPEC quotas. How could the cartel enforce discipline on other members if one of its key founding members was the poster child for cheating on quotas? The election of Hugo Chavez as president in 1998, however, brought a sharp reversal of Venezuela's posture toward restraints on production. Suddenly, Venezuela became a hawk, sticking with tough quotas in order to raise prices. The OPEC strategy was also aided by a steady growth in oil demand in the United States, due to a long period of low prices, and by a booming China with a growing appetite for energy.

The impact of the cartel became evident throughout the Bush years, as spot prices passed $30 a barrel, then $50, then $70, then $90. In his final year, oil has broken the long-thought-unapproachable $100 barrier. The American invasion of Iraq lowered oil production in that country, and saber rattling on Iran increased market nervousness in general about supplies from the Persian Gulf. Cartels do not succeed in most economics textbooks. But now, oil exporters are raking in the money without having to increase production, and OPEC is on a new roll.

Despite these problems, the mindset remained in many quarters that Congress should not increase the government's role in energy, since to do so would interfere in the free market believed to exist. Fortunately, Congress in 2007 recognized the fallacy of this argument and began to challenge OPEC's dominance of the world trade in oil.

I wanted to avoid this, but I must bring up the issue of elasticity. For oil markets to work, prices must be set by balances between supply and demand. If supplies are tight, prices will rise. If prices go up enough, they encourage an expansion of supply and contraction of demand. It also works in the other direction when there are energy surpluses. Thus, the market is constantly self-correcting.

But there is an important hitch. It may take quite a while for high prices to bring on greater supplies or reduced demand. If the responses are rapid, the market is elastic. If they are slow, the market is inelastic. This distinction is not just a matter of economic theory. If you are pulling up to the pump to buy gasoline, it makes all the difference in the world.

We know from experience that oil supplies do not react quickly to price. If prices are low, private oil companies will rarely find it economical to shut-in production. On the other end of the spectrum, if you are paying $3 for a gallon of gasoline, you cannot take comfort in the idea that your high price is going to suddenly bring some newfound oil to market. Moving through the stages of exploration, development, and production takes many years. In addition, oil companies have to proceed cautiously and take into account that prices might drop after they launch their projects. Government companies in a cartel may not want to increase production at all. As a result, a market response described in economics textbooks is not as likely, at least in the short run, in the real world.

Is demand for oil more elastic to price movements? It has been in the past. The price shocks from the oil crises during the Carter years played a major role in cutting U.S. demand for oil and ultimately bringing down prices. But the demand response to higher prices has been more muted of late. The price of crude oil in 2006 was almost five times that in 1998. Did the demand for gasoline drop, as my economics professor said it should? Exploding prices dampened the increase, but it sure did didn't stop it. Gasoline consumption rose during each of the eight years. Many of us who follow energy trends and believe they tend to be cyclical due to the laws of supply and demand have frankly been puzzled by this extreme case of inelasticity. If demand does not respond very much to price spikes, how can the market correct itself?

I think I now have an explanation. Commentators on high oil prices often tend to discount their importance because they are not hurting the economy. They explain that energy used to be a bigger share of the economy, and, therefore, rising energy prices in the past were more quickly translated into general inflation and slowing economic growth. Now that energy constitutes a smaller share, these adverse effects are less likely to occur. It sounds like good news.

But there is a downside. If energy is a smaller part of my personal budget, I might be able to ignore higher prices and keep on driving. And that is a problem. As energy becomes a smaller and smaller part of disposable personal income, we do not have to adjust our behavior to higher prices, and energy markets become less elastic.

It gets worse. China views oil as vital to economic growth and is not going to cut consumption if it feels it is needed to implement national policy objectives. Thus wealthy American drivers and Chinese five-year planners have something in common. They are not going to be deterred from a growing reliance on foreign oil just because the price has gone up.

There are two factors that discipline the OPEC oil cartel, as they have publicly stated. First, they fear a sharp drop in demand that would erode their market. Apportioning cuts among the OPEC producers is never easy. Second, they fear damage to the major industrialized economies. They have invested a substantial part of their oil revenues abroad and will suffer from any substantial damage inflicted by high oil prices. We might take encouragement when high oil prices are not damaging the economy, but so does OPEC.

We have a (largely unrecognized) problem here. If there is no drop in oil consumption and no damage to the economy, what will stop the cartel (and oil traders) from continuing to force up prices? Maybe prices will keep going up *until* there is a drop in consumption or damage to the economy. Talk about having to pick your poison.

Market forces are wonderful, but they aren't all they're cracked up to be when it comes to energy. There is an oil cartel out there; the affluence of the Western nations has blunted demand responses to high fuel prices; and China is plunging ahead unconstrained by many of the laws of supply and demand. The market has not followed the textbook so far, and needs some assistance from enlightened national policy.

TECHNOLOGY AND THE MARKET

Advocates of keeping the government from interfering in the economy sometimes grant that there is a legitimate role for government in spurring new technologies. It is hard to imagine the development of nuclear reactors or the Internet, for instance, without strong efforts organized by the government. The position of combining free markets with government stimulus of technology provides a political safe haven for politicians of many stripes. It was the predominant strategic position of both Democrats and Republicans until a new Congress came to Washington in 2007.

The numerous calls (since those of Richard Nixon in 1973) for scientific projects as intense as the Manhattan Project and the Apollo moon landing imply that the United States has the scientific ingenuity to invent its way out of its dependence on foreign oil. Yet after all these years of rhetoric about Manhattan and Apollo, the great solution to our dependence on foreign oil has yet to emerge. Is it possible there is something inherently wrong about comparing energy with the efforts to build the atom bomb or send a man to the moon?

I found the answer to this question deep in the archives of the Ford Presidential Library. President Ford and Secretary of State Kissinger, eager to convince allies in Europe and Japan (as well as the American people) that the United States was taking the recent energy crisis seriously, bragged publicly in 1974 that we had already spent more on energy research than on either Manhattan or Apollo. After these public boasts, the president asked for a more detailed analysis from Mike Duval, a trusted 35-year-old White House aide, to determine whether the claims were factually correct.

The former Marine officer and scheduler for President Nixon reported back that projected government spending on energy research and development already exceeded that for the atomic bomb or the moon landing. Duval suggested to the president, however, that the administration might be comparing apples and oranges. "[U]nlike space and defense, the private sector will be the main customer for the fruits of our energy R&D efforts," he noted. "In the case of space and defense, the main user, of course, is the government itself." The technologies advanced by government research would have to compete in the private market. Even with research efforts well beyond Manhattan and Apollo, there would be less assurance of success.[1]

The insight of the Ford advisor has been totally ignored ever since. Crop after crop of politicians have continued to call for another Manhattan or Apollo project for energy, ignoring the basic difference that the government is not the primary customer for alternative fuels. These fuels will penetrate the market only when energy consumers find their qualities and costs attractive.

We have plenty of evidence that an energy strategy confined to competitive markets and investments in technology will not work. It is the strategy that has been employed by recent Republican and Democratic administrations, and oil imports have continued to escalate. Yes, technology has improved. But it has been offset by demands for a wider range of energy services and increases in population. It is a path that has led in the past (and will lead in the future) to growing dependence on oil imports. We need to do more.

Any successful plan for energy must accommodate market forces. It also has to recognize the limitations of a totally unfettered market. We know from experience that a "markets only" or a "markets lite" (supply and demand plus government stimulus of technology) strategy is insufficient. We need to invest much more in new technologies than we do currently, but we must find additional solutions if we really want to win energy independence.

A TURNING OF THE SHIP?

It has been remarkable how little influence the high energy prices of the twenty-first century have had on energy supply and demand. Yet some recent evidence suggests that their influence is finally being felt and will become even greater in the next decade. If this is true, the market is going to make a belated contribution to energy independence—much less than suggested in the economics textbooks, but considerably more than it appeared to just a couple of years ago. As is so often the case in these matters, the truth lies somewhere between the two polar positions.

High prices do seem to be corralling American driving habits a bit. Annual driving distance per car dropped slightly in 2005, only the second decrease since 1980. The numbers also suggest that people are, to a limited extent, purchasing more efficient vehicles. These mini-trends were offset by population growth (which runs about 1 percent a year), but U.S. oil consumption has remained fairly stable over the past three years. This is hardly an energy revolution, but is still a lot better than the 15 percent increase throughout the 1990s. The growth in oil imports has also stopped, at least for a while. After foreign oil topped 60 percent of consumption for the first time in 2005, imports have dropped a bit, both in volume and percentage.

The Energy Information Administration's initial release of *Annual Energy Outlook 2008* foresees additional impacts from high oil prices. The agency projects that high prices will bring a modest rebound in U.S. oil production. From 2006 to 2020, output rises 22 percent. This returns production only to the levels of the late 1990s, but it is better than the continuous decline since the mid–1980s. It makes the battle for energy independence somewhat more winnable than it appeared just a few years ago.

The Energy Information Administration also projects some relief on the demand side, with oil consumption still rising, but much more slowly than before. Imports of oil in volume grow even more slowly. In share of consumption, imports drop to 55 percent by 2010 and remain at that level until 2020. In its 2001 *Outlook,* EIA had projected oil dependence in 2020 at 64 percent. Emissions of carbon dioxide also continue to grow, but more slowly than in previous forecasts.

These shifts in energy trends are due mainly to higher prices. The initial 2008 projections were completed before passage of the Energy Independence and Security Act of 2007. As a result, the impacts of recent policies were not included.

The market reactions to high prices, even in the long term, are not proportional to the magnitude of the price hikes. The market is not an elastic rubber band that reacts immediately to price shifts. It is more like a giant cruise ship that has slowed down and is trying to turn around. Ingrained patterns of consumption and state oil companies not investing in future production will continue to keep the market from emulating the graphs in the economics textbooks.

Still, even moderate corrections in the market are going to help in the battle for energy independence. Reversing the trends of growing reliance on foreign oil and emissions of greenhouse gases enough to make a big difference remains daunting. But at least we will be getting some help from reactions in the market. Efforts to put new energy policies in place will not have to confront trends moving inexorably in the opposite direction.

To build on this foundation, we will have to move beyond the partisan sound bites of energy debates in recent decades, remove our ideological blinders, and look for bold actions that attract the broad support of the American people.

Chapter 7

Seeing through the Ideological Blinders (of the Right and the Left)

Forging good energy policy requires accurate information and clear analysis. But attempts to find better policies are too often derailed by factual distortions and ideological thinking. Some people take comfort in seeing only the facts that support their ingrained positions. Similarly, if someone makes statements they disagree with (e.g., arguments for or against nuclear power), they stop listening, assuming that they will automatically disagree with everything else. I call this the problem of *ideological blinders* to make the point that unquestioned doctrines and political correctness often block out the ability to accurately grasp the whole energy picture. Ideological thinking can be lethal to good energy policy. We need to transcend the narrow visions of the Right and the Left if we want to declare energy independence.

People should bring their own values to the energy debate. How one prioritizes the natural environment, ranks personal freedom versus government action in pursuit of the common good, or chooses an ideal lifestyle can be a personal preference that is not necessarily susceptible to change by a new study on the issue. What I am talking about goes beyond adhering to one's value system. It is the proclivity to shut out useful information—a trait common on a whole variety of national issues, not just energy.

Like many problems of modern energy, the prevalence of ideological thinking is so enmeshed in our national consciousness that we rarely look for a better way to do things. On the major issues of our day, the television talk shows seem required to pick one commentator from the Left and one from the Right of the political spectrum. Without any genuine effort to find a common set of facts or disinterested analysis, such encounters frequently end up as shouting contests.

If we do not confront the problem of ideological blinders, we are unlikely to overcome the problem of energy dependence. Here are two reasons why.

❧

Ideological blinders stifle the intellectual honesty of attempts to take constructive action on energy. New facts on energy are constantly emerging. Sometimes an innovative technology performs better than expected; sometimes it proves to be a dud. Economic theories may fit current trends in the data or they may not. Sometimes going back to take a second look at historical data leads to insights missed during earlier inspections. On occasion, a trusted analyst produces new evidence on a contested matter. If we want to find the best energy solutions, we need to constantly look for new information and new insights. Since ideological thinking blinds us to new information and insights, it can steer us toward the wrong energy solutions.

There is a second problem with ideological thinking that is related to the political realities of getting action on any important matter of national policy. It takes votes from 60 out of 100 members (60 being the number to end debate of sometimes-controversial issues and move on to a final vote) to get major legislation through the Senate. This may be the most important fact to know about the American political system. The threat of a filibuster can torpedo many legislative endeavors. Getting political action, particularly in the Senate, requires going beyond narrow partisan or ideological groupings.

At those rare moments in history when significant new energy policy has come into force, Congress has followed a similar pattern. It bickers over the matter for a year or two, leaving the impression that nothing will get done (and it usually doesn't). Every once in a while, long into the process, things start to jell. Some bold ideas in the package get dropped, but enough remain to make the overall effort credible. The votes start to tumble in and the measure passes with a large majority that crosses partisan and ideological divides. An energy plan that starts out seeking just a narrow majority is doomed to failure. (I repeat: it takes at least 60 votes to get important legislation through the Senate.) We should adopt the goal of finding solutions with the potential for attracting broad support, and that requires getting rid of those ideological blinders.

Now, what are these blinders, and how do we get rid of them?

The Blinders of the Left

I do not want to suggest that there are millions of people out there on the Left thinking in total lockstep. Still, there is a clear set of ideas about energy that show up again and again on the nation's op-ed pages and on the floors of the Congress that seem impervious to evidence. There are two major elements to this ideology.

First, many on the Left in effect *rule out most sources of energy.* We cannot use coal because of carbon and other emissions, oil because it is found in fragile environments or unstable nations, nuclear because of the dangers posed by radioactive waste, windmills because they kill birds, or hydroelectric dams because they kill fish. In isolation, each of these arguments makes a lot of sense. In combination, they create an almost impossible situation.

Conservation can do a lot, and should be the first line of attack in efforts to use energy more rationally. Solar cells and collectors—very (but not totally) benign sources of power—also have a big role to play. But they cannot do it all themselves. Yet the opponents to most fuels do not acknowledge that their restrictions on fuel sources will eventually require severe adjustments in modern lifestyles (a legitimate argument if they are willing to make it).

Certain fuels are better than others, and we ought to use carrots and sticks to move to those with the least-adverse effects. But we also ought to be honest enough to admit that we will have to use some fuels that are less than perfect or else dramatically reduce our consumption of fuels to levels well beyond what is currently being discussed.

Second, the ideology of the Left often *castigates any increases in energy prices*. The historical record is replete with unproven attacks that energy industries were manipulating oil prices and gouging consumers. Complaints about price increases and the demonization of the energy companies have been with us for a long time. Rising prices—highly visible on large signs at many intersections—are noticed more by consumers than falling prices, and many of us learned in school of the ruthless ways of John D. Rockefeller when he built Standard Oil. During the oil crises of the 1970s, politicians and the public widely condemned the oil companies for causing the shortages. Responding to a question about Nixon's popularity during 1973 Watergate investigations, one Congressman from the Chicago suburbs quipped, "Compared to the oil companies, Nixon is in excellent shape. Compared to anyone else, he's got a lot of problems."[1]

I have studied that period carefully and concluded that the problem of gasoline lines was caused mainly by the Arab production cuts and inept allocation by the federal government. Based on my research, I concluded that the oil companies stretched out the oil available about as well as possible.

Oil companies are not above criticism, particularly for their propaganda campaign against the prevailing evidence on global climate change. And some energy companies have manipulated markets (lest we forget Enron in California). But accusations that oil companies illegally ignore antitrust laws and fix prices have produced scant evidence to support them over the years. On the whole, the major energy companies have obeyed the law.

Price increases are often best explained by the normal fluctuations of commodity markets or added costs, like paying for new environmental controls. Shouldn't energy prices rise and fall according to the balance of supply and demands, as do, for instance, prices for agricultural products? Shouldn't energy companies be allowed to pass on to consumers the added costs of, for instance, new environmental technology?

Creating successful energy policies requires that we recognize that energy fuels have external costs and their prices will have to rise. I have devoted considerable attention to describing the energy policies of presidents Ford and

Carter because I believe their stories contain an important lesson. Both told the American people energy prices needed to go up. Their candor set the stage for passing major energy packages that restored (for a while) energy independence. (Neither won a second term.) As then, keeping prices low discourages energy conservation and the growth of alternative fuels. Low prices keep us addicted to foreign oil. (Stick with me on this point. I'm going to explain later why higher energy prices do not need to be as bad as they are often perceived.)

The American automobile industry has come under considerable condemnation in recent years from the Left, some of which is deserved. Critics assert that the companies intentionally produce gas-guzzling automobiles and do not give consumers the choices they want. I have to chuckle a bit when I hear this accusation, in light of a personal story from a few years ago.

I mentioned in a 1999 energy speech that I had just test-driven the Honda Insight, the only hybrid electric car available in the U.S. market at the time and very fuel efficient. At the end of my remarks, an official from Toyota told me he would have the first Prius shipped to America outside of my office the next morning for a test drive. As I took the wheel, he apologized that this Prius, built for Japanese drivers, did not have the acceleration of the American model that would soon be available. Most American drivers, we both agreed, would not accept the more fuel-efficient but slower Japanese version.

Then, years later, someone in another audience rushed up after my talk with information on a scandal they had discovered. The Japanese model of the Prius got better gas mileage than the American; it must be a conspiracy of the oil companies. Actually, it was Toyota trying to anticipate the desires of American drivers.

When a large enough number of American drivers demand fuel-efficient cars, Detroit will build them. Publications like *Consumer Reports,* the *New York Times,* and the *Washington Post* editorialize in favor of fuel efficiency. Yet, when their test drivers rate cars with options for small or large engines, they almost always downgrade the fuel-efficient models because they do not have enough pep. They are clearly reflecting the preferences of many of their readers.

Foreign and U.S. auto companies are selling more efficient models abroad and less efficient models here, but not because of a grand conspiracy.

They are giving different national markets what they want. In the battle for high-mileage cars, we have found the enemy, and it is us.

Both the insistence that energy prices should never rise and the demonization of major corporations often provide excuses for avoiding tough decisions about energy. To get energy independence, we need more truth telling—from both sides.

THE BLINDERS OF THE RIGHT

The Right has its own doctrines and taboos. These also exclude new information on subjects where we are learning more all the time.

As a central tenet, ideologues of the Right tend to *abhor any government action that raises energy prices or slows economic growth*. This viewpoint effectively shuts the door on most new government measures to protect the environment or national security interests (unless they are part of the defense budget). The ideological Right vociferously opposes actions to restrain damage to the environment by energy industries. Then, when environmental protections like clean air and clean water demonstrate positive results and prove popular with the public, these pundits give the credit solely to the companies who complied (who certainly deserve some of the credit) and none to those in government who had the foresight to pass the requirements in the first place.

Ironically, the ideologues of the Right are emulating the ideologues of the Left. They are refusing to recognize the external costs of fossil fuels—the costs to national security, the economy, and the environment not included in retail prices. They preach the virtues of free markets, but do not acknowledge the fact that market prices can't send proper signals to buyers and sellers if they fail to reflect the costs to the broader society. This sloppy thinking about free markets by the Right blocks any thoughtful discussion about the trade-offs between various energy options and any effective action to win energy independence.

The Right buttresses its bias against government action with a very selective memory of historical events. According to their narrative, all the energy problems of the 1970s were solved by deregulating energy prices and distribution. As we have seen, deregulation did play a major role in moving energy trends in a positive direction, but it received a lot of help from government policies that promoted conservation and fuel-shifting away from oil. We have to remove the historical blinders from our history if we want to solve the problems of tomorrow.

Many ideologues of the Right also tend to *dismiss ideas they do not like with the simple assertion they were advanced by someone they do not like.* I could offer many examples, but the name Al Gore comes quickly to mind. When Gore brought new attention to the climate change issue with his movie and book *An Inconvenient Truth,* people with a different view were entitled to rebut the Gore position with countervailing arguments. In many cases, however, his critics simply dismissed his ideas on global warming with personal attacks on him. You could not believe what Gore said, they suggested, because he was just trying to gear up his presidential campaign. For many ideologues of the Right, having a long list of people they do not like becomes an excuse for not having to deal intellectually with any arguments they do not like. I'm sorry, but if we are going to solve America's energy problems, we actually have to think about them.

To get a declaration of energy independence, we need a declaration by energy independents—people who can think for themselves and rise above the sound bites of television punditry.

TURNING ON THE LIGHT BULB

Getting rid of the ideological blinders can be very liberating. Energy issues that were once puzzling become clear. People on different sides of arguments can suddenly find some areas of agreement. Let us look at one perspective on climate change that often gets lost because people on both sides of the debate avoid talking about it.

Were you aware that the harmful sulphate emissions that burn our lungs and are sharply curtailed in many countries also contribute to global cooling by shielding the earth from the impacts of the sun's rays? As a result, sulphates and some other aerosols offset, to some degree, the global warming effects of carbon dioxide and other greenhouse gases.[2]

Understanding the opposing effects of sulfur and carbon emissions helps unravel one of the major mysteries of climate change. Why did some scientists in the 1970s detect a trend toward global cooling that might lead to another ice age? In the early years of the Clean Air Act, when sulfur emissions were not controlled like they are today, some data did show a cooling trend, so people who foresaw another ice age were not just dreaming it up. But most atmospheric scientists at the time saw the big picture. As carbon emissions rose rapidly and sulfur emissions declined, the dominant momentum was in the direction of warming. These complex interactions help clarify the underlying science of climate change.

There is a second mystery we can now explain. The temperature reports from around the world clearly show a dominant trend toward warming, but not everywhere. Again, the cooling effects of sulfur are part of the answer. In regions with particularly high sulfur emissions, the effects of carbon emissions can be temporarily offset. There is a lot about the climate that continues to be mysterious, but we can understand a lot more about the science than some of the public dialogue might lead us to believe.

It is pretty clear why the ideologues of the Right do not want to talk about the interactions between sulfur and carbon emissions. It is much easier to dismiss the massive evidence of global warming if you keep citing a few scientists who several decades ago predicted global cooling or pointing to the relatively small number of places in the world that are not warming. (There are reasons other than sulfur why a particular area might be cooling.) As a result, you can pose as an independent-thinking contrarian by ignoring the impacts of sulfur.

The ideologues of the Left have different reasons for ignoring the impacts of sulfates. These emissions damage human health and are easy to explain to the public. It complicates matters to raise the role of sulfur in global temperatures. In a time of concern about global warming, the cooling effects of sulfur emissions might even be used as an excuse to downplay their harmful effects. But the price of ignoring sulfur has been high. Without this perspective, it is harder to explain what appear to be discrepancies in the warming data.

When we get rid of the ideological blinders, we can move toward some common understanding of what our problems really are and construct solutions that will actually be effective. We cannot tell people only what we think they should know.

LET'S NOT BE TEPID

Energy debates that cross partisan and ideological divides produce better ideas. They also offer brighter prospects for gaining consensus, winning the votes needed to implement them, and actually producing the desired results. We have to be aware, however, that a drive for agreement can sometimes produce solutions that fail to accomplish very much because they are too watered down. These might be viewed as non-solutions that make us feel good.

From time to time, commissions on energy are created to chart new directions for the future. The membership includes experts representing many points of view. Knowing many members personally or by reputation, I get excited about the final work product. Then, the results hit with a thud. Energy consumers would hardly notice if the recommendations were implemented or not. None of the major energy trend lines, from reliance on foreign oil to carbon emissions, would change very much. To get unanimous agreement, the reports avoid anything that might smack of controversy or, alas, alter business as usual to a significant degree.

If we recognize that reliance on foreign oil and larger accumulations of greenhouse gases are big problems, but offer only weak solutions, we are not doing much more than those who deny the problems exist. In a way, tepid solutions are even worse. They might convince some that we are making progress when, in fact, we really are not.

The passage of the Energy Independence and Security Act of 2007 provides encouragement that we can now get a broad consensus behind policies that will make a big difference. Surprisingly, several important measures were dropped, but what remained will actually begin to shift some of our major energy trends in a more positive direction. We cannot afford to be tepid on energy anymore.

I will be offering seven solutions that will lead to American energy independence. I know they can move energy trends even more toward where we need to be as a nation. I hope they can win support that crosses the ideological and partisan divides.

PART TWO

Seven Economically and Politically Viable Paths to Energy Independence

Chapter 8

Solution One: Store Massive Emergency Reserves

OIL DELIVERIES CAN BE INTERRUPTED FOR MANY REASONS—SAVAGE HURRICANES LIKE KATRINA AND RITA, STRIKES IN NIGERIA, OR (THE BIG GORILLA OF THEM ALL) CONFLICT IN THE PERSIAN GULF. WOULDN'T IT BE NICE IF WE HAD A BIG STOCK OF OIL IN RESERVE THAT WE COULD USE TO REPLACE WHAT IS LOST DURING THESE EMERGENCIES? WELL, ACTUALLY WE DO.

Deep in the salt caverns of Louisiana sit about 700 million barrels of crude oil (over 29 billion gallons after refining). It is called the Strategic Petroleum Reserve (the SPR, in energy circles), and that is a lot of oil. The delivery systems are tested from time to time, and they work. John Shages, who ran the program until recently, helped build one of the federal government's most reliable systems. Within two weeks of a presidential order, oil can flow at the rate of 4.4 million barrels a day to alleviate shortages of whatever derivation.[1] It gets better. Europe and Japan also require their oil companies to hold petroleum for emergencies. That's the good news.

The bad news is that these petroleum reserves, while adequate to deal with most emergency scenarios, cannot handle the huge potential losses from major catastrophes in the Persian Gulf. This makes a big difference, because the seven largely unindustrialized nations on the Gulf (Bahrain, Iran, Iraq, Kuwait, Qatar, Saudi Arabia, and the United Arab Emirates) contain well over half of the world's oil reserves, and the industrialized nations are highly dependent on their exports.

The emergency reserve is inadequate due to the failure to achieve the goals set when it was authorized in 1975 after the Arab oil embargo. Moreover, its basic rules were established more than three decades ago and are badly out of date. The petroleum reserve needs to be expanded and modernized to better contribute to energy independence.

❧

Improving our emergency petroleum stockpile is only one of many solutions that will be needed to create American energy independence. But its principles are perhaps the most ancient, going back at least to the book of Genesis. Joseph interpreted the Egyptian Pharaoh's dream with a prediction that seven years of agricultural abundance would be followed by seven years of famine. The recently released prisoner recommended that a fifth of the food during the time of plenty be set aside as a reserve "so that the country may not be ruined by the famine."

The biblical account does not mention whether any economists criticized Joseph's plan with the argument that free markets would be the best way to take care of the famine. But in the twenty-first century that argument is sometimes heard. We can learn from recent experience that Joseph was right. Markets cannot fully deal with major interruptions of supply. It is better to be prepared. Great oil emergencies arise from non-economic factors like wars, violent storms, and attempts to exert international pressure. It is too much to expect each individual and business to have a contingency plan to deal with an interruption of oil supplies from the Persian Gulf. But such should be expected of great nations.

How Did We Get a Strategic Petroleum Reserve?

In 1969, a group of consultants to the Oil Import Task Force established by President Nixon put forward a not entirely new, but nonetheless bold idea. Charles Rivers and Associates—out of Cambridge, Massachusetts— proposed building a government reserve of crude oil with a whopping five billion barrels (more than seven times the current reserve). At the time, the stockpile would have been large enough to replace the entire production of Saudi Arabia, the country with the world's largest oil reserves, for more than three-and-a-half years. The plan was designed to provide the United States with full supplies of oil, including the additional needs of the military, for a protracted war of at least three years, an important concern during the Cold War. With foreign oil then available at $2 a barrel, the consultants argued that the costs to purchase the supplies and build the necessary storage infrastructure, while substantial, were considerably less than other ways of dealing with oil insecurity.[2]

The oil industry blasted the Rivers proposal, and the Interior and Commerce Departments called it "not economically sensible." The final report of the task force ended up recommending that the strategic petroleum reserve only be considered, in effect killing the proposal.[3] By tabling an idea that might have revolutionized U.S. energy policy, the decision increased the potential that military force might become necessary to maintain access to Persian Gulf oil.

The Rivers proposal for a huge government stockpile of oil was remarkable in its timing. Until just a few years before, the reserve was not needed. In normal times, the Texas Railroad Commission had kept the state's oil production well below full capacity, allowing emergencies to be dealt with through surge production. A few years after the Rivers plan, the world price of oil had escalated sharply, making creation of a reserve with these volumes extraordinarily more expensive. A brief window of opportunity had been missed.

$$\mathcal{C}\!\!\sim$$

The Arab oil embargo gave the idea of a national oil stockpile new life in Congress, where Senator Jackson's support predated the boycott. President Ford, in his first State of the Union address in January of 1975, proposed a strategic storage program of one billion barrels of oil for domestic needs and 300 million barrels for national defense purposes. Though the petroleum reserve rated only one sentence in the speech and questions remained about how it would be paid for, the idea was a new presidential initiative, contrasting with Nixon's view of it as a political "hot potato" not to be even debated internally, let alone advocated as national policy.

The reserve became law in the Energy Policy and Conservation Act of 1975. The authorization agreed with Ford's proposal, setting a capacity of one billion barrels. It also established a goal of maintaining 90 days worth of imported oil and authorized an early storage program to purchase 150 million barrels within three years. Mindful of the jump in oil prices after the embargo and the fragility of the world oil market, the bill allowed considerable latitude on the schedule for future purchases.

The government began buying oil for the reserve in 1977. During the Carter years, 108 million barrels were deposited, short of the purchases contemplated by the legislation. After the loss of oil from Iran in 1979, the costs of oil jumped even more and the administration worried about putting additional demands on the world's diminished supplies. For a while, acquisitions were suspended, and the program lost momentum.

Ronald Reagan and Congress gave the reserve its strongest support from 1981 to 1985. During that period, 386 million additional barrels were stockpiled—well over half of the total volume in the reserve today. The results were impressive, and by 1985 had exceeded one original goal of the 1975 legislation. Because imports were declining, the United States now had 115 days of imported oil on hand, well above the ninety-day target. The SPR contributed another piece of good news to the transformation of the energy landscape from 1975 to 1985. National energy security was arguably in the best shape since domestic oil production peaked in 1970.

The presidencies of George H. W. Bush, Bill Clinton, and George W. Bush saw periodic additions to the oil reserve. However, the new volumes were modest and failed to keep up with a renewed surge in imports. Focus on balancing the federal budget took precedence over oil security in 1996 and 1997, when an energy-complacent Congress sold off 28 million barrels of federal oil to obtain revenue. The tepid support for the reserve after 1985 led to a sharp decline in its ability to replace a major shortfall in foreign deliveries. In 2007, it could supply only 56 days of imports, well below the original target and less than half of its potential in 1985.

Proving Its Value

Despite the weakened support for the reserve over the past two decades, it has made valuable contributions to oil stability on several occasions. Only once has the reserve been used for its primary purpose of compensating for the loss of oil from the Persian Gulf. After Iraq's Saddam Hussein invaded Kuwait in 1990, the world suffered a massive loss of oil from both countries. Part of the American response was a sale of 21 million barrels of oil from the strategic reserve and the announced commitment to release more if necessary. The withdrawals were modest by most standards and largely eclipsed by a huge ramp-up in production by Saudi Arabia. Still, Secretary of Energy James Watkins was correct when he said,

"We have sent an important message to the American people that their $20 billion investment in an emergency supply of crude oil has produced a system that can respond rapidly and effectively to the threat of an energy disruption."[4]

The reserve has also been used in less-publicized cases to help in domestic disruptions to the market, several resulting from the damage caused by hurricanes, which often hit Gulf Coast areas where the oil industry is concentrated. In many of these cases, oil was exchanged rather than sold and often resulted in more oil being returned to the reserve than was released.

Perhaps the greatest success of the reserve came in 2005, after Hurricane Katrina roared into the Gulf of Mexico and caused massive damage to offshore oil platforms and to terminals, pipelines, and refineries. To make matters worse, Rita followed closely behind. The release of another 21 million barrels of crude oil from the reserve helped calm the market for crude oil, but the more pressing problem was what to do about the loss of refinery products, gasoline, and diesel. Since the vast bulk of strategic reserves are unrefined oil, the unexpected blow to the refineries raised questions about how the crude oil available could be turned into products people could actually use.

Though little recognized, the American petroleum reserve has been linked to international oil-sharing agreements between the industrialized nations that become operative in times of emergency. Other members of the International Energy Agency hold their strategic stockpiles by requiring that their oil companies keep certain levels of products in reserve. After Katrina and Rita, these product reserves were released to offset the American shortage. Since the rush to help the United States did not fit the predominant national story line, there was little explanation at the time why gasoline and diesel were flooding into U.S. ports and providing considerable relief after a major blow to the U.S. energy infrastructure. (The differential in prices across the Atlantic also helped, but did not in itself explain the huge amount of products available.)

WHY ISN'T THE OIL RESERVE BIGGER?

The strategic petroleum reserve has, at times, received strong support from presidents and congressional leaders of both parties. So partisan bickering has not been a major hindrance to its success. But there are other problems.

National interest in energy swings back and forth between intensity and complacency, which creates a major hurdle for good energy policy, especially in the case of building an emergency oil stockpile. The desire to build the reserve is greatest during periods of crisis. But such times are the worst for purchasing oil that is going to be withdrawn from the market. First, prices are very high, greatly increasing the cost of the additions to stocks. Second, with oil already in short supply, purchases for the reserve make the shortage even more severe.

The best time to purchase oil for emergencies is when supplies are abundant and prices are low. (Joseph did not build Egyptian food reserves during the famine.) Unfortunately, times of plenty produce apathy among the public and their elected representatives, who no longer see the need for emergency reserves. A classic case came in the 1990s. Prices were low, creating an ideal opportunity to add to the SPR. Yet the reserves actually declined during the decade, a casualty of widespread disinterest in energy policy.

We have been lulled into complacency by more than low prices. During some periods, Saudi Arabia maintained excess capacity that it made available to deal with major interruptions in supply, most notably the 1990–1991 Persian Gulf War. But this capability helps only if the Saudis decide to absorb the costs of keeping excess capacity and if their interests coincide with the market's need for more oil. In fact, in recent years, their excess capacity has eroded. It is risky, in any case, to depend on another country whose positions may vary from our own. Even with the risks of relying on extra Saudi oil when it has only limited availability, many people have failed to see the need for a dependable U.S. reserve.

Another barrier to building a strong oil reserve is the set of Byzantine rules for the federal budget. Under current rules, any purchases for the reserve must be offset by specific cuts in federal spending, even though oil stocks are an asset likely to grow in value. The pressure on Congress is to fund immediate concerns rather than prepare for some emergency that might never occur. (Plus, the reserve has no special interests lobbying on its behalf.) The great purchases up to 1985 occurred when they were off-budget. Since they went on-budget, purchases have lagged.

The budget problem has been circumvented to some extent by a program called "royalty-in-kind," developed by the Department of Energy under Secretary Bill Richardson. Starting in 1999, oil companies paid their royalties for production on federal lands with oil rather than dollars. Since there were no federal expenditures, no offsetting budget cuts were required. The George W. Bush administration has supported the idea of royalties-in-kind, but the amounts involved are too modest to beef up the reserve to needed levels.

A third impediment to making the strategic oil reserve a robust weapon in the fight for energy independence is pressure from the Persian Gulf nations, on whom we depend for fuel. Saudi Arabia has, during the early years of the SPR, threatened the United States that it would cut its own production if the United States made additional purchases for the reserve. The threat makes a point. America cannot achieve energy independence without a reserve that is large enough to allow such pressures to be ignored.

GETTING THE SIZE RIGHT

If the current reserve is too small, what is the right size? The creators of the reserve had it about right. Adequate security under most scenarios requires storing at least 90 days of U.S. net imports. It is inconceivable that all imports would be shut off at the same time, but it is also quite possible that an interruption would last well beyond 90 days. So having enough to cover all imports for three months should provide considerable confidence that we can weather most severe scenarios. At the current rate of imports, that would mean a stockpile of a bit over one billion barrels (what Gerald Ford called for in 1975). We are not starting from scratch, but we would have to add about 45 percent to the current reserve.

In the real world, a reserve with 90 days worth of imports would cover the total production of Saudi Arabia for 110 days. That is a substantial cushion. It is not a total energy security package, nor does it help reduce greenhouse gas emissions. The new, larger reserve will need to be coordinated with the efforts of other major oil-consuming nations and combined with other policies that reduce oil imports.

Adding the additional oil to the reserve will not be cheap. Obtaining petroleum in the form of royalties does not fill it fast enough, so federal funds will have to be expended. At recent high price levels, getting to one billion barrels could carry a price tag of around $20 billion to $30 billion. In addition, the current capacity of the reserve is capped at 727 million barrels. As result, expanded stockpiling will quickly bring additional expenses for preparing new storage facilities.

In recent years, spending this much on the reserve and taking the expenses off-budget have not received serious consideration. In light of the current costs of war in the Middle East, however, the price of getting the reserve to one billion barrels may look more modest. It would be a prudent insurance policy against future economic disruptions or the need for military intervention in the Persian Gulf.

The real test for America will come if the world oil market gets less tight, as it always has in the past. Times of plenty and lower prices have generally produced public apathy about oil. Yet a drop in world oil prices (yes, it is possible) might provide a chance to go beyond one billion barrels in the reserve. If another opportunity presents itself to make massive additions, we should not let it slip by.

EXPANDING THE MISSION

The effectiveness of the current petroleum reserve is also constrained by the outdated rules governing its usage. Congress created the reserve to be released during times of emergency shortages. At the time, with federal price controls, a sudden drop in production was more likely to lead to visible shortages, as evidenced by the gasoline lines of 1974 and 1979. The mission of the reserve seemed clear.

The current situation is muddier. Influenced by the 1970s view of shortages, modern officials have said the reserve should not be used to influence price. Yet prices are often a leading indicator of imbalances in the market. Federal officials have been reluctant to use the reserve to deal with tight supplies resulting from OPEC cuts in production. Yet that is the most common problem in the twenty-first century. When OPEC ministers meet to discuss production quotas, Americans often can only observe as helpless bystanders. To make the reserve the effective tool it can be, we need to rethink the policy.

Greatly troubled by the loss of American influence in global energy markets, Alan Greenspan, as Chair of the Council of Economic Advisors in 1974, became a strong advocate of creating a strategic petroleum reserve. At an energy strategy session with President Ford in December, the future Federal Reserve Board chairman saw an oil reserve as a way to provide for unexpected interruptions and, perhaps more importantly, as a way for the United States to regain leverage in setting the world price of oil. Since the loss of America's excess capacity in 1970, he explained, the OPEC nations had been able to dictate prices. Armed with a strategic reserve, the United States could again be a major player. The idea of using the reserve to maintain leverage on world oil prices did not go much further. Now it is time to resurrect Greenspan's suggestion.

A new role for the Strategic Petroleum Reserve should be patterned after the Federal Reserve Board's governance of the monetary system. The Fed provides stability to the financial system by adopting countercyclical policies. In its own words:

> If the economy slows and employment softens, policy makers will be inclined to ease monetary policy to stimulate aggregate demand. . . . In contrast, if the economy is showing signs of overheating and inflation pressures are building, the Federal Reserve will be inclined to counter these pressures by tightening monetary policy.

For the Fed, the challenge is aligning aggregate demand with the economy's potential to produce.[5]

To follow the Fed model, the Strategic Petroleum Reserve should be inclined to release oil when prices are high and obtain oil when prices are low. If determining when oil prices are high or low sounds like subjective gobbledygook, the data challenges are no greater than those that face the Federal Reserve. It is possible to make reasonable judgment about the cost of bringing on new oil supplies. When the purchase price of oil is substantially above these replacement costs, the government should strongly consider shedding oil from the reserve. If the price falls below the cost of bringing on new supplies, the government should tend toward acquiring more oil for the reserve.

The history of the current federal stockpile provides an example of how a revamped policy might work. In October of 2000, the White House directed the release of 30 million barrels of oil from the reserve—the largest in history. Opponents argued the move was political and, coming just weeks before the presidential election, the timing did look suspicious. But the decision had considerable logic behind it. At the time, the price of oil was "backwardated," energy lingo used when futures prices are lower than current ones. The Clinton administration, taking advantage of the lower futures price, was able to guarantee that more oil would be eventually returned than was released through a contract with companies willing to absorb all the market risks. After several delays to take advantage of more backwardation in the market, 34.5 million barrels were returned during the first term of George W. Bush—an addition of 4.5 million barrels without cost to the government.

The legislation for the Strategic Petroleum Reserve should be modified to encourage such exchanges when they are helpful in balancing the market and allow the government to acquire additional stocks without cost to the government. Such actions could help achieve what Greenspan discussed in 1974.

THE PROS AND CONS

There are several fears about taking a more proactive approach to the management of the Strategic Petroleum Reserve that should be taken seriously. There are legitimate reasons to worry that decisions would be based on political considerations and that pandering to consumers might dampen incentives for oil production. Others might say, even if these objections can be overcome, the volumes involved are too small to make a difference in a vast world oil market.

The way to take decisions about the Strategic Petroleum Reserve out of politics would be to follow the model of the Federal Reserve Board's independent governance, which (for the most part) insulates it from politics. A board of energy experts with fixed terms of office should be appointed to run the reserve. If this sounds implausible, it should be noted that the Energy Information Administration, with its strong statutory protections, has been able to produce energy data and analysis independent of political pressures that might be exerted. The board for the petroleum reserve should make decisions based on data and market conditions, not on the election calendar. This would be a useful step in any case and should build confidence in the validity of reserve policies.

An effective board would not confine its actions to periods of public outcry demanding more oil be released to the market. There may be, as was the case in 1998 and early 1999, times when low oil prices fall below the costs of production. In such cases, a modernized policy for the petroleum reserve would suggest that the government become a buyer of oil. There will be inevitable outcries that the government is bailing out the oil companies. But we have learned from experience that economic signals that discourage oil production are bad for consumers in the long run. Proactive moves by the petroleum reserve, both when prices are high and when they are low, can become part of a viable balancing strategy that calms volatile markets and avoids dangerous extremes on both ends of energy cycles. They can also help offset criticism that the reserve creates a disincentive to produce oil.

The remaining question is whether intervention by the petroleum reserve in the market can have much impact in a world that consumes over 85 billion barrels of oil a day. We can observe how the local uprisings in Nigeria that threaten oil production (or other occurrences of similar magnitude) can have significant impacts on world oil prices. These interruptions are temporary and fall far below one million barrels a day. While it is probably not advisable for the U.S. reserve to react to every perturbation in global oil trade, the potential that the reserve would intervene more frequently than allowed by current policy should have a beneficial effect on the market and remove some of the panic that has prevailed in recent years. Similarly, when the reserve intervenes to buy oil when prices are too low, it sends a signal to the market that the nation's energy experts believe that prices will bounce back and has an impact that goes beyond the number of physical barrels involved.

Properly managed, a proactive petroleum reserve board would remove some of the volatility in recent markets that created confusing signals for both oil production and consumption. It could also facilitate the acquisition of additional oil at lower costs. It could, in addition, be part of a strategy of building a larger reserve capable of dealing with the worst-case scenarios that have not yet occurred but for which we spend money in other ways, such as military operations in the Persian Gulf. The new petroleum reserve policy is not just a dream. It is a practical economic approach with very few downsides.

Despite its virtues, a larger, more proactive Strategic Petroleum Reserve is not a silver bullet that solves all the problems of oil dependence. We must keep looking for other, larger bullets to achieve true energy independence.

Chapter 9

Solution Two: Drive the Car of the Future

Where can we take the biggest strides toward energy independence? Cars, trucks, and planes consume the great bulk of the oil used in this country. Consequently, transportation assumes primary responsibility for America's massive dependence on foreign oil. If we fix the transportation sector, we can fix the imported oil problem. Moving people and things around, moreover, is the largest and fastest-growing source of human-generated greenhouse gases. Any successful strategy for slowing climate change requires that we rein in these emissions. Failure to control the excessive use of oil in our vehicles is the biggest threat to energy independence.

Americans love their cars. They have an iconic status that goes beyond moving people from one location to another. But if we want to become less reliant on foreign oil, automobiles, as we currently know them, will have to change. They will have to acquire greater fuel efficiency and consume less gasoline per mile driven.

This is a problem we know how to solve, because we did it before. The historic energy legislation of 1975 required the doubling of fuel efficiency for new cars. Under the new Corporate Average Fuel Efficiency (CAFE) standards, the goal of 27.5 miles per gallon (mpg) was attained in 1988.[1] These efficiency requirements dramatically changed American automobiles and reduced dependence on foreign oil. So why did we stop?

Having achieved victory, we retreated from the energy battlefield. After 1988, the updating of the fuel efficiency standards stalled out. No higher standards were required, and even the existing standards were eroded by unexpected developments. The 1975 energy legislation had established a separate category of vehicles called light trucks, which Congress assumed would be used primarily for business purposes or by individuals that might have special needs like driving off-road. Under the rules initially adopted, these light trucks had to reach 20 mpg. Later, the auto industry began to offer vans and sport-utility vehicles (SUVs) that fit into the light truck category and qualified for the more lenient mileage standards. When drivers increasingly purchased vans and SUVs instead of cars, the overall average for new vehicles dropped, an outcome the original designers of auto efficiency standards did not anticipate.

Until 2007, Congress took no additional action to require that continuing improvements in auto technology be devoted to achieving better fuel efficiency. Neither were the rules for cars updated administratively, as encouraged by the 1975 legislation. Congress and the Department of Transportation did gradually update rules for vans, SUVs, and other light trucks. Rules adopted in 2006 by the Bush administration require these vehicles to meet a higher standard of only 24 mpg by 2011. Over time, the absence of new requirements for automobiles and the tepid federal response to the switchover to heavier vehicles allowed Americans to resume their increasing addiction to oil and become more dependent on foreign supplies.

To the surprise of many observers, congressional interest in modernizing auto efficiency rebounded sharply in 2007. In June, the Senate passed a bill requiring new cars, vans, SUVs, and other light trucks to become 10 mpg more efficient by 2020 (the ten-in-ten provision). At times, it appeared the legislation would be blocked in the House, where the powerful John Dingell of Michigan headed the Commerce Committee, which had jurisdiction over the matter. But all parties eventually coalesced around a version of the Senate bill. When stiff new mileage requirements were eventually adopted as part of the Energy Independence and Security Act, the votes in both houses were overwhelming. The national commitment to make new vehicles average 35 miles per gallon by 2020 took a major step toward reducing reliance on foreign oil and becoming more energy independent.

Because we have used mileage efficiency standards before to reduce America's oil consumption, we have a good understanding of what they can accomplish, the pitfalls we need to watch out for, and of strategies that can prove successful. What have we learned?

STANDARDS CAN CHOP GASOLINE CONSUMPTION

Corporate Average Fuel Efficiency standards passed in 1975 made limited impacts on the auto market during their first years of implementation. Memories of the Arab oil embargo and price shocks at the pump encouraged Americans during that period to purchase more fuel-efficient vehicles whether they were legally required or not. Drivers were also cutting back their driving distances to reduce costs, even though there was no legal requirement to do so. The big contribution of mandatory efficiency standards began in the early 1980s. Rulemaking by the Carter administration accelerated the ramp-up during Reagan's first term at the same time that lower prices led to a climb in driving distance and some drop-off in consumer preferences for fuel-efficient cars.

In 1977, the last year before CAFE standards went into effect, the average passenger car was pulling up to the pump about once a week and consuming 676 gallons of gasoline a year. Eight years later, consumption per vehicle had dropped 20 percent. Spread across the entire fleet, the impact was huge. The auto efficiency standards contributed to an overall drop in gasoline consumption (despite an increase in the number of vehicles) and in imported oil. More fuel-efficient vehicles helped make the United States, for all practical purposes, energy independent by 1985.

It took several years for the substantial benefits of CAFE standards to kick in. Similarly, it took a while for the positive impacts to fade. After the standards maxed out, the efficiency of the fleet continued to improve as purchasers of new vehicles traded in older, less efficient models. Enjoying much lower fuel prices, drivers in the late 1980s and 1990s began to log considerably longer mileage. Until 1992, these increases were more than offset by the still-increasing efficiency of the fleet. After that, consumption per vehicle trended up. This reversal, combined with a growing number of cars, not surprisingly produced an intractable climb in oil imports. The efficiency standards had achieved their purpose for a long time, but without updating they could no longer do the job.

The effects of the efficiency standards passed last year will also have lagged impacts. Within a few years, they will gradually start to constrain American oil consumption, and the effects will continue for a long time.

CRITICISMS OF STANDARDS HAVE SOME VALIDITY, BUT ARE MANAGEABLE

Fuel economy standards have for some time provoked fierce debates about the unintended consequences of energy policy. One major subject of dispute has been the *rebound effect*. Proponents of this theory make three points. First, more fuel-efficient vehicles reduce the cost per mile of driving. Second, this reduced cost leads drivers to log more miles. Third, the increase (rebound) in miles driven cancels out the intended goal of reducing the use of gasoline.

The argument seems logical if gasoline behaves like other commodities or according to the theories of economics textbooks. Actual data, however, suggest gasoline is different. Drivers lack readily available alternatives for transportation fuels. Moreover, given the purchase price of vehicles, insurance, and maintenance, gasoline is not a major factor in the overall costs of operating an automobile. Thus, drivers generally continue their regular driving patterns despite movements in the price of gasoline and adjust their budgets in other areas. This is important. If consumption is highly related to costs, efficiency standards would not work very well; gasoline taxes would be a more effective way to rein in gasoline consumption.

Careful analysis reveals some modest rebound effect. Although driving distances picked up when memories of the oil crises faded, distances in 1985 remained below levels seen before the Arab oil embargo. A 1999 study estimated about 20 percent of the benefits of fuel-efficient vehicles were lost over time due to increased driving mileage—fairly minimal in light of the overall benefits. The preponderance of evidence suggests that efficiency standards have been a viable approach to reducing gasoline consumption, but we must be aware that by reducing the cost per mile of driving, we will likely lose some benefits of the new law.[2]

The impact of efficiency standards on passenger safety stoked even greater controversy. Cars had to be downsized at first to meet demands for greater fuel efficiency, and drivers in small cars were more vulnerable in crashes. But vehicle weight works both for and against safety, and one study by the National Research Council (NRC) urged consideration of "the net effects of the safety gains to the occupants of heavier cars and safety losses that increased weight imposes on the occupants of the struck car, as well as other road users (e.g., pedestrians, pedalcyclists, and motorcyclists)." A later NRC study estimated that fatalities, on balance, increased in the range of 1 percent for each 100-pound decrease in vehicle weight.[3]

Rapid improvements in mileage efficiency did not always require downsizing of vehicles. By the early 1980s, manufacturers were able to employ new technology and actually increase horsepower while complying with mileage efficiency standards. After that, a direct connection between improved mileage and fatalities became increasingly difficult to detect. Moreover, other factors promoting safety came into play, such as improved automobile engineering, seatbelts, and crackdowns on drunk drivers. By 1985, fatalities per miles driven dropped 25 percent below those of just five years earlier. (In the early years of the twenty-first century, the United States was still suffering about 43,000 traffic fatalities a year. However, the rate of 1.4 fatalities per 100 million miles traveled was well below the pre-embargo level of 4.7 in 1970—a decline of 70 percent.)

But you do not have to slog through historical data and studies to determine whether fuel efficiency can be combined with high levels of safety. Look at current efficiency leaders like the Toyota Prius and the hybrid electric version of the Honda Civic. These high technology models earn praise for both their miserly fuel consumption and excellent crash protection. Perhaps even more significant, smaller economy cars like the Honda Fit and Nissan Versa, despite their shorter wheel bases, are getting good ratings in crash tests. It is clear people can drive cars that promote energy independence without jeopardizing their safety.

Another sore point over the adoption of CAFE standards resulted from the financial difficulties experienced by several major American auto manufacturers just as they were coming into force. This fed the ongoing argument that these companies should not have to absorb the capital costs of converting their facilities to produce more fuel-efficient cars.

In 2002, however, a National Research Council study found "little evidence of a dramatic impact of fuel economy regulations" on these manufacturers. It concluded, "General economic conditions, and especially the globalization of the automobile industry, seem to have been far more important than fuel economy regulations in determining the profitability and employment shares of the domestic automakers and their competitors."[4] In other words, despite the protestations of Detroit, the economic impacts of fuel-efficiency mandates on the American auto industry have been greatly exaggerated.

Behind these specific debates lies widespread skepticism about government interference in the market, including, in this case, decisions by motorists about what kind of cars they want to buy. Why shouldn't customers be allowed to favor horsepower and acceleration over fuel economy?

The dominance of laissez-faire economics has been so great that from 1996 through 2001 (the six years leading up to the 9/11 attacks), Congress banned the Department of Transportation from even considering updates to the CAFE standards. During this same period, the likelihood that the old standards would be repealed was greater than the adoption of new requirements reflecting improved technologies.

At the same time, an extreme form of free-market ideology led the United States and other industrialized nations to insist that the Chinese quit discriminating against gas-guzzling cars. As a price of joining the World Trade Organization in 2001, China was forced to scuttle its punitive tax on auto imports. Without the tax, the cost of cars (including those produced in China, which suddenly had to compete with imports) sharply dropped. People bought more cars because they were increasingly affordable— and additional fuel-thirsty, luxury models became available. The old taxes provided incentives to restrain the number of cars on the road, encourage mass transit, and block gas guzzlers. Pressure by the developed countries was a major step toward encouraging greater gasoline use, greater reliance on the Persian Gulf for supplies, and pushing up emissions of greenhouse gases in the world's most populous nation. Later generations will ask, "What were those people at the WTO thinking?"

A good free-market economist should acknowledge that the consumption of gasoline has external costs. Dependence on foreign oil creates costly obligations for our military and weakens our national security. Combustion of oil of any origin is changing the earth's climate. Moreover, individuals concerned about the security and environmental impacts of their cars cannot make much of a difference. If I buy a fuel-efficient car and the manufacturer is just building to the required average, I am effectively giving them room to sell another inefficient model. Finding effective ways to restrain excessive fuel consumption is a legitimate role of government, whether in the United States or China.[5]

Democrats have supported auto efficiency standards somewhat more than Republicans, but the issue has not been terribly partisan. When CAFE first passed in 1975 it was strongly championed in the Senate, not only by Democrats Fritz Hollings of South Carolina and Henry Jackson of Washington, but also Republican Charles Percy of Illinois (and then signed by Republican President Gerald Ford). The Republican leadership in the House led the assault on auto standards in the late 1990s, but Democratic President Bill Clinton chose to avoid a fight over the matter. In a key vote in June of 2007, the Senate passed a strong energy bill with significant CAFE improvements by a solid tally of 65 to 27. Democrats supplied most of the votes, but the two Democrats from Michigan voted nay, and the Republicans present split 20-20. Bipartisan national momentum for action on auto fuel consumption had turned in a more favorable direction. When the entire bill passed the Senate in December, there were only six votes against it.

STANDARDS NEEDED UPDATING

Auto efficiency standards in practice have never met the goals envisioned by Congress in 1975. The long failure to seriously update rules established well over three decades ago made them increasingly ineffective.

The Environmental Protection Agency requires new cars to display stickers indicating their fuel efficiency, but the numbers have generally overstated what drivers can expect. The stickers are occasionally updated, but EPA laboratory tests have a hard time keeping up with real driving conditions. As motorists increasingly prefer jackrabbit acceleration, speed limits rise, their enforcement lapses, car mileage deteriorates—factors the EPA was slow to acknowledge. To its credit, EPA has dramatically improved the accuracy of its stickers for the 2008 model year. Car buyers will now have a much better idea of the fuel efficiency they will actually get.

The numbers used by the Department of Transportation to enforce the standards are even further off base and greatly exaggerate the efficiency of the vehicles it regulates.[6] Because the DOT still makes no attempt to maintain accurate ratings, auto manufacturers do not have to meet the standards set in laws and regulations. Over the years, this oversight has made us more addicted to oil. This clearly is not like Lake Wobegon's children. In the American auto showrooms, most cars are *below* the required average.

The most obvious failure in the auto standards has been the inadequate response to the proliferation of light trucks. In the 1980s the Jeep Cherokee and the Dodge Caravan led the way toward larger, taller, and weightier vehicles that provided personal transportation but did not have to meet the stringent standards for passenger automobiles. Over time, more and more people made the switch from cars to vans and SUVs.

During Clinton's first term, the analysts at EIA pondered this growing phenomenon. The larger passenger vehicles, not counted as passenger cars under the law, appeared to be replacing old-fashioned station wagons, which were difficult to build as cars without creating difficulties meeting required efficiency averages. In our projections for the use of oil, we made the tentative judgment that people would purchase vans to accommodate the addition of children to the family but likely would return to traditional cars when the children left home. When that projection proved to be wrong, it became clear that vans and SUVs (often with a single person on board) would have an even greater impact than originally thought.

In addition, manufacturers came to realize they could build less-fuel-efficient vehicles by making minor adjustments in their designs. In 2005, Subaru raised the ground clearance for its Outback "sports utility wagon" from 6.1 inches to 8.7. The extra height qualified the vehicle, under the law, as a light truck with easier mileage requirements. Since then, bevies of new "crossover vehicles" have entered the market—they function as passenger cars but are exempt from those rules.

Then there's the Hummer. When the Carter administration wrote the original rules for light trucks, it was inconceivable that a vehicle over 8,500 pounds would be used for personal transportation. As a result, these very heavy vehicles were not covered by any mileage standards at all. Like lighter vehicles not classified as passenger cars, they were also exempt from the gas-guzzler tax. Thus, after the Hummer (a civilian version of the military Hum-Vee) went on sale in 1992 as a personal transportation vehicle, the best way to evade federal controls on gas-guzzling cars was to buy the most guzzling of them all.

The tattered auto standards also suffered from the tendency of some manufacturers to simply pay fines rather than comply with them. Two German car manufacturers, Mercedes-Benz and BMW, led the way in paying large fines year after year rather than meet the average fleet standard. American and Asian manufacturers have met the standards rather than pay fines.

The Bush administration rules of 2006 belatedly dealt with several of these problems. The rules for the small crossover vehicles require a few of them to meet standards as stiff as those for passenger cars. In addition, very heavy vehicles like Hummers were finally put under the regulatory regime. The new requirements will, however, not go into effect until 2011, almost two decades after Hummers became available to the public for purchase. Furthermore, court challenges have made the future of these rules uncertain.

The Energy Independence and Security Act of 2007 made some further progress by establishing averages that apply to all covered vehicles. From now on, it will not be possible to reduce the overall mileage of new vehicles by shifting from cars to light trucks. Manufacturers will find it more difficult to sell inefficient crossover vehicles to escape the higher standards for cars.

In general, rulemaking on auto efficiency by the Department of Transportation has been a failure. With only minimal press scrutiny, rulemaking provides an ideal venue for industry lobbyists and lawyers to exert maximum influence. For roughly 20 years, the efficiency of automobiles has failed to keep pace with available technology. In the original 1975 legislation, Congress set most of the standards for passenger cars through 1985 by law and allowed only a limited role for rule-making during the first 10 years. As time has gone on, the wisdom of that decision has become increasingly clear.

The new mileage-efficiency law allows more latitude for rulemaking than the old one, so the chronic lassitude at the Department of Transportation must be addressed. The Department could increase the effectiveness of the law by bringing its ratings up to date and making them more reflective of real driving conditions. It could also stymie the intent of Congress by not phasing in the 2020 standards in steady increments, as required by the law. During the period of implementation, it will make a big difference whether the Department reports to a president who is sympathetic or hostile to tough mileage-efficiency standards.

TECHNOLOGY OFFERS THE KEYS TO SUCCESS

Tweaked for more than a century, the internal combustion engine is a modern marvel. Year after year it can offer some combination of greater size, more horsepower, and reduced fuel use. Improvements in auto technology played a big role in the success of the CAFE standards during their first two decades of implementation.

Four technologies in passenger cars went from rare to common during this period, helping improve fuel efficiency while at the same time making these vehicles better in other ways. *Front wheel drive* improved handling and traction, while at the same time facilitating weight reduction due to the elimination of certain drive train components. *Fuel injection* helped make fuel combustion more efficient, reduce dangerous emissions, and improve engine responsiveness. *Lock-up torque converters* in automatic transmissions reduced slippage and increased efficiency. *Four-valve-per-cylinder* engines improved both performance and fuel economy.[7]

Do past improvements in auto technology mean we have run out of ideas about how to go further? The bad news is that, even today, only about a fifth of the potential energy in automobile fuels is used to actually propel the vehicle. The rest is lost mainly from waste heat in the exhaust, standby idling, mechanical friction, and the need for cooling systems. But this low conversion efficiency is actually the good news. There is a lot more that can be done to improve the cars we drive.

One highly publicized technology that currently occupies only a niche section of the market is the hybrid electric car. Increasingly feasible because of advanced computer controls that allow the car to shift seamlessly between battery and combustion power, these vehicles (like the Toyota Prius) can capture kinetic energy as they slow down (*regenerative braking*). Hybrid electrics can also shut down during idling, a valuable feature in urban traffic. In the coming years, we will undoubtedly see the cost of hybrid technology come down and the effectiveness of the batteries go up. Increasingly affordable hybrids offer a very promising path to building the autos of the future, which will make us less reliant on foreign oil and lower the emissions of greenhouse gases.

While the Japanese (and to a lesser extent the Americans) were pushing hybrids, the Europeans expanded the use of direct-injection diesel engines to promote fuel efficiency. These vehicles offer a flat torque curve that enhances drivability and can achieve fuel consumption improvements of about a third over current gasoline engines. Diesel engines have had trouble in the past meeting customer expectations for pollution mitigation, but the new models are burning much cleaner and starting to meet stringent American requirements. Diesel technology offers another attractive path toward solving our energy problems and might at some point be combined with batteries to make hybrid diesels.

The problem is not the lack of better technologies. Using advanced, low-friction lubricants can cut fuel consumption by 1 percent. Better controls on the intake valves (*variable valve timing*) can make a difference of 2 to 3 percent. The list goes on and on.

With all this room to adopt advanced technologies, why haven't we solved the problem of dependency on foreign oil, even without federal efficiency standards? Understanding the answer to this question is a vital key to declaring energy independence.

In the first place, as new technology becomes available, auto designers face many choices. Do they use the gains primarily for upping the horse-power to increase weight and speed while keeping mpg stable? Or do they emphasize reducing fuel consumption and keep horsepower constant? For the past two decades, there has been no doubt about what designers and their customers would choose.

The top-selling Ford Taurus typified the trend for many autos in the last two decades. The sedan was introduced in the 1986 model as a 188-inch-long, 3,050 pound vehicle. Over more than two decades, it became longer outside, roomier inside, heavier, safer, faster, and more powerful. Only one major feature stayed unchanged. Mileage efficiency remained virtually identical to that of the earliest models. Similar to other manu-facturers, Ford devoted none of the numerous new technologies added to improve mpg.

The official data confirm the bulking up of American autos we have observed with our own eyes. The EPA reports in *Light-Duty Automotive Technology and Fuel Economy Trends: 1975 through 2007* (September 2007) that the average light vehicle in 1987 weighed 3,221 pounds and rated 118 horsepower. By 2007, weight stood at 4,144 pounds (up 29 percent) and horsepower at 223 (up 89 percent). During the same period, vehi-cle mileage dropped from 22.0 mph to 20.2 (down 8 percent). Improved technology kept the mileage from falling even more, but could not stem the rush for weight and power.

We should not underestimate the desire to have faster and faster acceleration of still-heavier vehicles in the future as well. (Is this a male trait?) Such trends will continue to offset the potential gains in mpg from advanced technologies. Nor should we underestimate the likely demand for new features that make a car feel like a home. (Is this a female trait?) "I think a vehicle today has to be your most favorite room under your roof," said Robert Nardelli, the new CEO of Chrysler, in 2007. "I really believe . . . it has to bring you gratification, it has to be tranquil. It's incidental that it gets you from Point A to B."[8] Air conditioning in autos, though originally introduced in the 1939 Packard line, did not boom in popularity until the 1960s and 1970s. In the future, will we be adding to vehicle weight with coffee makers, refrigerators, and microwave ovens purchased from Chrysler rather than Home Depot?

When we project the potential for even faster acceleration and features that add to vehicle weight, we have to recognize the likelihood that manufacturers will be offering high-tech hybrid and diesel vehicles with low mpg. This means that hybrid cars do not necessarily equate to green cars. Attention should be paid less to the hybrid badge put on the car by manufacturers and more to the EPA efficiency stickers on windows.

The other constraint on new technology is cost. Advanced systems raise prices, especially when they are first introduced. These costs may or may not be justified by reduced fuel bills or customer appreciation of enhanced features. But these benefits need to be added to others, like lower world prices for oil due to slacker demand, stronger national security, and enhanced environment.

The politically popular way to push higher-technology automobiles is to push voluntary partnerships between industry and government, or to advocate tax credits. So far, every such partnership has been a smokescreen to avert attention away from proposals that would actually produce results. It is one thing to build a prototype for an auto show that looks like it will solve all our problems; it is quite another to penetrate the market.

What about using tax credits for advanced autos to stimulate market penetration? The potential costs of these credits are so great that they are usually designed to cover a period of only several years. As a result, they do not affect production levels very much and often end up subsidizing people ("free riders") who were going to purchase the car anyway. As a result, they do not create the long-term incentives needed.

Mandatory efficiency standards have great appeal because they are at the same time technology neutral and a strong impetus in bringing new technologies to market. Federal standards do not specify how they will be met. Hybrids, diesels, or some other unanticipated technology might rise to the challenge of achieving higher mpg. Some customers will prefer cars with expensive technologies that combine generous sizing, fast acceleration, and provide efficiency. Others will opt for small, but safe cars that get exceptional mileage but do not cost more than average. Governments should establish parameters that meet national objectives and allow considerable latitude on how manufacturers can meet customer expectations.

THE PATH AHEAD

To achieve energy independence, the United States must again achieve steady improvements in the fuel efficiency of new automobiles, and with the new Energy Independence and Security Act, we are off to a good start. Because we have lost two decades when we could have continued to make progress, we need to set the bar for implementation as high as possible and get started right away.

The new CAFE standards raise that bar a full mile-per-gallon a year. In contrast to what was discussed just a couple of years ago, that is a bold move. Congress deserves a lot of credit for pushing through a substantive requirement in the face of substantial opposition.

I don't want to carp, but we've ignored mileage efficiency for a long time. In the last two years, the need to act on oil dependency and global warming has become much clearer. The technologies of hybrid electric, diesel engines, and direct injections are progressing faster than we thought they would. Customers facing high gasoline prices are giving greater priority to vehicle efficiency. Shouldn't we really be doing more?

I propose that automakers be required to raise mpg at the rate of a mile and a half a year, not just the mile per year in the energy legislation. Based on what we now know about the need for energy independence, this requirement should go into effect as quickly as possible and continue on almost a permanent basis. By 2020, this rate of progress brings to market a "freedom car" with a combined average of 40 mpg across the fleet of new vehicles. Unless some major trend lines surprise us (always a possibility), we will probably want to go to 55 mpg by 2030.

The problem, of course, is that Congress, having so recently taken action, is unlikely to reenter the fray over mileage standards for several years. This is where the president comes in. A commander-in-chief committed to auto efficiency (and national security) can adopt rules quickly and make the Department of Transportation's rating accurate. These administrative changes could provide the equivalent impact of raising the standard higher with additional legislation.

There is a big question overhanging ambitious goals on mileage efficiency. How much will they disrupt the auto market? People want to have fun driving and also have the ability to purchase vehicles at reasonable prices. At the least, requiring 40 mpg vehicles by 2020 will make it difficult for manufacturers to continue the race toward faster acceleration and greater weight. Their challenge will be to find new electronic features that will get customers into their showrooms (whether in the physical or cyber worlds).

A look at cars already on the market provides some assurance that high-mileage cars can be attractive to customers. The Toyota Prius and the Honda Civic Hybrid are not large cars, but they are packed with features. According to the updated 2008 EPA mileage ratings, the Prius gets 46 mpg and the Civic 42. Thus, assuming no further technology developments (extremely unlikely), the Prius could meet my proposed average up to 2024. But the expected progress in batteries alone will substantially increase the design options for these hybrids.

What about SUVs? One hybrid sold as the Ford Escape, the Mazda Tribute, or the Mercury Mariner gets 32 mpg, good enough to meet the proposed average up to 2014. The Ford SUVs have been attractive to politicians, who want to prove their green credentials and buy American. To be clear, these vehicles do illustrate the trade-offs car buyers will face in the coming years. Moving from two-wheel drive to four-wheel drops mileage by four mpg. That is a hefty loss of efficiency to get an off-road vehicle. In the future, decisions to get four-wheel drives will be made more carefully, more often confined to people who actually do drive off-road or encounter icy conditions while driving.

The most interesting fuel-miser automobile available in the 2008 model year is not a hybrid. It is the Mercedes-Benz E320 Bluetec—a midsize luxury car that spurts from zero to 60 mph in 6.6 seconds. It is a high torque wonder that can tow a heavy load. Got to be a gas-guzzler, right?

This new direct-injection diesel from Mercedes gets 26 miles per gallon in the latest EPA rankings. Even with numerous features that work against saving fuel, that is slightly above the current national vehicle average. Similar E-Class cars from Mercedes without diesel engines average 19 mpg. These are $50,000-plus vehicles, but the incremental cost of diesel technology is only about $1,000. Notice that is an improvement of 7 miles per gallon (37 percent) for a mere $1,000. Diesels can play a big role in providing much better fuel efficiency at a reasonable cost, especially in cases where its superior torque can service customers wanting to haul a boat or toss a deer in the back.

About half of the new cars sold in Europe these days are diesels. Americans have been slow to adopt this old technology, due to performance and pollution issues. But numerous refinements developed in Europe have eliminated most of these concerns. The Mercedes Bluetec already meets the new ultra-low American emissions standards (by using its AdBlue liquid-based additive) and is slated to soon meet the even more stringent California standards. Mercedes also plans to quickly expand its diesel Bluetec technology into other models that can meet tough American environmental standards.

There are other, more exotic auto technologies on the horizon that may be used to meet stricter CAFE standards, and some of them will undoubtedly work well enough to reach market. Hybrid electrics and diesels are the "birds in a hand" that can get us a long way toward 40 and 50 mpg vehicles. Though some optimists think a full range of technology advances at reasonable prices will offset the need to downsize the American fleet, I cannot offer such an assurance. In fact, there will likely be fewer 6,000-pound light trucks at the auto dealer. Still, if the option of large vehicles is there for drivers who really need them, the safety tests from smaller vehicles continue to provide positive results, and our neighbors are bound by the same efficiency rules as we are, some downsizing of the fleet should be acceptable to achieve national objectives.

Bold national programs can sometimes get derailed by details that turn out to be more important than expected. We need to adopt several measures to ensure that our ambitious new auto efficiency standards actually achieve their objectives. For instance, the potential for avoiding stricter standards by paying fines needs to be sharply curtailed. The Energy Independence and Security Act continues to give the option of fines for manufacturers who do not meet efficiency standards. The major option to get actual compliance with the standards, then, lies with public opinion. Those who repeatedly violate the standards should be singled out for scrutiny and identified as special contributors to reliance on oil and global warming.

For the first time, the new law allows some trading of efficiency credits among automakers. This provision allows producers of cars above required standards to sell credits to those below. While still allowing some manufacturers to escape full compliance with the standards, the net effect will be much better than fines. The overall average will still be met. Allowing individual companies to focus on what they do best will also encourage the use of advanced technologies and make compliance more economically efficient.

$\sim$

Unfortunately, we cannot confine our efforts to reduce the amount of oil used by transportation to the vehicles covered by the CAFE standards. We will also have to deal with large trucks and planes. We will also need to expand American options for mass transit. Getting started right away on cars, vans, SUVs, and other light trucks will set a path that can be emulated, to some degree, in these other areas.

We should also ask whether, even with more efficient vehicles, we need to be using petroleum products at all. All alternatives to oil have their own costs; there is no free lunch here. So we will still need to develop highly efficient vehicles, no matter what fuels them. Still, as we are about to see, there are some attractive non-oil options out there.

Chapter 10

Solution Three: Bring Alternative Fuels to Market

W e do not have to use petroleum products (gasoline and diesel) to power our automobiles, vans, SUVs, and trucks. The range of other options is impressive. We could power our vehicles with hydrogen, liquids produced from coal or plants, natural gas, batteries, and even more exotic alternative fuels. If we displace the oil burned in our automobiles with these alternatives from the United States, we lessen our dependence on foreign oil. We do not have to continue our addiction to oil, wherever it comes from.

In the real world, alternative fuels have a hard time competing with oil products. Gasoline and diesel are easy to transport, whether at sea, overland, or underground. They are also dense fuels—that is, they get a lot of mileage from the volume stored in your gas tank. These factors help keep costs down and give vehicles greater driving ranges than possible with other fuels. In addition, the infrastructure of the oil industry is well established, making it hard for startup alternatives to compete. As a result, we have plenty of alternative fuels that are technically feasible but cannot break into the market.

The ground has shifted dramatically over the past few years, in favor of alternative transportation fuels. Most notably, the Energy Independence and Security Act of 2007 phases in hefty mandates for displacing gasoline with ethanol. Make no mistake: the greater role for liquid fuels made from plants has been written into law and is definitely coming. We will be reducing our use of gasoline, but we need to be sensible about it. Are we moving too fast? Are we moving too slowly? Are there better options? The challenge for energy independence is identifying the alternative fuels with the greatest benefits, then finding economic ways to get them into cars across the country.

Some Also-Rans

Most alternative fuels for vehicles sound exciting upon first hearing. On closer inspection, however, we find that several are impractical, have serious adverse side effects, or are too far off into the future to provide much immediate value.

Hydrogen

Hydrogen gets rave reviews in many quarters. When consumed, it releases no pollution or greenhouse gases. It is lightweight and has no detectable odor. The universe is filled with abundant hydrogen. It fuels NASA space shuttles. Many scientists are bullish about the future of a hydrogen economy. George W. Bush made hydrogen a cornerstone of his first energy plan. When people first hear about hydrogen, it almost sounds too good to be true.

Well, there is a very big catch to the hydrogen hype, often omitted in briefings on the subject. Hydrogen does not exist in nature as such. Therefore, it must be produced by some process that uses energy. Like a battery, hydrogen stores the energy until it is needed. As a result, the environmental and other problems associated with normal energy use are transferred from where the hydrogen is consumed to where it is made. Over time, hydrogen may be produced in benign ways, but most of these benefits would accrue more broadly than just to hydrogen. Given this perspective, hydrogen loses its luster as a miracle fuel.

There are other problems with hydrogen as well. Its relatively low energy content per unit of volume makes it troublesome to transport and use. It is also highly explosive under pressure. A transition to a hydrogen economy would require massive changes in the national infrastructure for fuel delivery, making it difficult to identify likely paths to market penetration. Because it is a clean storage mechanism, hydrogen may someday play a major role in creating energy independence, but not in the coming decades.

Synfuels

Synthetic fuels are created when coal is chemically altered to make gaseous and liquid fuels. This process takes the most abundant fossil fuel and converts it to the more useful forms of its fossil cousins. It is not some pipedream. Germany's synthetic fuel plants produced enough liquid fuels from coal during World War II to replace half of its lost petroleum deliveries until Allied forces virtually wiped out its synfuels facilities.

Inspired by the German success, the Interior Department in 1947 proposed another Manhattan Project—a massive effort costing $10 billion to produce two million barrels a day of synthetic fuels within five years. The next year, Congress voted to extend a much less-expensive synfuels program supported by President Truman. About the same time, the *New York Times* opined, "The next ten years will see the rise of a massive new industry which will free us from dependence on foreign sources of oil. Gasoline will be produced from coal, air, and water." By the next year, Interior was operating a demonstration plant and claiming that synthetic fuels could be produced much cheaper than conventional oil.[1]

Following lulls in national interest, presidents Johnson, Ford, and Carter (with the assistance of coal-state congressmen) tried to revive interest in synfuels. But they kept running into a persistent problem. Synfuels were, in fact, more expensive than conventional oil. Converting solids to liquids costs a lot less if Mother Nature does it. Proposals to provide risk-free price protection to synfuel producers were never adopted. Without them, there were never sufficient incentives to sustain massive investments in the technology.

In recent years, synfuels have faced an even bigger obstacle than high prices. Coal-based transportation fuels emit a great deal more carbon dioxide than gasoline. Still, the Bush Department of Energy continues to encourage China to develop coal-based transportation fuels, a strategy that would aggressively speed global warming. Again, future generations will ask, "What were those people thinking?" With what we know about global warming, we should not be moving to fuels that increase greenhouse gases in the United States or China. Coal can technically displace oil, but there are much better ways to achieve that objective.

Both hydrogen and synfuels show that technical feasibility is just one challenge facing alternative fuels. We want the next generation of fuels to meet the triple goals of promoting national security, economic efficiency, and environmental protection. We're looking for *threefers*.

THE WINNERS WILL BE. . .

Getting fuels from plants may strike you as moving backward. Wasn't it a sign of advancement when we cut back burning wood and moved on to the combustion of more powerful fossil fuels? In the modern world, however, people are increasingly looking at energy from plants to save us from our dependence on foreign oil. The plants we can grow for fuel are right here at home, not from unstable regimes in dangerous places. They can reduce the contribution of fuels to global warming. Moreover, we already know how to convert them into liquid fuels for vehicles. They already provide over 4 percent of the total gasoline pool, and their contribution is growing rapidly.

Right now, the biofuels we have are not the biofuels we want. To maximize their benefits, we need to move beyond their predominant form at present, ethanol produced from corn kernels. We can make greater progress on declaring energy independence if we turn the focus to cellulosic ethanol and biodiesel.

Ethanol

President Carter, with the strong support of legislators from agricultural states, launched the modern era of ethanol production. The technology available at the time turned the starch found in corn into sugar, which was then fermented into alcohol. Blenders mixed 10 percent alcohol with 90 percent gasoline to create what at the time was called "gasohol." During a decade of major energy crises, gasohol gave great promise for replacing foreign oil with a fuel that was both home-grown and renewable.

Unlike many other initiatives of the period, the incentives created for ethanol have retained their political support over time and survived pretty much intact. On average, every gallon of gasoline with a 10 percent blend of alcohol qualified for a five-cent tax break, boosting the value of a gallon of pure ethanol by fifty cents.

Ethanol has received many other forms of government support over the years. These include federal tax credits for producers and stiff tariffs protecting against foreign competitors. Oil companies are required to use ethanol as an oxygenate. Federal energy legislation in 2005 set minimum requirements for ethanol use in future years. Some states offer further incentives. Ethanol is our most costly national energy program (well over $2 billion a year and growing rapidly).

Added to previous government support for ethanol, the 2007 energy legislation sharply upped the requirements for ethanol use. These goals are not optional, and they are very substantial. Congress has required the use of 1.3 million barrels a day of ethanol by 2015 and 2.4 million barrels a day by 2022. By comparison, last year the United States consumed about 9.3 million barrels of gasoline a day. New ethanol production will displace a big chunk of future gasoline demand.

In the early years of this ethanol production, most of the new ethanol will be produced from corn kernels, but corn-based ethanol has a problem its proponents would like to ignore. It is an energy-intensive crop. Because of the tilling of cropland, fertilizers, water pumping, and tractor mileages needed to grow corn, many gains in displacing petroleum with ethanol are offset. Moreover, distillers generally use natural gas for the energy needed to convert the sugar to alcohol. Most of the advantages in reducing petroleum dependence and carbon emissions get lost, in fact, making ethanol subsidies from the government too substantial for what is delivered (at least from an energy point of view).

We do not have to make ethanol from energy-intensive crops like corn. We can produce it from fast-growing trees (willows or poplars) or switchgrass (a prairie grass that grows to the height of a tall human without the need for much watering). We can also use the waste from other crops grown for other purposes. These include corn stover (leaves and stalks), forest product residues, and bagasse (the remains of sugar cane stalks after the juice has been removed). Cellulosic ethanol consumes much less energy during production. As a result, by turning to noncorn sources of ethanol, we can dramatically improve the gains for national security, the economy, and the environment.

Cellulosic ethanol also has a catch, but one that is being resolved. Cellulosic plants demonstrate, in the words of the Department of Energy, "recalcitrance to processing to ethanol." Better techniques are needed to break down the complex polymer composites that trap the sugars. In hindsight, we have not given enough support to research on cellulosic ethanol. But it is widely assumed by energy analysts that we are on the verge of seeing economically viable cellulosic ethanol plants.

In November of 2007, Range Fuels broke ground in southern Georgia for what it hopes will be the nation's first commercially successful cellulosic ethanol plant. Funded by capital from Silicon Valley, the facility will employ a proprietary two-step thermochemical process that uses heat, pressure, and steam to convert biomass (likely wood chips) into synthesis gas, which is then passed over a proprietary catalyst and transformed into ethanol suitable for fueling vehicles.

A lot of national ethanol policy (and, indeed, national energy policy) rests on the results of the early cellulosic ethanol facilities. If they prove commercially viable, we will be able to move much more quickly toward energy independence. Plants for cellulosic ethanol will still require much greater capital than those for corn-based ethanol, but it is assumed that they can become cost effective because the crops utilized are much less expensive.

The Energy Independence and Security Act recognized the need to move to cellulosic ethanol. The Act requires that 15 percent of ethanol production should come from cellulose by 2015. In 2022, the percentage rises to 44 percent. Since cellulosic ethanol is not yet in commercial production, these are clearly stretch targets.

We know a lot about how vehicles run on ethanol, but certain key information is still lacking. Ethanol is generally sold as a 10 percent (E–10) or an 85 percent (E–85) blend. The rationale for these levels is not well demonstrated. There may be other blending levels that provide better performance.

This is an important consideration. The new 2008 rankings by the Environmental Protection Agency show that new vehicles running on E–85 get a quarter to a third less miles per gallon than their gasoline counterparts. It is easy for auto manufacturers to make flex-fuel vehicles that can run on E–85 or on gasoline, but drivers will decide which fuel to put in their tanks. With mileage losses of these magnitudes, E–85 may be a policy overreach and a commercial bust. The search should begin for other, more viable blending levels.

Biodiesel

Diesel engines can also run on biofuels. Biodiesel is particularly important strategically, because more fuel-efficient diesel cars will be entering the

American market, and petroleum refineries will have a hard time keeping up with the demand for distillates. So biodiesel can help us switch from oil to a renewable fuel and expand the possibilities for driving vehicles with better mileage.

Biodiesel is different in some respects from traditional diesel, but in most respects performs better. It does not run as well in cold climates, but many issues with biodiesel can be ameliorated with innovations in blending. It is easy to make and not very capital intensive. The big limitation is finding a large and affordable supply of the animal and vegetable oils needed to produce it. Due to this problem, current production of biodiesel is almost negligible compared to corn-based ethanol (though also growing rapidly).

Biodiesel is produced mostly from what is called *yellow grease* (generally waste oils from restaurants) and soybean oil (a surplus product from the oil meal–crushing industry). These waste products can (with existing federal subsidies) contribute several percent of the total diesel fuel market. On the whole, they make biodiesel (with its federal subsidies) economically competitive with diesel from petroleum. Other waste products, like shaved chicken fat, might make added contributions. But it will likely prove difficult to move much beyond the initial threshold created by the limited volumes of waste oils. Virgin soybean, rapeseed, and sunflower oils can be produced in much greater quantities, but they double the costs of the feedstocks and require extremely high subsidies. It is not surprising that the Energy Independence and Security Act contains only modest goals for biodiesel.

The economics of biodiesel production is greatly influenced by local situations. But it should be national policy to encourage as much biodiesel as possible from waste oils. Even in somewhat limited quantities, these biofuels can make an important contribution to energy independence. The new energy legislation also mandates more research and development on biodiesel, which will be needed if this technology is going to make major advances.

HOW TO MOVE AHEAD

At the beginning of 2007, the country had a commitment to increase its ethanol production, based on generous financial incentives and modest requirements for future production. By the end of the year, Congress had passed much more robust ethanol requirements and tilted them more in the direction of cellulosic ethanol. Based on the remaining uncertainties about ethanol, Congress took its boldest steps on ethanol.

The Bush administration, under Energy Secretary Samuel Bodman, has put more emphasis on cellulosic ethanol research than any predecessor since the Carter years. But national goals for this still-untested alternative fuel are very bold, and even more aggressive federal investments will be needed to make the scientific advances necessary to meet them.

The combination of market responses to high energy prices, mandates for more fuel-efficient cars and light trucks, and new requirements for ethanol will contain future demand for oil products and probably even reverse it. With the passage of the Energy Independence and Security Act of 2007, we have ended an age of energy complacency and begun to dig ourselves out of dependence on foreign oil. But our addiction to oil will be tough to break, and we will need to do even more if we want to achieve true energy independence. In the future, might we get less of our transportation fuel at the gasoline pump and more from electric outlets in our garages?

Chapter 11

Solution Four: Plug into an Electric Future

We plug in our cell phones and laptops. With batteries recharged, these weapons of the road warrior can operate pretty much anywhere, anytime without being connected to a power source. Why can't we do that with our cars and trucks? Why would we want to?

The motivation to embrace electric-based transportation is clear. Our national goal should be reducing reliance on oil, particularly foreign oil. Unfettered international trade makes sense for most goods and services, but not for oil. Our heavy reliance on oil from troubled places leads to the indirect financing of terrorists, heavy military commitments to protect access, and the possibility that producers can put a stranglehold on our economy and national security. Running our personal and business vehicles on domestic fuels would completely change the national security equation.

Since we have already backed most oil out of electric generation, the power we get from our electrical outlets derives mainly from domestic sources—coal, nuclear, natural gas, and hydropower. If we continue to increase the use of wind and other renewable sources of electricity, we will still be utilizing power we do not have to import.

Like liquid fuels from plants, electric power offers an attractive option for breaking our bondage to foreign oil. Like other proposals for new ways of producing and using energy, we need to examine the electric car option carefully. If we understand the risks and opportunities, we can not only make better decisions about whether we want to move to an electric future, but also how we can get there.

THE PATH WE'RE ON

Since the early days of the auto industry, using batteries rather than gasoline for power has been technically feasible. Indeed, for light vehicles operating where any exhaust fumes are frowned upon—like carts at airports and golf courses—battery-powered vehicles are in wide use today. But the gasoline-powered combustion engine won the battle for auto supremacy on American roads. Once entrenched in the market, the traditional oil-consuming car became hard to displace.

California attempted to bring all-electric cars to market with a 1990 mandate that auto manufacturers eventually produce some zero-emission vehicles, a standard that could only be met by cars that run on batteries. Under pressure from auto manufacturers, the state dropped the requirement in 2003, provoking a debate about whether all-electric vehicles were the wave of the future or a pipedream. A 2006 documentary film *Who Killed the Electric Car?*—narrated by Martin Sheen and featuring Hollywood stars Mel Gibson and Alexandra Paul—argued that car companies conspired to kill off a product with many attractive features and a long line of potential customers. The companies rebutted that people expressed interest in the cars, but declined to actually lease them (they were not available for purchase), so there was no way to make them profitable.

The death of the all-electric car in California has failed to dampen enthusiasm for running our cars and trucks with electricity instead of oil products. The recent successes of hybrid-electric vehicles demonstrate both the national security and environmental advantages of relying more on electricity and a path toward greater reliance on electricity in the future. Since the first model to achieve popular acceptance, the Toyota Prius, entered the American market in 2000, these high-mileage vehicles have set the pace for reducing oil dependence and emissions of greenhouse gases. At the same time, they have proven remarkably reliable for a new technology and extremely popular with the people who buy them. In 2008, surveys by *Consumer Reports* ranked the Prius the top car in customer satisfaction for the fifth year in a row. Drivers did not just rate this hybrid best in class. It was number one among all vehicles of any size at any price.

Other manufacturers are now producing hybrid vehicles, sometimes with licenses to the technology bought from Toyota. While not every model has sold well, the trend for hybrids is definitely on an upward trajectory. The new mileage requirements in the Energy Independence and Security Act of 2007 will provide even more impetus to the expansion of hybrid options.

It is easy to forget how new the hybrid technology is. As a still-recent development, it has plenty of potential to get even better. Batteries in hybrids have already improved and will undoubtedly continue to progress. The issues are similar to those for the batteries that run those cell phones and laptops. We want batteries with small size, low weight for portability, and high levels of safety. We also want longer life to reduce the need for frequent recharging or replacement. Combining these features can be challenging, even for devices with small power requirements. Developing batteries for vehicles heavy enough to provide safety and fast enough to meet customer requirements faces even bigger hurdles, but the momentum is in the right direction.

CONNECTING TO THE GRID

Currently, the batteries in hybrids are recharged primarily from regenerative braking, which converts the kinetic energy of the car into electric energy as it slows down. But oil use and the size of conventional propulsion systems can be further reduced by repowering higher-capacity batteries from the electric grid. In the coming years, plugging into the grid could increase the electric share of an auto's power needs while retaining an engine that burns oil as a smaller complement or backup. Further down the road, as technology continues to improve, plugging in might even bring the return of the all-electric vehicle. Oil consumption could shrink to zero.

A recent study by Pacific Northwest National Laboratory estimated that converting 73 percent of America's 220 million vehicles to plug-in vehicles (that still have a small gasoline engine) would displace up to 6.5 million barrels of oil a day. Another optimistic study of the potential for plug-in electrics assumed they would make up half of annual car sales around 2025.[1] These levels of market penetration are quite rosy given the changes that will need to occur. Still, we are talking about a technology that within a couple of decades can reduce oil imports in the magnitudes of *millions* of barrels a day. Combined with improved fuel-efficiency standards and a rising share of ethanol, drawing transportation energy from the grid makes a significant contribution to slashing oil imports and enhancing national security.

The national security advantages of ending our addiction to oil are obvious, but what about the economics and the environment? Do we have a *threefer* here?

❧

The economics for plug-ins looks favorable. The demand for electricity varies greatly over a 24-hour day. It generally runs highest when people are awake. That is when they need indoor lighting and run their appliances. The refrigerator and electric heater (in winter and when natural gas is not the preferred fuel for space heating) run at night, but except in rare cases that load will hardly tax the capacity of electric generators. Thus, in the words of the Department of Energy lab study, "The U.S. electric power infrastructure is a strategic national asset that is underutilized most of the time."[2]

The time people are generally asleep happens to be ideal for recharging car batteries. They are obviously not driving their vehicles and are not going to get impatient if the process takes a while. Since there is excess capacity at the time, electric companies will not have to build new plants to accommodate nighttime recharging (or even use their expensive peaking plants running occasionally) to handle heavy loads. That starts to make the economics look very good. But there is more.

The need for power during off-peak periods may also help improve the economics of intermittent power. Wind currents at night generate power, but have limited value because of the low demand during that time. If we can shift auto recharging to nighttime and synchronize it to when currents are strong, we could eventually increase the value of that noncarbon-emitting wind power. We will need a smarter grid that better matches supply and demand, but it should be economical to build one.

In short, we can recharge our electric cars at night when electric demand runs well below what baseload and other nonpeaking plants can produce. So electric companies do not have to build new plants to accommodate a very large number of plug-in vehicles, which helps them better use their capital investments. Customers will get very inexpensive off-peak rates, lowering their overall energy bills. While we're displacing oil and enhancing national security, we're saving money. So far, connecting to the grid is a very attractive *twofer*.

❧

Will plugging in, as some studies have indicated, also eventually reduce emissions of greenhouse gases? The answer is maybe. It seems logical that controlling emissions at a few hundred central electric generation facilities would be easier than controlling emissions of millions of individual vehicles. But plug-ins will not be utilizing noncarbon-emitting nuclear plants, since even during periods of low demand, most nuclear power is generally already being fully utilized. As a result, we need to be concerned about the amount of power for our vehicles that comes from carbon-spewing coal plants.

Two serious studies on environmental impacts (one from the Pacific Northwest Laboratory and the second from a partnership of the National Resource Defense Council and the Electric Power Research Institute) provide encouraging results. The lab study concluded that national "total greenhouse gases are expected to be reduced by a maximum of 27% from the projected penetration of plug-in vehicles." In the industry/environmental study, seven of eight scenarios for 2050 showed plugs-ins producing less carbon than hybrid vehicles and less than half as much as conventional vehicles. But I am not reassured on the environmental issue yet.

The lab study attributes the major savings from plug-ins from the efficiencies of regenerative braking. But there's no need to hook up to the grid to get those benefits, since they are fully achievable in unconnected hybrid vehicles. As a result, these efficiencies shouldn't be attributed to electricity from the grid.

The industry/environmental study assumed that conventional vehicles would gain efficiency only from market-based incentives and not from any new government policies. By contrast, it assumed even in its most carbon-intensive electric generation case there would be additional policy incentives from a carbon cap or tax. Not assuming any policy drivers for unconnected vehicles when they are assumed for electric generation makes the study a comparison of apples and oranges. Plug-ins certainly have the *potential* to be less carbon intensive than today's conventional and hybrid vehicles. It is less clear whether they *will* be.

The differences in assumptions became even more troublesome several months later, after Congress mandated mileage efficiency (carbon reduction) standards for vehicles well beyond those contemplated in the study, and electric industry lobbyists successfully supported a filibuster in the Senate that blocked the major part of the energy package to make electric generation less carbon intensive (the renewables portfolio bill). To get the benefits identified in both studies, electric generation will have to be reformed in ways that some companies are supporting and others are fighting.

On the whole, the case for plugging in a greater amount of vehicles to the grid is strong. We get immense national security and economic benefits. We might eventually get a *threefer*. From what we know now, however, we need to carefully monitor the environmental impacts to see if the reality matches the models.

ENVISIONING A PLUG-IN FUTURE

Several things have to happen if we are going to transition to cars powered more by electricity and less by oil. First, we need to get time-of-day pricing in place, so drivers will have appropriate incentives to switch to cheaper, off-peak power on the electric grid. It is a win-win situation for everyone.

At the same time, battery technology needs to improve. Moving a car requires a lot of torque and energy. Companies right now are working on increasing the energy density and safety of lithium batteries (and even more exotic projects), and they will likely finds ways to get more power and life from smaller systems. As batteries advance, manufacturers can offer new models of cars that increasingly rely on electricity.

The all-electric car can penetrate the market only if there are readily available locations for recharging. This infrastructure was being built in California and some other urban areas until the large experiment with electric cars died out. The backbone for recharging stations will be the home garage, so drivers can take advantage of off-peak rates at night. These outlets should have timers or communications to grid operators that allow recharging at times of lowest demand on the system.

In an ideal world, the power should be able to flow both ways. When the electric system goes down, people could then keep their computers and refrigerators running for a while with electricity from their car batteries. In levee-wobbly New Orleans, residents have rushed to buy diesel generators as protection against another hurricane that ravages electric lines. I do not find the storage of diesel fuel in the garage a very appealing idea, so why not, instead, take advantage of that powerful battery that will be sitting in your car?

We can supplement home outlets with others at places where people spend enough time to get a full recharge. These could include airports, office complexes, and shopping malls.

Our transition to all-electric cars will likely include a stage during which two-car families have a very clean electric vehicle with very low fuel costs for commutes and other short trips and a second gasoline or hybrid-powered vehicle for longer distances. But the transition does not have to stop there.

It takes much longer to recharge a battery than to fill a gasoline tank. Unless there are major breakthroughs that allow much quicker recharging, the time required will not be acceptable to drivers on the road. We will have to get creative about how to service drivers who need a power boost on long trips.

I have argued for many years that the answer was not recharging batteries at service stations, but swapping one battery for another. The driver would trade in a spent battery for one ready to go. Depending on the weight of the batteries, a crane of some sort might be needed for the replacement process. If batteries get light enough or modular, taking the used batteries out and putting in new ones might eventually resemble how we replace the toner in our printers.

This scenario has many attractive features. First, a fresh battery could be substituted in less time than it takes to pump a tank of gas. Second, proprietors could manage the recycling of the batteries and their toxic chemicals. Third, service stations could recharge the batteries at times when overall electric demand is low and prices are cheap.

I have tried to identify potential deal-breakers in a transition to more-electric or all-electric cars. Some of the challenges remain formidable, but any insurmountable technical or commercial hurdles seem unlikely, especially given the incentives for achieving success.

What should we be doing right now? Expanded research and development on battery technology is a must. We need to get time-of-day pricing in place around the country. We should be installing 240-volt outlets that can fast-recharge automobiles in the garages of our homes.

STRATEGIC PLANNING FOR ELECTRICITY

Oil almost disappeared as a fuel for electricity after the early 1980s. Despite changed circumstances, advocates for solar and nuclear energy continued to claim they could help end our dependence on foreign oil, but this was only the case if there was a way for electricity to play a greater role in transportation. Now that electric vehicles are making a comeback, all the issues of electricity are back on the table in the battle to win energy independence.

If we are going to add transportation vehicles to the machinery powered by electricity, we need baseload power that is clean, dependable, and economical. Currently, coal and nuclear plants do the heavy lifting, providing the power that runs 24/7. It is hard to imagine major economies prospering without an expansion of one or both of these old standbys. But they each have major problems that need addressing.

We have found ways over the years to dramatically curb most major pollutants that come from coal, but the big gorilla of carbon dioxide emissions threatens the future viability of this abundant fossil fuel. As stricter controls on carbon emissions are imposed, we will have to either reduce coal use or find ways to mitigate its impacts on global warming. This can be done, at least in theory, by gasifying the coal to generate electricity, capturing the carbon dioxide, and injecting it back underground. The sequestration of carbon will likely work best when it is deposited in underground caverns, such as depleted oil fields. There is an attractive symmetry in injecting carbon emissions into reservoirs drained of their carbon fuels, but electric plants will need to located next to these reservoirs or rely on new underground pipelines to transport the carbon to sequestration sites.

Though it has been evident since the 1970s that the use of coal would have to adjust in order to meet the need to slow global warming, efforts to develop sequestration options have lagged. Neither coal industries, electric companies, nor the federal government have shown much sense of urgency on this issue. Furthermore, in January of 2008, the Bush administration withdrew its support for the major technology for carbon separation, based on high costs, leaving the planning for reducing carbon emissions from coal in tatters. If coal is going to compete effectively in a carbon-constrained world (and power those plug-in vehicles), the work on sequestration will need to transform from today's tepid efforts into a major national priority—and very soon.

Nuclear power plants can operate safely. The management of nuclear facilities has improved dramatically since the 1970s, when the popularity of the nuclear option dropped precipitously. (The poor performance and economics of nuclear power plants led to a stop in new orders, even before the 1979 Three Mile Island accident.) Constraints on carbon emissions will improve the economics of nuclear power versus coal, its major competitor. The federal government is willing to subsidize some new nuclear plants built in the coming years. The prospects for nuclear power are brighter than they have been in many years. From a long-range perspective, the major impediment to boldly moving into a nuclear future is the problem of waste.

The United States has failed to develop a permanent repository for its nuclear waste. There are strong local pressures, particularly in Nevada, against siting a nuclear dump, and experts are divided on whether we have identified the best techniques for isolating the waste for the long periods required. It is possible to recycle nuclear waste, as is done in many places in the world. This approach reduces the need for permanent storage but increases the chances that nuclear materials can be used for weapons. Both the United States and the international community face stiff challenges in finding safe solutions to the nuclear waste puzzle.

Highly efficient natural gas plants can also provide baseload power, but electric companies are worried about the future supplies and prices of natural gas. The improved economics of importing liquefied natural gas may ease these concerns in the coming years.

Beyond the issue of baseload power, the electric industry needs to diversify to alternative forms of energy, particularly those that do not emit carbon dioxide. In 2007, twenty-four states required that some portion of their electricity come from renewable energy such as biomass, wind, or solar. These mandates—often called *renewable portfolio standards*—are successfully boosting output from renewables around the country and providing valuable opportunities to assess the strengths and weaknesses of the various options.

In December of 2007, the U.S. Senate fell just one vote short of the 60 needed to stop the filibuster against a national requirement that 15 percent of electricity come from renewable resources by 2020.[3] Opponents argued that this part of the broader energy bill not only costs too much, but penalizes states not particularly suitable for solar or wind power. The success of these arguments was surprising, since earlier in the year an Energy Information Administration study of an earlier version of the renewable portfolio standard had found otherwise.

Most states have good options for adding renewable energy to their electricity mix. The argument that all states needed to have above-average access to sunlight and wind currents was shaky, since EIA projected that biomass—which is very plentiful in many of the states that fought the mandate—would be the primary way to add renewable energy.

In the EIA study, the cumulative cost of $18 billion to end users sounds large, but given the volume of electricity sold and the 25 year period, it is a reasonable price to pay. The average cost of a kilowatt-hour (KWH) of electricity would increase by 1 percent (that's percent, not cent). In 2030, for instance, a KWH would run 8.21 cents with the requirement for renewables, compared to 8.05 cents without. The increased share of renewable energy reduces carbon emissions from electricity 7 percent below their projected level in 2030, achieving a major goal of the proposal. Even without accounting for all the external costs of energy, this is a great bargain.

The renewable portfolio standard already has majority support in both houses of Congress, so it will likely be an anchor provision in the next round of energy legislation.

Energy-efficient appliances and lighting provide a third path for strengthening the U.S. electric system. Even during the era of energy complacency, the Department of Energy passed rules mandating greater efficiency as authorized by the National Appliance Energy Conservation Act of 1987. Strict provisions for new refrigerators and air conditioners, for instance, have helped to slow (but certainly not reverse) the steady growth in electricity demand.

Title III of the 2007 energy package greatly strengthened national requirements for energy-efficient appliances and lighting, although this was somewhat overlooked amid the heated debates over auto standards, the renewable portfolio, and energy taxes. In 130 pages of highly technical language, Congress set higher standards for major appliances, streamlined processes for future rulemaking, and ordered the phase-out of most incandescent lighting. The net effect of these provisions will be a major decline in electricity demand coming from residential and commercial buildings.

After years of federal lethargy, the country is again moving toward making our electric system more diverse, efficient, and green. We are approaching the day when electricity can increasingly substitute for the oil currently burned in our cars and other vehicles. If we don't drop the ball, we will take the next steps to make these national goals a reality. We will be making America energy independent.

I have proposed many mandates for promoting energy independence, but mandates cannot do the whole job. We also need broad-based economic incentives. Unfortunately, "economic incentive" is a polite way of saying "energy taxes."

Chapter 12

Solution Five: Adopt Energy Taxes Liberals and Conservatives Can Like

It would be wonderful if we could make America energy independent without imposing heavy new taxes on energy. Energy taxes are one of those hot-button issues that experienced politicians strive to avoid. Unfortunately, we cannot sidestep a fresh look at energy taxes, despite their controversy. We have dug ourselves into a deep hole of energy dependence. After decades of delaying any significant response to our energy addiction, we will have to fight this battle on many fronts.

Europe and Japan adopted steep taxes on gasoline (currently ranging from about $2 to $4 a gallon) as their principle oil strategy after the energy crises of the 1970s. The United States chose the more politically palatable path of auto efficiency standards. American drivers do pay federal and state gasoline taxes, but these are devoted solely to building and maintaining roads (with a small set-aside for mass transit). The federal tax now stands at 18 cents a gallon, but, controlled for inflation, it has fallen below the level *before* the 1973 Arab oil embargo.[1]

During 2007, Congress passed serious energy proposals and considered many others. By contrast, any discussion of energy taxes was rare. It would be easy to conclude that we consider taxes to spur energy conservation to be un-American.

We are not going to achieve any success with a simple call for new energy taxes. We cannot remain blind to the harsh objections to them, whether political or theoretical. We have to construct a proposal that is both politically viable (remember those 60 votes needed in the Senate) and likely to achieve the intended results.

THE CASE FOR . . .

Aren't four solutions enough? We have already provided for (assuming the proposals are implemented) an emergency stockpile of oil with greater capacity, vehicles with much better gas mileage, liquid fuels from plants that displace petroleum products, and the shift of more cars to electricity. Can't we just stop there? We have already proposed major steps toward energy independence, but we are not there yet.

So far, we have not provided any incentives for living closer to work and cutting down miles to commute. We have not done anything to encourage mass transit or other methods of reducing the amount of solo driving in individual vehicles. To some extent, more fuel-efficient cars might even encourage people to drive longer distances, because the variable cost-per-mile has declined. With a 60 percent dependence on foreign oil, Americans need to do more than gradually decrease their use of oil. We need big cuts. If we make a strong effort to slow climate change, we will eventually have to get by on well under half of the oil we use today. It is hard to imagine this happening without energy taxes, or some functional equivalent.

The appeals of energy taxes (is that an oxymoron?) are their wide coverage and the flexibility of the responses to them. A gasoline tax, for instance, would apply to the entire market and avoid the loopholes found in other energy solutions. But a gasoline tax is also flexible, since it allows several strategies for drivers. They can buy more efficient cars than required under federal standards. They can take steps to cut back their driving mileages. They can do both. They can do neither. Many advocates for energy taxes hope they will encourage people to live closer together, thereby reducing driving and increasing walking and the use of mass transit. But maintaining a suburban lifestyle with super-efficient cars using alternative fuels can still get the job done.

The conservative side of the energy debate has often viewed energy taxes as the lesser evil of available policy options. When I reviewed the records of the Nixon and Ford presidencies, I was surprised to find that Treasury Secretary William Simon, who became a major spokesperson for the conservative wing of the Republican Party, was a strong inside advocate for gasoline taxes (and at hefty levels for the time). Simon thought taxes discouraged discretionary driving and were less intrusive on the economy than regulation. He greatly preferred gasoline taxes to auto efficiency standards.

Over the years, Simon and other conservatives have acknowledged that the prices paid for gasoline do not fully reflect their environmental and national security costs. Taxes are a reasonable way to incorporate these external costs.

Outside the political arena, support for a gasoline tax is surprisingly strong. When energy problems reassert themselves in the national consciousness, the first response of many liberal editorial boards and policy analysts is a call to hike the gasoline tax. The principle is rather fundamental. If you want people to smoke fewer cigarettes or burn less gasoline, you charge them more for it.

Heavy gasoline taxes in other industrial countries have helped constrain the runaway growth in gasoline consumption seen in the United States. Why can't it happen here?

THE HURDLES

Many economists complain about the *regressivity* of gasoline taxes. That is, poor people spend a bigger percentage of their incomes on energy than rich people do. Therefore, if you have a low income, a larger portion of that income goes to new energy taxes, like the one on gasoline. With energy taxes, the poor will have to make the greatest adjustments, while the rich can just pay the tax and continue without any change in behavior. As a result, regressive taxes are generally regarded as unfair. Regressivity is a big problem for energy taxes, but one that can be handled.

Historians record the political unpopularity of gasoline taxes. Few pieces of legislation for higher gasoline taxes to reduce energy consumption have made it to the floors of Congress for a final vote, but the results have always been similar. Al Ullman got a 23-cent-a gallon gasoline tax out of his House Ways and Means Committee in 1974, due in part to the

Arab oil embargo that ended just a year earlier. It did not just lose. It crashed on the house floor, 345–72, even though it had the support of most of the leadership. In 1980, the year after the Iranian Revolution and the Soviet invasion of Afghanistan, Jimmy Carter vetoed congressional repeal of his 10-cent-a-gallon tax on imported oil. He did not do as well as Ullman. The votes of 68–10 in the Senate and 335–34 in the House provided the first override of a Democratic president since Truman and one of the congressional low points of the Carter term.

The political hurdle for energy taxes is linked to their regressivity. Consumer groups object to their impact on those with low incomes, and liberal members of Congress have been the most strident opponents of gasoline taxes. When conservatives join the attack, the forces against energy taxes become overwhelming. Those in office today now know that proposing energy taxes is playing with fire. As a result, the idea has a very small constituency in Congress.

❧

Some economists would also observe that energy taxes have an unknown elasticity. That is, we do not really know how much consumers will adjust their behaviors in response to higher prices. It is easy in the economics textbooks. If you have higher prices for something, you get lower demand. But with energy that response does not seem to be very strong. People reduce their energy consumption in the face of higher prices, but not very much.

Consumers, up to a point, regard their driving habits and indoor temperature levels as pretty much nonnegotiable issues. As a result, if energy prices jump, they cut their spending on nonenergy items rather than on gasoline or electricity. The increase in gasoline consumption during the last eight years, while prices were skyrocketing, illustrates how inelastic the relationship has become.

The problem is getting worse. As energy becomes a smaller portion of disposable income, people become increasingly resistant to changing their patterns of energy use in response to price changes. We identified inelasticity as a problem in relying on the market to solve energy problems, but it is also a problem for tax fixes. To change behavior, any energy tax, and the gasoline tax in particular, will have to be very hefty and sustained over a long period.

So, what do we have here? Some pundits think energy taxes are a good idea. But they are unfair, extremely unpopular, and we are not even sure they will work if we pass them. Is it worth continuing this discussion?

Even if short-term responses to higher prices are minimal, sustained price signals from energy taxes can affect the choices people make about the cars, homes, and appliances they buy and hold on to for many years. They can even affect the efficiency of products brought to market.

Taxes are not a quick fix, but long-range strategy needs a tax component. To overcome the hurdles, though, we have to get everything right to pass them into law and to make sure they work.

THE KEY INGREDIENT

What is the critical factor in whether a gasoline tax can pass and be effective? It is what is done with the proceeds. Those who favor such a tax generally have a long list of energy projects they want funded. The eyes of many legislators light up when they see opportunities for additional appropriations. But we should not spend the money from the gasoline tax. We should rebate it back to the American people. All of it.

Since energy taxes are regressive, it is a good idea to use the proceeds to replace another regressive tax. A leading candidate would be the payroll tax for Social Security. This rebate would solve the regressivity problem. (Of course, we have to find a mechanism to rebate the money to people who do not pay social security.) The rebate also offsets the negative impacts of the tax on the economy.

The trade-off of gasoline taxes for payroll tax cuts makes sense on several levels. Don't we want to tax things we do not like more than things we do like? Reducing a tax on labor and replacing it with proceeds from a gasoline tax rejiggers the national incentive system in a positive direction, especially when labor is domestic and most oil is foreign.

The rebate should help win popular support, though that is far from a sure bet. With the rebate, it is easier to argue that the gasoline tax is fair and does not raise the net tax burden of the American people. We must note, however, that Simon, Ullman, and Carter all favored rebating revenues and could not get their proposals passed. But in none of these previous cases was the rebate aggressively sold to the American people. Most Americans were unaware the rebate was even part of the package. A new effort to pass energy taxes requires presidential leadership. Only a trusted leader speaking on prime-time television, putting great emphasis on the rebate (and the need to become energy independent), has a chance of selling an energy tax package to the American people.

In his recent book on energy policy, former State Department official David Sandalow proposes sending rebate checks to arrive just before the July 4th Independence Day holiday.[2] This dramatic effect could help convince people that the rebate is real, though the amounts will be small at first until the tax ramps up.

In a way, the rebate also increases the chances that the taxes will actually cut gasoline consumption. The gas tax cannot be just a token thing. The idea that a small tax will cut gasoline use in any significant way has been strongly contradicted by the relationship between price and consumption in the past decade. We do not know the exact point at which taxes change consumer behavior, but we are talking a dollar a gallon and up. If the early experience with rebates convinces people that the trade-off of higher energy taxes and lower payroll taxes is a good one, the door will be open to the adjustments needed to make the energy tax effective. If the rebates fail to win public confidence, Americans will lose the energy tax component of a national energy strategy, making success more difficult.

A presidential proposal for a gasoline tax can point to another advantage. Because we have not dealt effectively with growing oil demand in the face of OPEC production quotas, we are paying a higher- than-market price (in effect, a tax paid to OPEC). An effective gasoline tax would cut demand, likely lower pretax prices, and reduce this OPEC tax. This adds to the benefits from the lower payroll tax.

There will be winners and losers from shifting labor taxes to energy, making legislative approval difficult even in the best of circumstances. To achieve fairness, it will be necessary to phase in a gasoline tax gradually. This will give people time to adjust to the new realities. The pace of implementation should not adversely diminish the impact of the tax, at least not to a large extent, since the prospect of a higher tax can affect (almost as much as a tax in place) the priority customers give to the energy efficiency of equipment they purchase.

So what is the bottom line? We need to raise the gasoline tax by 20 cents a gallon each year over the next decade. That adds two dollars, which sounds high to us but is still low by the standards of other industrialized nations. The *entire* amount needs to be rebated, so that the taxes are on average a wash. To the extent the tax proves effective and stifles demand, the pretax price of gasoline will go down. The average citizen then makes a net gain. What a deal!

Expanding the oil tax beyond gasoline brings additional benefits in cutting dependence on oil. We need to reduce the demand for all oil, not just gasoline. As a result, we will have to eventually extend the tax to petrochemicals (and other industrial production based on oil) as a second tax strategy for winning energy independence.

The risks of this broader tax are also greater than for a tax just on gasoline. A tax on American industries would put them at a competitive disadvantage with foreign competitors and might even convince them to transfer more of their operations abroad. If they move outside of the country to escape energy taxes, they are still putting excessive demand on world oil supplies and emitting greenhouse gases, defeating the purpose of the tax. This is what economists call the problem of *leakage*. The adverse effects of energy use are simply relocated rather than reduced. To level the playing field and combat leakage, we will need to tax manufactured imports based on the oil used to produce them.

CAPS AND TRADING

We can tax oil consumption or greenhouse emissions, but there is an alternative. Right now, there is a broad consensus among experts (including people with very divergent views on global warming) that we can best control climate-changing emissions by imposing general caps on all emissions and allowing trading of carbon credits among those over and under the quotas to encourage the most cost-effective reductions.

Taxes and caps are really two sides of the same coin. With taxes, the size of the levy is known, but the impact on oil consumption or emissions is not. With caps, you get the opposite situation. The levels of consumption or emissions are known (if the caps are enforced), but the resulting price is unknown. Some have proposed that with emissions caps the government guarantees a price at which it will sell carbon credits—in effect, an escape hatch. Guaranteeing that prices will not exceed a certain level is probably a political necessity during the initial ramp up (while kinks in the system are being worked out), but it makes cap and trade little more than a tax by another name.

The advantage of carbon trading is that it provides even broader coverage and greater flexibility for the market than taxation. If reductions in carbon emissions, emissions of other gases, and protection of carbon-absorbing plants can be included in an omnibus trading system, the lowest cost solutions are likely to be selected first by the market. Economic efficiency reduces conflicts between constraints on carbon emissions and economic growth. There is another big advantage for cap and trade. It is not called a tax, even though it raises prices. Better labeling makes this idea less objectionable in the political arena.

During the 1990s, cap and trade was sold as the cure-all solution that would ease the way for compliance with the Kyoto treaty and later limitations on carbon. Writing actual rules to establish cap and trade systems has proved difficult, however. The chore is terribly complex, especially when applied around the planet.

The science of climate change creates immense challenges for a new economic system designed to slow it. At the current stage of knowledge, it is hard to establish exact exchange rates between carbon emissions, other gases, and reforestation. Moreover, it takes great ingenuity to avoid paying people for what they were going to do anyway (e.g., not destroy a rain forest), the so-called *free rider* problem.

Then there is the problem of establishing the responsibility for complying with the cap. For emissions from automobiles, does it lie with the driver of the car, the manufacturer of the car, the refiner of the gasoline, or at the wellhead? Senators Joe Lieberman (D-CN), John McCain (R-AR), and Senator John Warner (R-VA) and their staffs have done yeomen's work trying to craft legislation that will resolve these issues. The path to final passage will still be confusing to the public and rife with opportunities for private interests to out-lobby public interests.

Cap and trade has also been a hard sell internationally. The very idea of caps implies starting from some historical level from which cuts are made. This has led the industrializing nations to worry that, at some point, the extreme variations in per capita energy use between them and the industrialized nations will get locked in. This would be devastating to the developing nations, whose energy use will need to grow if they are going to raise their standards of living. Similarly, the poorer countries fear that the wealthy nations will be able to purchase the declining pool of carbon credits, denying them needed energy resources. International negotiations on slowing climate change try to address the concerns of developing countries. But as long as the dominant concept is cap and trade, countries like India and China will be reluctant to join in (even when the United States agrees to mandatory caps).

We must also recognize that a cap-and-trade system raises energy prices and has the same regressive impact as conventional energy taxes. As a result, the government should auction credits to emit the allowable amounts of carbon and rebate the proceeds through the payroll deduction for Social Security. Since the costs for carbon credits will be borne by both individuals and companies, the rebate should be divided between the employees' and employers' contributions. As with taxes, this scheme would allow the price of credits to reach high levels and still hold the public harmless to some extent. Government officials should make it clear to the public that the big increases in energy prices are not because the companies are ripping them off. It is because fuels have very high environmental and national security costs.

Unfortunately, there is another way to do cap and trade. The government simply reduces the amount of carbon allowed. Companies are grandfathered in at their reduced quotas based on historic levels. Under this system, the regressive nature of higher prices is not offset, and companies obtain greater revenues from the imbalance between high demand (for energy resources) and a shrinking resource (the ability to emit carbon). Energy companies could become the new OPEC, using higher unit prices to gain more profits, despite decreasing volume. The issue of how to cap and trade has hardly surfaced in the national debates over climate change outside of Washington, but it is vital to establishing a system that is fair and that works over the long haul.

We live in a political world, and energy companies have great clout in Washington. As a result, some grandfathering of carbon emitters may be necessary during the early years of transitioning to carbon constraints in order to pass the necessary legislation. Most climate-change bills currently in play start with substantial grandfathering and phase in the greater use of government auctions over time. Economic results will improve as proceeds are captured by the government and rebated to the public.

FINDING THE RIGHT PATH

Cap and trade offers many advantages over other systems for slowing climate change and will also have the side benefit of limiting dependence on

Middle Eastern oil. Slogging through the tough details in creating domestic legislation and international agreements based on cap and trade is a valuable endeavor, but we need also to recognize the immense difficulties involved and offer fallback positions in case efforts to adopt cap and trade falter. We will need old-fashioned taxes (with new-fashion rebates) to deal with both the national security and environmental aspects of energy independence.

For the coming years, I recommend a three-pronged approach to deal with oil dependence and climate change. We can cut oil dependence and carbon emissions from transportation vehicles most simply with a combination of mileage efficiency standards for automobiles and trucks, cellulosic ethanol, and taxes on oil. This brings up the hated word—*taxes*—but these mechanisms are well understood, and national leaders can sell them to the public based on their combined national security, economic, and environmental benefits. This approach can be a *threefer* with political appeal.

Cap and trade applies best to the electric industry. The trading of sulfur credits has proven successful and given companies general confidence in cap and trade. There are several strategies in the Senate for this approach—the Feinstein-Carper bill, which caps emissions from the electric sector in 2015 at 2001 levels and has been endorsed by several large electricity companies, or a version of the broader Lieberman-Warner bill, which has been the focal point for discussions about comprehensive cap and trade. It is important to recognize that the cuts in these bills are calculated from expected higher future rates rather than 1990 levels, so they do not come close to requiring the progress that will eventually be needed. After years of inaction, however, it is better to get started with legislation that contains real impacts instead of waiting for perfect solutions.

We are left with the problem of other gases. These are easier to deal with, because in some cases there are other products that can be substituted or the solutions (like plugging leaks in natural gas pipelines) are relatively cheap. We will have to treat these gases separately, but in general we should phase them out over time rather than throw them into a complicated trading system.

Both the tax strategy and the cap-and-trade strategy will have dramatic impacts on the public. If we want to use them, national leaders will have to explain them clearly and avoid the normal temptation to spend the proceeds on pet projects. Many economists are willing to help in the effort to defend the need for energy/carbon taxes. Former dean of the Chicago business school, Nixon-Ford Treasury Secretary, and Reagan Secretary of State George Shultz wrote in an op-ed last year, "In many respects, a straight-out carbon tax is simpler and likelier to produce the desired result [than cap and trade]. If the tax were offset by cuts elsewhere to make it revenue-neutral, acceptability would be enhanced."[3] If we are going to win our energy independence, we cannot give up the tax option.

But if we are all patriotic Americans, why does it take financial incentives to get us to do the right thing?

Chapter 13

Solution Six: Make Energy Conservation a Patriotic Duty

W e have not heard much from our national leaders in recent decades about the importance of conserving energy, nor have we been told that we have a patriotic duty to think differently about how we use the fuels that sustain daily life. As a result, we have given up a national tradition of accepting individual sacrifice when needed to achieve important national objectives.

We justly celebrate our national resolve in winning World War II, an effort that required great sacrifice on the battlefront and the home front. We lost over four hundred thousand troops during the brutal conflict. Civilian sacrifices were mild by comparison, but substantial in their own way. People accepted rationing of gasoline and other strategic commodities. They grew their own fruits and vegetables in local gardens. Women reported for double duty, keeping families together and taking on shifts at local factories. Companies profiteering from the war were hauled before congressional committees, where they were castigated by (among others), future President Harry Truman. Everyone was expected to pitch in to defeat the enemy.

Presidents of the 1970s drew analogies to World War II as they tried to cope with the great energy crises of the time. Carter in particular spoke repeatedly about the need for sacrifice and conservation to win what he called "the moral equivalent of war." Both Nixon and Carter urged the public to drive less and slower, adjust their thermostats, and turn off unnecessary lighting to save energy—and, for a time, the public responded. Ford and Carter were even willing to accept the politically unpopular path of higher energy prices to spur conservation.

Ronald Reagan ridiculed the idea of resetting thermostats, which he equated to being cold in the winter and hot in the summer. Talk of energy conservation or sacrifice to solve energy problems quickly disappeared from the presidential lexicon. Reagan's great popularity and an era of low energy prices led his successors to eschew mentions of energy conservation or sacrifice, as well.

When I joined the Energy Department in 1993, I was told by a senior Clinton official that we did not talk about energy conservation; we were for *energy efficiency*. Conservation and efficiency are two related but different concepts. Individuals and companies achieve energy efficiency by buying improved equipment that reduces energy consumption. The higher initial capital costs are repaid from lower energy bills. Those who advocate sole reliance on energy efficiency imply that we do not have to worry if energy services keep rising because of expected improvements in energy technologies. In other words, we can invent our way out of our energy problems.

The problem in the 1990s was that demand for new energy services outstripped gains in energy technologies. As a result, we saw a sharply escalating dependence on foreign oil and emissions of greenhouse gases that has continued to the present. Calling for energy efficiency helps, but until we include the external costs of energy into market prices, it is insufficient to win energy independence.

Conservation is energy efficiency plus. Conservation implies buying energy-efficient equipment *and* examining whether we are wasting energy with oversized vehicles and buildings, rapid auto acceleration, excessive indoor heating and cooling, and elevator rides between adjacent floors. If we had not dug ourselves so deeply into the holes of oil dependence and human-induced climate change, energy efficiency might be enough. Energy efficiency is too tepid for modern realities. We need the more robust challenge of energy conservation.

Politicians of both parties during the 1990s feared a backlash if they called for any energy sacrifices. Given the low prices at the time and general complacency about energy, it wouldn't have made much difference if they did talk about energy sacrifice.

Vice President Richard Cheney's statement in 2001 that "conservation may be a sign of personal virtue, but it is not a sufficient basis for a sound, comprehensive energy policy" was widely interpreted as mocking calls to reduce energy use. Still, the word *conservation* did make a bit of a come-back in the new millennium. With war in the Persian Gulf and soaring oil prices, the Bush White House uses the word conservation more than his predecessor. But unlike Clinton, Bush has not acknowledged that oil con-sumption or greenhouse gas emissions should actually come down.

Given the great threats of wasted energy to our national security, our economy, and our planet, it is time to revive a national dialogue about the need for energy conservation.

RETHINKING THE NATIONAL INTEREST

Let's review what is at stake when we talk about energy. We have troops fighting—and losing their lives—in the Persian Gulf to protect our access to the oil there. Emerging countries like China acknowledge that their future successes will be tied to their ability to obtain oil. Oil imports make a major contribution to America's large trade deficit and give the oil-exporting countries great leverage over the strength of our currency and economy. Soaring oil prices contribute to inflation, limiting the options of the Federal Reserve Board in dealing with an economic slowdown. Emissions from carbon fuels are warming the planet at an accelerated pace. Why isn't taking action against our country's overuse of oil considered a patriotic duty?

Well, it is. The United States has prospered because it developed its once-dominant supplies of oil, which contributed to its rise as a world power. The vitality of the U.S. economy gave us the staying power to win wars, whether armed conflict or cold wars. American influence has rested not just on its armed and economic might. The United States has also advocated powerful ideas like democracy, human rights, free markets, and clean air and water. If we abandon the energy fight, we will have to accept less influence and respect in the international community. We will also bequeath to our children and grandchildren a more dangerous world.

Many of our solutions so far—ranging from energy-efficient cars to alternative fuels to energy taxes—are effective ways to advance the national interest. They are ways to build a stronger America. They are patriotic duties.

So far, I have not talked much about the role of individual and busi-ness responsibilities in the fight for energy independence. This discussion intentionally has come after chapters on the need for the government to pass laws and appropriate money to solve our energy problems. Many calls for voluntary actions by individuals and businesses have, unfortunately, presented them as substitutes for government action. This tendency has made me wary of putting too much emphasis on nongovernmental solutions. But we must not discredit the role patriotic citizens and businesses can play. We need federal and state laws and expenditures, but there is still an important complementary role for voluntary actions.

When individuals and corporations alter their daily practices or long-term purchases to use energy more wisely, their actions have immediate impacts. Unlike the tortuous struggle to pass federal energy legislation, voluntary actions become effective right away. Moreover, it is more difficult to pass good energy legislation when public behavior is moving in the other direction. We have seen from historical experience that it is easier to pass major energy reforms when the public and corporations are already taking steps to conserve energy. The battle to win energy independence cannot be won solely by our elected representatives in Washington or by international agreements.

GIVING NATURE HER DUE

The availability of cheap energy with prices that do not reflect the external costs of national security and environmental damage has tended to overly isolate people in wealthy societies from the forces of nature. Two examples illustrate how, in many ways, we have lost the knowledge of our ancestors.

A visit to Charleston, South Carolina, is a much-anticipated event, and not just because of the she-crab soup at local restaurants. I marvel at the grand homes built in the eighteenth and nineteenth centuries. These people showed great awareness of the orientation of the sun and the direction of wind currents, and it pays off in buildings that conserve energy.

The grand early Charleston houses almost always face south, often with a large porch. The windows and porches capture the light of the low-setting winter sun, providing natural heating when most needed. In the summer, the heat gain from the southern exposure is much less. With the sun higher in the sky and porches offering shade, the direct sunlight and increases in heating are minimized. Doors and windows in these houses are also planned to maximize the flow of westerly winds, providing further relief during sweltering summers. Today, even energy-efficient builders tend to ignore the orientation of the sun and prevailing winds in their designs. It is much easier to replace the forces of nature with extra electricity, most likely generated from coal.

As a second case in point, in an era of cheap energy, we have paid less attention to the science of locomotion and to designing aerodynamic cars with high gasoline mileage. In an affluent society, it is often easier to ignore better body lines that reduce air drag and just pay the extra fuel costs. Many people purchase off-road vehicles not to actually drive off road, but to have the potential to do so. Riding higher above the ground, these vehicles lose mileage efficiency from their poor aerodynamics. Four-wheel-drive in off-road vehicles provides another feature rarely needed but that is an additional drain on fuel efficiency. Ignoring the orientation of the sun in contemporary architecture and the role of air in slowing moving objects contributes to our modern energy dependence.

Nature has momentums that require energy to reverse. It takes more energy to attain than to maintain the speed of any automobile or truck. The faster the acceleration, the greater the energy consumed. It takes more energy to change than to maintain the temperature of a house. With a bit of adaptation to the rhythms of nature, we can reduce the amounts of energy we consume. But in the modern era, energy has been so cheap and abundant that we think nothing about the consequences of jackrabbit starts or keeping our thermostats at constant temperatures year round, ignoring the direction of temperatures outside.

Greater sensitivity to the forces of nature and the real price of energy leads us to adopt more energy-efficient (and safer) driving habits. It also encourages us to adapt to seasonal ambient temperatures in our homes and offices. Give it a try. After an initial adjustment period, there is little sacrifice involved, and we are all contributing to energy independence.

THE PATRIOTIC AUTO SHOPPER

If you own a fairly fuel-thrifty car, you do not need to rush out to buy the most efficient model currently on the market. It takes energy to manufacture an automobile. As a result, keeping one on the road for a long time can help reduce energy consumption. But when you decide you need to upgrade your transportation, the energy part of the equation is simple.

Those stickers in the window required by the Environmental Protection Agency pretty much tell the whole story. The labels with the big numbers indicate the expected fuel efficiency of the car in the city and on the highway. Even if the stickers do not always reflect actual driving conditions (they are getting better), they do accurately show the relative mileage of most vehicles. If you pick the models with the highest numbers, you are taking effective action to reduce oil imports and the emissions that cause global warming.

You can largely ignore the technologies the cars use. We may want to buy an electric-hybrid or diesel model because we have heard they are more fuel efficient. In most cases, they are. But even a hybrid or a diesel can be turned into a gas guzzler if the manufacturer works at it. Do not get distracted. Go for the high mileage efficiency numbers.

Then there is Section 105 of the Energy Independence and Security Act of 2007. Starting in 2009, the EPA stickers will also have to include the greenhouse gas and other emissions likely over the life of the automobile. The new labeling is somewhat redundant, since there is a direct correlation between the fuel consumed and the emissions of carbon dioxide. Still, most consumers will be surprised to learn the amount of greenhouse gases their driving spews into the atmosphere. The environmental labeling will provide additional information to the patriotic shopper on which car to buy.

The major constraint on buying the most fuel-efficient models comes from the need to transport a large family or equipment. The most fuel-efficient car, the Toyota Prius, can comfortably seat five adults, but will not meet the needs of every driver. It is still important to ask what features you will really use and how often. If the need for a large vehicle is rare, it may make more sense to rent one when necessary rather than drive a bigger-than-needed vehicle all the time. If you do not drive off road or in icy conditions, you do not need fuel-robbing all-wheel-drive.

If you make a realistic assessment of your vehicle requirements and then buy the most efficient model that provides them, you are conserving energy, cutting oil imports, and slowing climate change. We'll know we're making progress when the norm in our neighborhood is not who parks the largest vehicle in their driveway, but who has the most fuel-efficient model.

It also makes a big difference how you and your neighbors drive your new autos, vans, SUVs, and trucks. As you leave the new-car lot, do not rush to test how fast you can get from zero to 60 miles per hour. That is going to waste a lot of the fuel you are trying to save. Hopefully, you have one of those new gauges on the dash that provides constant monitoring of mpg. Get your kicks out of seeing how high you can keep that number. If you're a prudent driver, you might be able to beat the estimates on the EPA sticker. Driving to conserve is fun. It reduces reliance on oil. It is part of being a patriotic driver.

THE PATRIOTIC HOME BUYER

Picking a new home is more complicated than buying a car. We have no single measure to determine how much your choice will contribute to energy independence. Moreover, houses last a very long time. There are six important questions to consider when buying a new home.

First, you want to emulate those home buyers in early Charleston. You need to check out the orientation of the house. *Maximum exposure to the southern sun* and *minimum exposure* on the east and west sides to the rising and setting sun is best. You will get the most natural heating in the winter and the least in the summer. Your choice, on the surface, makes little difference. If you do not buy the ideal house, someone else will. But homebuilders tell me buyers do not ask about passive solar design, which reduces their incentive to follow the example of early Americans. If more buyers would ask these questions, we would get more houses that conserve energy.

Second, look for new homes with an *Energy Star* rating. The Environmental Protection Agency, Department of Energy, state energy officials, and homebuilders have formed partnerships to establish standards for insulation, high-performance windows and doors, high-efficiency heating and cooling systems, and energy-saving appliances and lighting that exceed conventional building codes. The estimated energy savings range from 15 to 30 percent. That conserves a lot of fuel. If you want to upgrade a previously lived-in home, consider buying Energy Star appliances, which can reduce the use of energy and water.

Third, how do you feel about *sharing walls?* When you live in an apartment, condominium, or townhouse, you have less exposure to the elements. That reduces the work your cooling and heating systems have to do. Choosing multifamily housing can produce sizeable savings in energy. It is another way to conserve.

Fourth, when looking at your prospective domicile, ask whether there is space you will not use very much that still needs to be heated and cooled. Underutilized space is a major source of wasted energy. The Energy Information Administration currently projects that the average American home will grow from 1,776 square feet in 2006 to 1,941 square feet in 2020. (The area of commercial building space is estimated to increase at an even faster pace.) The continuous upsizing of American buildings overwhelms the gains from more efficient appliances (and other advances in equipment that reduce energy consumption when space is held constant). The biggest savings come when we combine energy efficiency with the *right-sizing* of our space requirements. Right-sizing is another way to conserve energy that requires some alterations in the usual way of building homes, but it does not have to sacrifice quality. It does require more serious thinking about what is and is not needed to create a great home.

Fifth, the *location* of your new home will have a great impact on how much you have to drive. Living close to work or near a mass transit station can substantially reduce the fuel burned for commuting. Proximity to restaurants and other services further cuts the need to drive. Some communities offer the opportunity to walk rather than drive to complete daily chores. This results in fuel savings (and better health from regular exercise).

Sixth, you may want to jump to the head of the pack and order features that are still *on the cutting edge.* More people in California these days are installing photovoltaic cells on their roofs to capture sunlight that can be converted into electricity. It is a major long-term investment, but it can dramatically cut the need to take energy from the grid and help achieve energy independence. The garages of the future will also need plugs for electric-powered vehicles. Get ready for the future. Order that plug for your new house. Be the trendsetter on your block.

Your new energy-efficient house may cost more than an inefficient alternative, but will pay off in reduced operating costs over the long haul. But there should be an additional incentive for energy patriots. Our country has dug itself into a deep energy hole and you can help get us out. If you live in the Northeast where the use of heating oil is common, your better insulation helps cut our dependence on oil and reduces the emission of greenhouse gases. If you live elsewhere, you are still reducing the emissions of greenhouse gases, and you are freeing up the electric system for those new plug-in electric cars.

THE SUSTAINABLE BUSINESS

In energy circles, the name Ray Anderson is held in high regard. Anderson is the chairman of Interface, Inc., a large global carpet tile company headquartered in Atlanta, Georgia. The carpet business is an intense user of petroleum products, and until 1994, Anderson saw his company's energy and environmental responsibilities largely in terms of complying with federal, state, and local laws.

At that point, he was struck ("galvanized," is his term) by the need for corporations to contribute to a sustainable environment, one in which people were not on a path to depleting and despoiling the earth's resources. The new strategy for Interface became *reduce, reuse, reclaim, recycle,* and *redesign.* In concept, this meant viewing corporate practices as cyclical rather than linear. In practice, Interface harvested used carpets, recycled old petrochemicals into new materials, and converted sunlight into energy.

Anderson's company has reduced the use of fossil fuels by 45 percent and greenhouse emissions by 60 percent, while increasing sales 49 percent. Sustainability has been good for the company balance sheet, but that was not the original point. Anderson was consumed by a vision of taking a longer-range view of the planet, which also turned out to be profitable. The motivation transcended simple short-term economics. Anderson has not received the Presidential Medal of Freedom (yet), but he is a major warrior in the battle for energy independence.

Major corporations operate all over the world and base their appeal on ideas that can cross national borders. Hence, they talk less in terms of nationalistic goals and more in terms of broader concepts like sustainability. Patriotic appeals for conservation and corporate commitments to sustainability share important ideas. Traditional economics divorced from moral duties does not spark the innovation necessary to deal with long-term challenges. Conversely, a devotion to ethical behavior without producing a good bottom line will lead to corporate destruction. Ray Anderson has shown that ethical responsibility and good economics can support each other.

Many corporations are looking for energy *threefers.* Those massive delivery trucks on our highways offer great targets of opportunity. One of the fastest-growing sources of energy use is the increasing driving distances for freight trucks, which EIA estimates will grow at a rate of 1.7 percent a year and reach 304 billion miles by 2020. If businesses reduce the amount of fuel consumed in moving goods over our national highways, they help reduce our addiction to oil and protect the environment.

Wal-Mart, in 2006, launched a massive program to encourage environmental sustainability, slash energy consumption, and reduce waste. Several initiatives targeted conservation of transportation fuels. The company has announced a goal of using hybrid trucks to double the efficiency of its fleet in 10 years. It also estimates that requiring suppliers to cut the size of packaging by 5 percent can take 213,000 trucks off the road and save 1.6 million barrels of diesel fuel a year. Just the transportation part of Wal-Mart's program can move national energy numbers in significant ways. These are serious commitments.

Other corporations are undertaking similar efforts. The grocery firm Safeway Inc. is converting its fleet of 1,000 trucks—each of which is expected to travel 110,000 miles a year—to cleaner burning biodiesel blends. United Parcel Service (UPS) is partnering with the Environmental Protection Agency to get new hydraulic hybrid commercial trucks on the road. In urban driving conditions, EPA estimates that these advanced vehicles can increase fuel efficiency by 60 to 70 percent over trucks that run solely on diesel fuel.

These corporations have many motivations to change their business practices. "We set out to do [sustainability] as an obligation, a good-works effort," said Wal-Mart CEO Lee Scott. "But we discovered the truth: The real reason to do this is for the business itself." Reducing waste protects the environment *and* cuts the cost of doing business.[1]

Voluntary actions of corporations like Wal-Mart have global impacts. As a result, they influence international energy use, even when the world's governments cannot agree on concerted actions.

The influence of international corporations sometimes works in unexpected ways. The surprisingly broad support in 2007 for stricter U.S. mileage efficiency standards stemmed in part from support by Japanese automaker Nissan, which has production facilities in Alabama and Tennessee. Representatives from those states provided key votes in getting the previously controversial measure through Congress. Companies doing substantial business in Europe and Japan, where energy policy has been more aggressive in recent years, have helped nudge the United States into stronger action. Now that the United States is arising from a long period of energy complacency, its companies can also exert influence in countries that are lagging in their efforts.

Individuals and corporations who want to do good and save money by conserving energy will play vital roles in reducing reliance on oil and the emissions of greenhouse gases. They are an important part of solving our massive energy problems but they cannot substitute for strong government leadership.

Chapter 14

Solution Seven: Throw Some "Hail Marys"

Several of my solutions for energy independence are tested and ready to go. We have created the Strategic Petroleum Reserve and auto efficiency standards before to make our nation more energy independent. There is no reason we cannot use them again, in conjunction with other solutions, to win a new energy independence. Other ideas—like massive requirements for biofuels, energy taxes, and caps on carbon—take us into less-charted waters, but seem well worth the risks, given the magnitude of the energy challenges ahead.

If energy dependence was just a national (rather than a global) problem, these solutions might be sufficient. But we need to also be looking for some big technical leaps forward. The world of advanced energy research and development is exciting, but fraught with risk. Many highly touted new technologies simply are not going to work, because they have persistent bugs that block successful operation or cannot find a pathway to commercial market penetration. In addition, some use the prospects of some future silver bullet technology as an excuse to not take immediate action with the tools that are already available to reduce oil dependence and dangerous emissions.

Our ability to find high-tech solutions is hampered by the United States' neglect of energy research and development in recent decades. Even with U.S. troops committed in the Persian Gulf and $3 a gallon gasoline, federal expenditures (controlled for inflation) remain below those before the Arab oil embargo. If we just follow the money, we can conclude that recent presidents and Congresses have not cared that much about new energy technologies. To make matters worse, politics often trumps strategic planning in determining where those scarce research dollars go. It is time to get serious. Corporate lobbyists skewing research dollars to low-priority technologies deserve the same opprobrium of the contractors who were skewered for profiteering off of World War II.

Scientific research leads to unexpected places. Sometimes, important discoveries are made by accident. Other times, promising ideas just do not pan out. Even if most projects fail to produce significant results, occasional successes can more than justify expenditures on robust research efforts.

We have fallen behind in the effort to win energy independence. I have already offered a game plan for marching down the field using tested strategies. But we may need to throw a few long passes down the field into the end zone. Even if they might fail, the benefits of completing them are so high that the effort is more than justified. We need to keep searching for the breakthrough technologies that can transform energy markets.

SETTING PRIORITIES

For years, we have devoted scarce research dollars to projects with limited strategic value. We know we can turn coal into liquid transportation fuels, and at times we have spent a lot of money trying to perfect the process. Unfortunately, the environmental impacts of converting to synfuels would be highly adverse, so these research dollars are essentially wasted. During his first term, President George W. Bush diverted research from other areas to support hydrogen technologies. In this case, there is no plausible scenario for extensive use of hydrogen in the energy economy in the coming decades. It makes more sense to select other priorities for research.

During Bush's second term, his Energy Secretary, Samuel Bodman, improved the administration's research portfolio, and a broader consensus emerged in industry and energy circles on where research money should be targeted. Here are five priorities that should have wide support.

First, displacing oil with ethanol should be a top national goal, but making alcohol fuels from corn kernels, as is done today, has only limited benefits. Moving to *cellulosic ethanol* greatly expands the kinds of plants that can be utilized and gives us the strategic and environmental benefits we are looking for. The technology is still immature, meaning there is plenty of room to improve. Congress has set tough future requirements for the inclusion of cellulosic ethanol in the national fuel mix. We need a very robust research agenda to meet (and hopefully exceed) those goals. The United States has excelled in research on plants over the years, and we should be able to dominate this technology.

Second, *better batteries* offer many ways of moving more aggressively toward energy independence. For transportation, more efficient batteries can enhance the performance of hybrid electric cars and open up opportunities to power them from the existing electric grid. Batteries can help cure our addiction to oil. By storing power for when it is needed, improved batteries can help us better utilize intermittent sources of power like wind and solar in dispersed locations. There is broad agreement that battery technology is ripe for continued progress.

Third, meeting aggressive targets for slowing global warming would be a lot easier if we could *separate, capture,* and *sequester* carbon emissions from coal. Without this technology, we will likely lose the coal industry as we know it today, despite the abundant resources that remain. We generally know how this can be done, but there are a lot of issues to be worked out and not a lot of time to get the job done. Development of the needed technology suffered a major blow when the Bush administration withdrew its support for advanced coal power plants in 2008. Even when the technology is up and running, it will be deployed only if national policy puts a price on carbon emissions that creates the needed economic incentives.

Fourth, we must figure out the best way to *bury nuclear waste.* An influential 2003 study of nuclear power at the Massachusetts Institute of Technology argued for disposing of, rather than recycling, spent nuclear fuel discharged from nuclear reactors, but acknowledged the current failure to site repositories that would isolate the waste for the required many thousands of years. The study recommended that federal research concentrate on deep borehole technology that would dispose of waste in much deeper crystalline rock. This new approach would provide better isolation from water penetration and potential volcanic or seismic activity. Deeper burial of nuclear waste creates its own set of problems, but still offers a good option on a very difficult issue.[1]

Fifth, *photovoltaic cells* (PVs) offer another technology option that can play a larger role in the energy mix. Solar cells are expensive and require a lot of space for the amount of energy produced. On the other hand, they can produce power at times when air conditioning loads are high and energy is especially needed. They can also produce electricity without the line losses typical with central generation. Plus, the cost and efficiency of cells are steadily improving. In November of 2007 the Department of Energy announced that, to advance the technology, it was spending $21 million for PV projects at 15 universities and six companies. This is, unfortunately, not a level of support that will allow the United States to regain the world leadership in solar technology that it enjoyed in 1980.

On the whole, these priorities for research are well recognized and likely to produce steady progress. But are there other technologies not being discussed that might offer strategic breakthroughs in achieving energy independence? I hesitate to put major emphasis on big technology advances. They often fizzle out when confronted with the realities of energy markets. They can often distract attention away from more practical things we can do in the short run to implement the technologies we already have. But I do see one thing on the horizon that might be a game changer. We do not know at this stage whether it will actually work, so it may be a long shot. That is why I compare it to the "Hail Mary" pass at the end of a football game, when the potential gain makes it worth a heroic effort.

A New Source for Biodiesel

As we have seen, diesel engines can make a great contribution to energy independence. They burn fuel much more efficiently than traditional spark ignition engines. They are particularly well suited for heavy vehicles, or those with a need to tow hefty loads or make long trips. Most environmental problems with diesels have been worked out, and their incremental costs are well worth the fuel savings. But there is a problem. Where are we going to get enough diesel fuel to run a growing number of these fuel-saving vehicles?

The world market for diesel fuel is currently under strain. Oil refineries are having trouble producing enough distillate to keep pace with the expanded use of diesel vehicles in Europe. Diesel prices have risen faster than those for gasoline, and the new, improved diesel vehicles are just starting to enter the American market in significant numbers. This gap between supply and demand could be filled by diesel produced from plants, but, as we have seen, the feedstocks for biodiesel are sorely limited.

The next big thing in energy technology could be biodiesel produced from algae. From what we know now, it is microalgae that have the best characteristics for converting sunlight into oil that can then be turned into biodiesel. That is like the phytoplankton found in the world's oceans or the green algae growing in swimming pools. If microalgae can be grown economically in sufficient quantities, it can transform the whole world of transportation. We can expand the production of diesel vehicles without having to worry whether there is enough fuel for them. The fuel itself will not be coming from the unstable Persian Gulf, nor will it add to the globe's layer of greenhouse gases.

Why haven't we heard more about this opportunity before? Is it too good to be true? I have earned a reputation as somewhat of a debunker of overly rosy technology scenarios, but biodiesel from algae is an area that should attract very serious attention from the government and private investors. And the sooner this happens, the better.

Growing algae for fuel is another example of a road not yet taken. This story demonstrates yet again the heavy price we still pay for the energy complacency of the 1990s. After the Congress led by Newt Gingrich swept into Washington, the Department of Energy algae fuels program started during the Carter administration was abolished for lack of funding. During its 18-year existence, the DOE effort tested over 3,000 strains of organisms before narrowing the species under consideration for fuel production down to about 300 with the best characteristics. (After the federal program was terminated, these were moved to the University of Hawaii for further study.) Based on test sites in Hawaii, California, and New Mexico, scientists determined that open ponds had the best characteristics for large-scale, long-term production of algae, as well as achieving very high rates of utilization for injected carbon dioxide.[2]

In the intervening years, the case for biodiesel fuels has become stronger and the wisdom of canceling the algae program more dubious. Due mainly to European manufacturers, diesel vehicles have improved dramatically in the twenty-first century. The prospect of efficient diesel engines powered by biofuels offers a powerful one-two punch for breaking reliance on ever-growing amounts of petroleum. Since biodiesel blends easily with petrodiesel, the transition to greater use of plants for fuel can be achieved without great disruptions to the existing infrastructure.

The potential for biodiesel cannot be realized without going beyond today's mainstream thinking to find alternatives to waste oil (too little of which is available to make a big difference) or crops like soybeans (too expensive and consumptive of natural resources). The simple cell structure of algae allows them to utilize sunlight and water efficiently in relatively small amounts of space. Estimates of algae production per acre vary widely because of the early stage of research. It appears that within a given area, algae can yield at least 15 times as much oil as soybeans.

An important side benefit of algae-based fuel is their use of carbon dioxide. When algae farms are located next to power plants, they can harvest emissions from exhaust stacks, contributing to clean power in a second valuable way. Because of under-investment in research and development, this idea remains more concept than reality, but GreenFuels Technologies, founded by MIT professor Isaac Berzin, captures the synergy between carbon capture and biodiesel production. The project is funded by venture capital, and others are getting started.

Much of the other work on building algae farms is conducted in the states included in the earlier DOE program. Current projects tend to use bioreactors to grow the algae, which avoids some of the problems of DOE's open-pond approach but which also substantially increases capital costs. Funding comes from sources as diverse as Utah's Science and Technology Research Initiative and the Royal Dutch Shell Oil Company. Even the Department of Energy is rekindling its interest in biodiesel from algae.

There are clearly opportunities to improve our understanding of molecular biology and genetic engineering in ways that improve the efficiency of algae production. It also appears that most major bugs in operating algae farms can be worked out. This leaves the ever-important consideration of costs. In the era of low-priced oil, it appeared that algae-based biodiesel might not be cost-competitive with oil-based fuels. In a time of high-priced oil, and with the need to put a price on carbon emissions, it is hard to imagine that algae-based biodiesel cannot prove successful in energy markets.

Once it has been more fully tested, the production of biodiesel from algae can be replicated in other nations as a way to reduce pressures on the world oil market and reduce emissions of greenhouse gases. The physical requirements for algae farming are quite reasonable, making it more attractive to other countries with less agricultural land than the United States (unlike corn-based ethanol, for instance). For nations with low labor costs and limited access to capital, cheaper open-pond technology might prove more suitable than bioreactors.

Although I normally resist the hyperbole that often surrounds energy technologies, I must say I agree with Utah State University chemistry professor Lance Seefeldt when he calls making biodiesel from algae "perhaps

the most important scientific challenge facing humanity in the 21st century."[3] Given the limited amount of research and testing that has been
done so far, this technology must still be considered a "Hail Mary," but
one that has a good chance of success.

Why aren't we doing these things already? Hasn't the need been clear?
Eventually, the great issues of energy are determined in the political arena,
and that is a big hurdle to achieving energy independence.

PART THREE

Securing Our National Future

Chapter 15

What We Need from National Leaders (and from Voters)

I s the term *political leadership* an oxymoron? As I studied the history of energy policy, I encountered instances when our leaders took paths that were politically popular, but wrong. The behind-the-scenes stories reveal leaders taking us into situations they knew would eventually hurt the country. They did it anyway. This is not the kind of leadership that is going to produce energy independence.

The classic case of choosing politics over what is good for the country is President Nixon's decision to impose wage and price controls and government allocation of fuels despite having information his actions would eventually prove counterproductive. Reading the decision memo on whether to give in to congressional pressure for allocation is a chilling experience.

The key document of September 21, 1973, (just weeks before the Arab oil embargo, but after the Watergate investigations intensified) informed Nixon that voluntary allocation of oil had failed, but creating a mandatory program would make matters even worse. The authors wrote "most of your advisors fear the effects of further regulation of a major industry and the creation of another major government bureaucracy." They added that "few believe that a mandatory allocation program will contribute to the resolution of the supply problem." They noted some relief might come from a gasoline tax, a public campaign advocating conservation, or delayed implementation of the Clean Air Act.

Nonetheless, two key advisors argued "a mandatory program is inevitable and we should get out in front of Congress on the issue." Another, who had been arguing against mandatory allocation for months, fell back on the position, "Right or wrong, people believe the Government can and should act by instituting such a program."[1]

Choices between expert and popular opinion often require resolution by the chief executive. But the dichotomy is usually presented in shades of gray. For Nixon's decision to implement mandatory allocation, the choice had little ambiguity. Most advisors believed such controls were counterproductive. Nixon himself had vehemently condemned mandatory allocation in private and public for years. Yet measures like price controls and allocation were popular with the public and Congress and, therefore, considered politically necessary. The bandwagon for the mandatory allocation that brought about the next year's lengthy gas lines was resisted to the end by just a few top officials, including Treasury Secretary George Shultz.

℮∽

George Shultz has popped up at several points in this book. A distinguished academic economist and a member of three presidential administrations, the Republican elder statesman possesses a well-seasoned view of the governmental process. For half a century, he has observed firsthand the obstacles to getting the government to take wise actions on energy and other national matters. He offers the clearest explanation I have seen on why politicians are so reluctant to tackle tough issues.

Shultz once noted how politicians regard policy differently than do economists, observing:

> Policymaking often confronts a problem of lags . . . After the politician correctly perceives a problem and makes the best long-term decision, conditions don't improve immediately. Where does that leave him while waiting for results—defeated at the polls?[2]

In recent years, I have heard former Vice President Walter Mondale make a similar point, in blunter terms. "In the Carter administration," he remembers, "we talked about the short-term pain and the long-term gain, and boy did we emphasize that short-term pain!" However it is stated, the likelihood that the positives and negatives of a president's policies will be felt most after he or she leaves office creates a major challenge for the American political system.

THE TIME LAGS OF ENERGY

The problem of time lags has bedeviled the fight for energy independence for a long time. Shultz discussed the lag issue in connection with his dissenting role in Nixon's wage and price controls, generally considered the most disastrous economic policy of the 1970s and a major impediment to balancing energy supply and demand. Nixon imposed controls in 1971 knowing they would probably restrain inflation in the short run and help him secure reelection, while increasing dependence on foreign oil and creating economic havoc in the long run. Carter took a major step toward decontrol of oil prices in 1979 in an attempt to dampen excessive demand, amid warnings from many advisors (which turned out to be correct) that prices would jump up in the short run and lower his poll ratings. On both occasions, the long-term results of the policies became evident well after the voters cast their verdicts on the respective presidents.

Auto efficiency standards—the most reliable single policy for dealing with the problem of oil dependency—provide another clear example of the problem of time lags. After legislation is passed requiring higher standards, several years are needed to implement the rules. Then, the rising requirements are phased in over a decade. The gradual turnover of the fleet also delays the impact of the new rules. It usually takes several years for the standards to produce any benefits at all, and even longer to see substantial reductions in oil use. Meanwhile, the auto companies have to invest capital right away to retool for the production of more efficient automobiles. By the next election, we are experiencing the short-term pain, but none of the long-term gain.

Climate change illustrates an especially difficult case of lagged impacts from innovations in energy policy. The gases that produce global warming remain in the atmosphere for decades, and landmass and oceans react slowly to changes in ambient temperatures. Getting significant reductions in oil imports from requiring more efficient automobiles requires several years. It takes decades to see impacts on temperatures and sea levels around the world. It is remarkable that politicians even try to tackle the tough problems of energy.

We might assume that historians eventually correct the record and, even if belatedly, give politicians due credit for their courageous actions or abnegations of duty. Actually, most historians rarely delve very deeply into matters of this complexity. That is why we have taken a fresh look at the roots of modern energy policy.

President Carter enjoyed declining oil imports, in part because of the opening of the Alaska oil pipeline. The heavy lifting required to get national policy in place for the pipeline took place in 1973, due to Nixon's Interior Department and mainly Scoop Jackson's work in the Senate. I often hear Carter credited for auto mileage efficiency standards, but the bill passed in 1975, when Ford was president. Similarly, I frequently see the end of oil price controls and the appointment of Paul Volker to head the Federal Reserve Board attributed to Reagan, yet Carter launched price decontrols in 1979, the same year Volker was appointed.

Until major energy legislation passed in December of 2007, the nation took no significant steps to promote U.S. energy independence after Reagan's completion of oil price decontrols in 1981. But the leaders during that period of energy complacency were able to coast, to a large extent due to the tough energy policies of the 1970s. It is all part of the problem of time lags, which do not provide much political incentive to tackle tough problems. Are there ways to overcome the problem of time lags? There are days I have my doubts, but I do have a few suggestions that can take us to where we need to be.

CHANGING THE POLITICS

With the problem of time lags, conventional political thinking is not going to produce genuine energy independence. All good ideas about reducing oil dependence and greenhouse gas emissions eventually have to get enough political support to make their way through the legislature and be signed by the president. How can this happen, if political incentives encourage the quick fix?

One key is *paying more attention to Congress*. We tend to invest our national hopes and dreams in the election of new presidents. Yet the commanders-in-chief are limited in many ways. They only get four or eight years in office, not very long in the larger scheme of things, particularly when dealing with issues like oil dependence or climate change. They do not get to vote when laws or budgets are passed. They often become absorbed in foreign policy and lose focus on domestic issues. Journalists, historians, and the public like to concentrate on what happens in the Oval Office, but that perspective does not always produce the best understanding of how things get done in Washington.

Commentators sometimes compare the passage of laws to making sausage—with both, you enjoy the product more if you do not watch it being made. A bill becomes a law only after going through a legislative maze that almost defies understanding by outsiders. Yet it is the members of Congress who stay in Washington for many years and can take on long-term projects. It is the members who are in the room when the decisions are made about whether the provisions of bills will just be rhetorical statements or have real teeth.

Leadership on recently passed tough new standards on auto fuel efficiency came from six longtime lawmakers with direct involvement in the great energy debates of the 1970s. This provision in the Energy Independence and Security Act of 2007 was shepherded through the Senate Commerce Committee by its Democratic chair, Daniel Inouye, and ranking minority member, Republican Ted Stevens. Inouye became Hawaii's first member in the U.S. House of Representatives in 1959. As the first Japanese American in the House, he was asked by Speaker Sam Rayburn to raise his right hand for the oath of office—but could not do so, since he had lost that arm in combat in World War II. He won election to the U.S. Senate in 1962, where he was joined by Stevens from Alaska in 1968. Both participated in the great energy debates following the Arab oil embargo. Hawaii's vulnerability to rising ocean levels and Alaska's melting permafrost have made both senators particularly sensitive in recent years to the dangers of global warming.

The sponsors of the auto efficiency provisions of the act, Dianne Feinstein and Olympia Snowe are more recent members of the Senate, but have long demonstrated a keen interest in energy. Democrat Feinstein became mayor of San Francisco in December of 1978, the same month that oil production in Iran collapsed. A few months later, California became the first state to suffer massive shortages of gasoline and long lines at the pump. Republican Snowe was elected to the House from Maine in 1978, just in time to join the renewed energy debates in Washington. Unlike most members, Snowe maintained a strong interest in energy, even during the decades of public complacency. Feinstein was elected to the Senate in 1992, Snowe in 1994. They fought for six years to get their bill requiring better gasoline mileage passed.

During the 2007 debates over auto efficiency in the House, John Dingell Jr. of Michigan (a defender of American automakers) and Ed Markey of Massachusetts (a champion of strict standards) were viewed as major protagonists within the Democratic Party. Dingell won election to the House in 1954 and was arguably the most influential member in crafting the energy legislation of the 1970s. Markey got his seat in 1976, just in time for the great energy debates of the Carter years. Having testified before both men, I was certain they would be part of a final grand energy strategy that they had been working toward for several years. Not surprisingly, they did join together to support the Energy Independence and Security Act, with strong provisions for auto efficiency.

Inouye, Stevens, Feinstein, Snowe, Dingell, and Markey take divergent positions on a wide variety of issues. However, in December of 2007, they were all patriots on behalf of energy independence.[3]

In every election cycle there may be a handful of congressional races that can tip the political balance, for decades, for or against energy independence. It makes a great deal of difference who wins the White House. For energy policy, though, who controls Congress makes even more difference.

A second key to getting energy independence is *increasing the political involvement of young people.* Good energy policy requires the ability to avoid the lure of quick fixes and to adopt long-term perspectives. Some politicians will always promise to lower your fuel bill, despite the necessity to increase energy prices to secure the kind of economy and environment we need for the future.

Young people have a special outlook on the future impacts of today's actions. They are the ones who will, for the longest time, reap the benefits and failures of our current choices about energy. Decades from now, they will live in a country still dependent on Persian Gulf oil and on a planet whose climate is rapidly changing, or they will enjoy hard-won energy independence. It is the young who should be most concerned about the challenges posed by the Shultz idea of time lags. They are likely to be around when the lagged impacts arrive.

Yet participation in electoral politics increases with age, leaving the younger generation with less clout. Politicians know who votes and tailor their positions accordingly. Thus, long-range perspectives often get shortchanged.

The excuse for nonparticipation is that elections do not make a difference, and with partisan redrawing of congressional districts, that is sometimes the case. But in every election cycle there are critical Senate races that offer clear differences on energy independence. The results of these races are often felt for decades. In the 2008 presidential race, the leading candidates all talked about energy independence, but did not all offer the same solutions. Those who will be most affected by dependence on Persian Gulf oil and climate change need to take the energy-independence battlefield.

Young people can do more than get involved in the political process. I have talked to several parents recently who are modifying their views on energy and the environment because of conversations they have had with their kids. I have also read press accounts of influential Americans going through the same process for similar reasons. I know this is anecdotal evidence, but I do think the younger generation can provide a long-range viewpoint that a lot of people need to hear.

We also need a different type of politician. Our third key to energy independence is *finding elected officials who dare to lose.* If the sole goal of elected officials is securing reelection, they cannot transcend the problem of time lags. It will always be easier to give the public energy rhetoric rather than energy action. Talk is cheap. Action creates winners and losers and often brings that short-term pain.

Some civil rights legislation and the 1977 Panama Canal treaty passed because some members of Congress risked losing their seats to cast affirmative votes. That kind of courage could well be needed to deal effectively with oil dependence and climate change.

There is no surefire way to identify political candidates who, once in office, will put the long-term interest of the country over personal job security. But we have to work at examining what they pledge to do about energy independence and whether they have the courage to act, even when benefits will come well after the next election.

The most important key to obtaining energy independence pertains to both voters and politicians. Both need to be *working for what is best for their children and grandchildren.* The idea of intergenerational responsibility is an old one. The British politician and philosopher Edmund Burke said in the eighteenth century that great things could not be accomplished in a single generation. Therefore, society should be "a partnership not only between those who are living, but between those who are living, those who are dead, and those who are to be born." Unfortunately, the dead and those yet to be born do not get to vote (at least in most jurisdictions). Those who can vote need to look out for those who will inherit the planet we bequeath them.

Consideration of future generations has spurred progress on other epic challenges. On the final day of the 1978 Camp David peace talks between Israel and Egypt, with the negotiations at an impasse, President Carter presented Israeli Prime Minister Menachem Begin souvenir photographs personally signed to each of Begin's grandchildren. Carter remembered, "We were both emotional as we talked quietly for a few minutes about grandchildren and about war." After the meeting, Begin called Carter to say that he would agree to new language on a critical sticking point, allowing the accords to be quickly completed.[4] Carter remains convinced that it was that discussion of grandchildren and the prospects for future wars that led to the peace agreement between two long-time enemies.

Future stages of dealing with oil dependence and global warming will require accepting some short-term pain, taking on powerful organizations with vested interests, and hammering out international pacts in which all parties do not get exactly what they want. It may be, in the end, a universal regard for grandchildren that turns stalled negotiations into successful agreements.

Acknowledgments

I would like to thank all of the energy experts at the Energy Information Administration who during my tenure there tutored me on the many facets of energy, and on the discipline needed to make all the numbers add up. The Energy Information Administration frequently reminds people that it does not make policy recommendations, so I am wearing a very different hat in this book, where I make numerous policy recommendations.

The many professionals who manage key archives on the history of energy policy have made my explorations both productive and enjoyable. The staffs at the Nixon Materials Project, the Ford Presidential Library, and the Carter Presidential Library all provided great assistance during my visits. While I did not visit the Eisenhower or Truman Libraries, I made good use of their materials. Diane Windham Shaw gave me excellent access to the William Simon papers at Lafayette College, and Jeff Sundstrom made it possible for me to examine the previously overlooked records of the American Automobile Association.

I owe a debt of gratitude to many friends, relatives, and professional colleagues too numerous to mention for their encouragement, advice, and feedback. All of the above are excused from having to agree with my conclusions.

My agent, Helen Rees, played a critical role in making this book possible. Senior Editor at Wiley, Richard Narramore, stuck up for the reader in suggesting innovative ways of presenting new ideas. Tiffany Groglio and Deborah Schindlar shepherded the book through to its final form.

My wife, Anita, deserves my special gratitude for assistance at every stage of the process.

Notes

Two major sources of information for this book are easily accessible on the Internet. All statements of presidents in office can be found in *Public Papers of the Presidents,* whether in hard copy or online. Specific citations beyond dates are no longer necessary, since statements can be easily word searched. Similarly, this book relies heavily on data from the Energy Information Administration, which are easy to find at the agency's web site, www.eia.doe.gov. The availability of historical monthly data online has greatly facilitated the ability of everyone to look more closely at major energy trends.

INTRODUCTION

1. Alan Greenspan, *The Age of Turbulence: Adventures in a New World* (New York: Penguin, 2007), 463.

2. OPEC oil ministers have asserted (at times to me personally) that the existence of oil stocks indicate that the world market is adequately supplied. However, the OPEC quotas restrict production of the world's lowest-cost reserves and put considerable pressure on high-cost frontier areas to fill the gap. The reluctance of OPEC producers to increase output rests less on fears of oversupplying the market than on a desire to keep prices from falling.

3. *The 9/11 Commission Report* (New York: W. W. Norton, 2004), 169–72.

4. Thomas L. Friedman, "Who Will Succeed Al Gore?" *New York Times,* October 14, 2007.

CHAPTER I   AMERICA'S PLUNGE INTO RELIANCE ON FOREIGN OIL

1. Those interested in a long analysis of the history of oil should consult Daniel Yergin's *The Prize: The Epic Quest for Oil, Money, and Power* (New York: Simon & Schuster, 1991).

2. Craufurd D. Goodwin, "Truman Administration Policies toward Particular Energy Sources," in *Energy Policy in Perspective: Today's Problems, Yesterday's Solutions,* ed. C. D. Goodwin, (Washington, DC: The Brookings Institution, 1981), 68.

3. Goodwin, "Truman," 147–48.

4. United States Cabinet Task Force on Oil Import Control, *The Oil Import Question: A Report on the Relationship of Oil Imports to the National Security* (Washington, D.C.: Government Printing Office, 1970), 34.

5. Cabinet Task Force, *Oil Imports,* 20–21.

6. Shale oil reserves in America were larger than those for conventional oil, but required crushing the deep sedimentary rock surrounding the oil, intense heat to liquefy it, and massive amounts of water.

7. Bush to Flanagan, November 17, 1969, and Bush to Dent, November 24, 1969, Box 40, RG220, Nixon Materials, National Archives and Records Administration (NARA).

8. H. R. Haldeman, *The Haldeman Diaries: Inside the Nixon White House* (New York: Berkley Books, 1995), 138.

9. Paul Volcker and Toyoo Gyohten, *Changing Fortunes: The World's Money and the Threat to American Leadership* (New York: Times Books, 1992), 101.

10. Nixon Tapes, Conversation No. 794–2, Nixon Materials (see Chap. 1, n. 7).

11. Steve Wakefield and Duke Ligon to Chairman of the Oil Policy Committee, "Major Oil Import Problems Requiring Immediate Attention," February 11, 1973, Box 24, DiBona files, Nixon Materials (see Chap.1, n. 7).

12. Data produced by the American Automobile Association taken from its press releases, found in the AAA Library, Heathrow, Florida.

13. Transcript by Radio TV Reports, Inc., February 4, 1973.

14. *Oil Daily,* September 13, 1973.

15. Henry Kissinger, *Crisis: The Anatomy of Two Major Foreign Policy Crisis* (New York: Simon & Schuster, 2003), 89.

16. FRM SECSTATE TO AMEMBASSY JIDDA, October 12, 1973. State Department cables of this period can be accessed on the web site of the National Archives and Records Administration, www.archives.gov.

17. Kissinger, *Crisis,* 239 (see n. 15).

18. FRM AMEMBASSY JIDDA TO SECSTATE, October 17, 1973 (see n. 16).

19. FRM SECSTATE TO USINT CAIRO, November 7, 1973 (see n. 16).

20. Henry Kissinger, *Years of Upheaval* (London: Weidenfeld & Nicolson, 1982), 658–66.

21. Haig to the President, June 6, 1973, Box 89, PPF, PSF, Nixon Materials (see n. 7).

22. Gallup Opinion Index, January, 1974, No. 103, 9.

23. Fiedler to Shultz, December 3, 1973, Simon Papers, Lafayette College Special Collections, 16:31; Carlson and Colvin to Director, December 14, 1973, Box 66, CEA Records, Ford Presidential Library.

24. *Time,* November 19, 1973.

25. FRM AMEBASSY JIDDA TO SECSTATE, January 3, 1974 (see n. 16).

26. Richard Nixon, *RN: The Memoirs of Richard Nixon* (New York: Simon & Schuster, 1978), 985.

27. Kissinger, *Upheaval,* 947 (see n. 20).

28. Information on Fuel Gauge reports from press releases and supporting materials in the AAA Library, Heathrow, Florida.

29. Lursch to Hill, January 24, 1974, Simon Papers, 17:33 (see n. 23).

30. Gallup Opinion Index, February 1974, No. 104, 2; March 1974, No. 105, 9. In previous polls, respondents could pick two problems, resulting in higher numbers for leading items than the new approach, which allowed for only one.

31. Haig to President, Box 90, PSF; and January 28, 1974 and January 30, 1974, Box 24, Kissinger Telcons, Nixon Materials.

32. Richard B. Mancke, *Squeaking By: U.S. Energy Policy Since the Embargo* (New York: Columbia University Press, 1976), 33–34.

33. One exception is Yanek Mieczkowski's *Gerald Ford and the Challenge of the 1970s* (Lexington: University of Kentucky Press, 2005), which devotes four chapters to energy.

34. Congressional Quarterly, *Congress and the Nation: A Review of Government and Politics in the Postwar Years, 1973–1976* (Washington, DC: CQ Press, 1977) 233–35; Peter Milius, "Democrats Fault Ford Tax Rebate," *Washington Post,* January 21, 1975.

35. "Abdication by Congress," *New York Times,* June 13, 1975; "The Energy Bill," *Washington Post,* June 23, 1975.

36. "Increase in Taxes Approved by Swiss," *New York Times,* June 9, 1975; J. W. Anderson, "Saving Gasoline, German Style," *Washington Post,* October 7, 1976.

CHAPTER 2 A FORGOTTEN VICTORY GIVES HOPE: HOW AMERICA SOLVED ITS LAST ENERGY CRISIS AND CUT OIL IMPORTS IN HALF

1. Edward J. Mitchell, ed., *Energy: Regional Goals and National Interest* (Washington, D.C.: American Enterprise Institution, 1976), 79.

2. *Congress and the Nation,* 239–40 (see Chap.1, n. 34).

3. Friedersdorf to the President, November 24, 1975, Box 51, PHF, Ford Library.

4. Zarb to the President, December 16, 1975, Box 12, Schleede Files, Ford Library.

5. "Signing the Oil Bill," 22; Simon, *A Time for Truth* (New York: Reader's Digest Press, 1978), 79–81.

6. Rosalynn Carter, *First Lady from Plains* (New York: Ballantine, 1985), 157.

7. Jimmy Carter, *Keeping Faith: Memoirs of a President* (New York: Bantam, 1982), 96–97.

8. Rickover to the President, April 12, 1977, Box 17; Speech Draft, Box 18, PHF, Carter Presidential Library.

9. Central Intelligence Agency, "The Impending Soviet Oil Crisis," March, 1977, and "The International Energy Situation: Outlook to 1985," April, 1977, Box 19, PHF, Carter Library. The CIA was wrong about the Soviet Union, which never became a net importer of oil, but right about Saudi Arabia, which never came close to reaching the production levels predicted by most analysts at the time.

10. Box 18, PHF, Carter Library.

11. "Results of Harris Poll," April 22, 1977, Box 28, Moore files, Carter Library.

12. Reston, "Carter's Best Week," *New York Times,* April 24, 1977.

13. William Stevens, "Auto Makers Generally Endorse Energy Proposals, But G.M. Terms 'Guzzler' Penalty Tax 'Simplistic,'" *New York Times,* April 22, 1977.

14. Robert Hershey, "Oilmen Attack Lack of Incentive in Carter Plan to Increase Output," *New York Times,* April 22, 1977; "What Price Energy?," *Newsweek,* May 2, 1977, 12.

15. Safire, "On Breaking Promises," *New York Times,* May 2, 1977; Carter Library.

16. Kraft, "An Old Pol with a Touch of Class," *Washington Post,* August 4, 1977; *Time,* August 15, 1977.

17. "On Energy, a Grave Defeat," *Washington Post,* December 15, 1977.

18. "At Last, the Energy Bill," *Washington Post,* October 16, 1978.

19. Schlesinger to the President, January 4, 1979, Box 114, PHF, Carter Library.

20. Vance to Carter, January 26, 1979, Box 39, Plains Subject File, Carter Library; J. P. Smith, "Lower Saudi Exports May Cause World Shortage," *Washington Post,* February 6, 1979.

21. George H. Gallup, *The Gallup Poll: Public Opinion 1979* (Wilmington, DE.: Scholarly Resources, 1980), 176–77.

22. Larry Kramer, "Administration Attempts to Stem Trucking Strike," *Washington Post,* June 23, 1979; "Guardsmen, Police Protect Trucks Against Strike Violence," *Washington Post,* June 24, 1979; Daniel Horowitz, *Jimmy Carter and the Energy Crisis of the 1970s—A Brief History with Documents* (Boston: Bedford/St. Martin's, 2005), 88.

23. *The Gallup Poll 1979,* 201 (see n. 21).

24. A careful study of the Bonn summit and its impacts can be found in W. Carl Biven, *Jimmy Carter's Economy: Policy in an Age of Limits* (Chapel Hill: University of North Carolina Press, 2002).

25. Blumenthal to Carter, March 16, 1979, Box 123, PHF, Carter Library.

26. Based on Eizenstat's handwritten meeting notes, as quoted in Biven, 172–74 (see n. 24).

27. *Carter's Economy,* Biven, 174 (see n. 24); Eizenstat and Schirmer to the President, March 26,1979, Box 250, Eizenstat files, Carter Library.

28. "Briefing for Solar Energy Ceremony," June 20, 1979, Box 278, Eizenstat files, Carter Library.

29. Yergin, *Prize,* 706–11 (see Chap. 1, n. 1); Kenneth Pollack, *The Persian Puzzle: The Conflict Between Iran and America* (New York: Random House, 2004), 182–88; Youssef Ibrahim, "Iran and Iraq Fill the Airwaves With Angry Rhetoric," *New York Times,* October 7, 1980.

30. Peter Kihss, "Oil Decontrol's Impact Assailed in Jersey, New York, and Connecticut," *New York Times,* January 29, 1981.

31. "Industry Welcomes Decontrol; Small Refiners, Dealers Worried," *New York Times,* January 29, 1981.

32. Notes of Michael Duval, August 28, 1974 (emphasis in the original), Box 4, Duval Papers, Ford Library.

33. M. A. Adelman, *The Genie Out of the Bottle: World Oil Since 1970* (Cambridge, MA: The MIT Press, 1995), 196–97.

Chapter 3   Lapsing Back into Oil Addiction: Retreating from Battle under Presidents Reagan, Bush, Clinton, and Bush

1. Elizabeth Drew, *Portrait of an Election* (New York: Simon and Schuster, 1981), 114.

2. David A. Stockman, *The Triumph of Politics: Why the Reagan Revolution Failed* (New York: Harper & Row, 1986), 61.

3. "Back into the Energy Bazaar," *Washington Post,* April 8, 1979.

4. National Science Foundation, Division of Science Resource Statistics, *Federal R&D Funding by Budget Function: Fiscal Years 2001–03,* August, 2002, Table 25.

5. Margot Slade and Wayne Biddle, "Watt Unleashes Oil Explorers, To Some Dismay," *New York Times,* July 7, 1982.

6. Ronald Reagan, *The Reagan Diaries*, ed. Douglas Brinkley (New York: Harper-Collins, 2007).

7. George Shultz, *Turmoil and Triumph: My Years as Secretary of State* (New York: Scribners, 1993), 927; Vance and Richardson, "Put the U.N. Into the Persian Gulf," *New York Times,* October 20, 1987.

8. Schultz, *Turmoil,* 929–34.

9. "Weinberger Statement on the U.S. Attack in the Gulf," *New York Times,* October, 20, 1987.

10. Shultz, *Turmoil,* 935–39 (see n. 7); Reagan, *Diaries,* 507 (see n. 6).

11. Bill Clinton, *My Life* (New York: Knopf, 2004), 494.

12. Author's notes from ceremony marking the twenty-fifth anniversary of the Department of Energy, shown on C–SPAN, October 8, 2002.

13. *Federal R&D Budget Authority,* Table 25. Comparisons across time are possible only through 1997 because of a discontinuity in the data series.

14. The price of oil is measured in many ways. In most cases, I use "refiner acquisition cost." OPEC price bands are based on selling price in producing countries, which runs somewhat lower. The most visible price of crude oil is the daily spot price, which is highly volatile and can reach higher levels than refiner acquisition costs. These distinctions rarely affect general conclusions about major energy trends.

Chapter 4   Blood and Treasure: The Heavy Cost of Dependence on Middle East Oil

1. The only mention of oil, in fact, was a one-sentence warning to Iraqi military and civilian personnel to not destroy the country's oil wells, if they did not want to be prosecuted as war criminals. See Address to the Nation on Iraq, March 17, 2003.

2. Steve Everly, "U.S. Considered Using Radiological Weapons, 1950 CIA Document Shows," *Kansas City Star,* February 19, 2002; Various National Security Council memos, Box 180, PSF, Truman Presidential Library. Contingency planners rejected the use of nuclear materials because they believed the Soviets would negate the strategy by forcing Saudis to work in contaminated areas.

3. Eisenhower to Dillon Anderson, July 30, 1957, and Eisenhower Diary, March 3, 1959, *The Papers of Dwight David Eisenhower,* ed. L. Galambos and D. van Ee at

www.eisenhowermemorial.org/presidential–papers/second–term/documents (emphasis in the original).

4. Warren Bass, *Support Any Friend: Kennedy's Middle East and the Making of the U.S.–Israeli Alliance* (New York: Oxford University Press, 2003), 127–32.

5. William Bundy, *A Tangled Web: The Making of Foreign Policy in the Nixon Presidency* (New York: Hill & Wang, 1998), 133–34; Nixon, *RN*, 133 (see Chap. 1, n. 26); Address to the Bohemian Club, San Francisco, July 29, 1967, from The Nixon Presidential Library, Nixon Papers, Yorba Linda, California.

6. Emile A. Nakhleh, *Arab–American Relations in the Persian Gulf* (Washington, D.C.: American Enterprise Institute, 1975), 42–45.

7. Nixon tapes, Conversation 475-23 (see Chap. 1, n. 10)

8. Kissinger, *Upheaval*, 879–80 (see Chap. 1, n. 20); See also *New York Times,* November 23, 1973.

9. The State Department and the National Archives have put the diplomatic cables from this period online, where they are word searchable. See http://aad.archives.gov/aad/series-description.jsp?s=4073&cat=all&bc=sl.

10. The unified command is located at MacDill Air Force Base in Tampa, Florida, due to the inability to find a permanent location in the Gulf region. An excellent account of the development of the new military strategy can be found in William E. Odom, "The Cold War Origins of the U.S. Central Command," *Journal of Cold War Studies Vol. 8, No. 2,* (Spring 2006): 52–82.

11. National Security Directive 54, National Security Archive, George Washington University.

12. The other signers to join the Bush administration were Elliot Abrams, Richard Armitage, Jeffrey Bergner, Paula Dobriansky, Zalmay Khalilzad, Richard Perle, Peter Rodman, William Schneider, Jr., and Robert Zoellick. Documents cited are available on the web site of the Project for the New American Century. See www.newamericancentury.org.

13. Ron Suskind, *The Price of Loyalty: George W. Bush, the White House, and the Education of Paul O'Neill* (New York: Simon & Schuster, 2004), 129.

14. Rachel Bronson, *Thicker Than Oil: America's Uneasy Partnership with Saudi Arabia* (New York: Oxford University Press, 2006), 194–95.

15. David S. Cloud, "U.S. Needs 'Long-Term' Presence in Iraq, Gates Says," *Washington Post,* September 27, 2007; Margaret Coker, "Navy Patrols Vital to Iraq Oil," *Atlanta Journal-Constitution,* October 22, 2007.

16. Vivienne Walt, "Petro Showdown: Iraq's Ethnic Groups Don't Agree on Much," *Time,* September 17, 2007.

17. Congressional Budget Office, "Estimated Costs of U.S. Operations in Iraq and Afghanistan and of Other Activities Related to the War on Terrorism," October 24, 2007.

Chapter 5   Fossil Fuels and Global Warming: A Dangerous Experiment with the Planet

1. Council on Environmental Quality, *Global Energy Futures and the Carbon Dioxide Problem* (Washington, DC: Government Printing Office, 1981), iii–iv, found in Box 34, Domestic Policy Staff Energy and Natural Resources files, Carter Library.

2. *Global Energy Futures,* 28.

3. Though the IPCC began publishing its Fourth Assessment reports in hard copy late in 2007, they are most quickly and easily accessible at its web site, www.ipcc.ch.

4. BBC News report, September 18, 2007.

5. My list includes what might be feasible in the coming decades. In addition, some have recently suggested the possibility of the human creation of a cooling layer in the atmosphere—a substantial challenge to human engineering.

6. *Congress and the Nation: 1997–2001* (Washington, DC: Congressional Quarterly Press, 2002), 354.

7. Al Gore, *Earth in the Balance: Economy and the Human Spirit* (New York: Houghton Mifflin, 1992); Christine Todd Whitman, *It's My Party Too: The Battle for the Heart of the GOP and the Future of America* (New York: Penguin, 2005), 170–78.

8. Thomas Fuller and Graham Bowley, "At Bali Conference, Signs of Compromise," *New York Times,* December 15, 2007.

9. "Kyoto by Degrees," *Wall Street Journal,* June 21, 2005.

10. Nicholas Stern, *The Economics of Climate Change: The Stern Review* (New York: Cambridge University Press, 2007), ii.

11. Kenneth J. Arrow, "Global Climate Change: A Challenge to Policy, *Economists' Voice* (June, 2007): 5 (see www.bepress.com.ev.); William Nordhaus, "A Review of the Stern Review on the Economics of Climate Change," *Journal of Economic Literature,* Vol. 45 (September 2007): 687–88.

12. Greenspan, *Turbulence,* 456 (see Intro., n. 1).

13. Bjorn Lomborg, "Chill Out—Stop Fighting Over Global Warming—Here's a Smart Way to Attack It," *Washington Post,* October 7, 2007.

14. This articulation was suggested by Harvard business professor Richard Vietor during discussions at a November 2007 energy conference at the University of Houston.

CHAPTER 6   THE MAGIC AND LIMITS OF MARKET-BASED SOLUTIONS

1. Duval to Jones, March 28, 1975, Box 4, Duval Papers, Ford Library.

CHAPTER 7   SEEING THROUGH THE IDEOLOGICAL BLINDERS (OF THE RIGHT AND THE LEFT)

1. Republican Edward Derwinski, quoted in Jack Germond, *Fat Man in a Middle Seat: Forty Years of Covering Politics* (New York: Random House, 1999), 114.

2. For relative impacts, see *IPCC, Fourth Assessment Report, Climate Change 2007: The Physical Science Basis,* 32, 96.

CHAPTER 8   SOLUTION ONE: STORE MASSIVE EMERGENCY RESERVES

1. Considerable information on the Strategic Petroleum Reserve can be found at its web site, http://www.fossil.energy.gov/programs/reserves/.

2. Details on the proposal can be found in James C. Burrows and Thomas A. Domencich, *An Analysis of the United States Oil Import Quota* (Lexington, MA: Heath Lexington Books, 1970), 177–79.

3. Douglas Bohi and Milton Russell, *Limiting Oil Imports: An Economic History and Analysis* (Baltimore: The Johns Hopkins University Press, 1978), 197–98; Henry Kissinger, *Upheaval,* 855–56 (see Chap. 1, n. 20).

4. http://www.fossil.energy.gov/programs/reserves/spr/spr-drawdown.html.

5. The Federal Reserve System, *Purposes and Functions* (Washington, DC: Board of Governors of the Federal Reserve System, 2005), 18.

CHAPTER 9   SOLUTION TWO: DRIVE THE CAR OF THE FUTURE

1. Through rulemaking, the standards were reduced to 26 mpg for 1986. They again reached 27.5 in 1990, where they have remained ever since.

2. David L. Greene, "Fuel Economy Rebound Effect for U.S. Household Vehicles," *The Energy Journal* (July 1, 1999): 1–2.

3. National Research Council, *Automobile Fuel Economy: How Far Should We Go?* (Washington, DC: National Academy Press, 1992), 57; National Research Council, *Effectiveness and Impact of Corporate Average Fuel Economy (CAFE) Standards,* (Washington, DC: National Academy Press, 2002), 24–29. Also see Robert B. Noland, "Motor Vehicle Fuel Efficiency and Traffic Fatalities," *The Energy Journal* (October 1, 2004) and National Highway Safety Administration, *Traffic Safety Facts 2004,* 15.

4. *Effectiveness and Impact,* 22 (see n. 3).

5. China was also, of course, trying to protect a domestic industry.

6. Cheryl Jensen, "Mileage Ratings Are Still Estimates, Though Closer to Reality," *New York Times,* September 16, 2007.

7. *Effectiveness and Impact,* 17–18 (see n. 3).

8. Michele Maynard, "At Chrysler, Home Depot Still Lingers," *New York Times,* October 30, 2007.

CHAPTER 10   SOLUTION THREE: BRING ALTERNATIVE FUELS TO MARKET

1. www.fossil.energy.doe/aboutus/history/syntheticfuels_history.html; Goodwin, "Truman," 152; 428 (see Chap.1, n. 2).

CHAPTER 11   SOLUTION FOUR: PLUG INTO AN ELECTRIC FUTURE

1. Michael Kintner-Meyer, Kevin Schneider, and Robert Pratt, "Impacts Assessment of Plug-In Hybrid Vehicles on Electric Utilities and Regional U.S. Power Grids, Part 1: Technical Analysis," *Journal of EUEC* (Vol. 1, 2007), available at http://www.euec.com/journal/documents/pdf/Paper_4.pdf; Electric Power Research Institute and National

Resources Defense Council, *Environmental Assessment of Plug-In Hybrid Electric Vehicles* (Electric Power Research Institute, July 2007), available on institute web site, www.epri.com.

2. Kintner–Meyer, "Impacts," 1 (see n.1).

3. Because of exemptions in coverage and various methods of compliance, the requirement in practice would likely require that no more than 10 percent of electricity be generated from renewables.

CHAPTER 12   SOLUTION FIVE: ADOPT ENERGY TAXES LIBERALS AND CONSERVATIVES CAN LIKE

1. John S. Duffield, *Over a Barrel: The Costs of U.S. Foreign Oil Dependence,* (Stanford, CA: Stanford University Press, 2007), 65.

2. David Sandalow, *Freedom from Oil: How the Next American President Can End the United States' Oil Addiction* (New York: McGraw Hill, 2007), 212.

3. George P. Shultz, "How to Gain a Climate Consensus," *Washington Post,* September 5, 2007.

CHAPTER 13   SOLUTION SIX: MAKE ENERGY CONSERVATION A PATRIOTIC DUTY

1. Kai Ryssdal, "Can Wal–Mart Save the World?" *Marketplace,* National Public Radio, November 16, 2007; Mindy Fetterman, "Wal–Mart Grows 'Green' Strategies," *USA Today,* September 25, 2006.

CHAPTER 14   SOLUTION SEVEN: THROW SOME "HAIL MARYS"

1. John Deutch and Ernest Moniz, *The Future of Nuclear Power: An Interdisciplinary MIT Study* (2003), at http://web.mit.edu/nuclearpower/.

2. John Sheehan et al., *A Look Back at the U.S. Department of Energy's Aquatic Species Program: Biodiesel from Algae* (Golden, CO: National Renewable Energy Laboratory, 1998).

3. "Using Pond Scum to Fuel Our Future," *Energy Daily,* February 5, 2007. For additional information, see Michael Briggs, "Widespread Biodiesel Production from Algae," University of New Hampshire Physics Department, 2004; Mark Clayton, "Algae—Like a Breath Mint for Smokestacks," *Christian Science Monitor,* January 11, 2006.

CHAPTER 15   WHAT WE NEED FROM NATIONAL LEADERS (AND FROM VOTERS)

1. Love and Ash to the President, September, 21, 1973, and Clarke to Kehrli, September 27, 1973, *Simon Papers,* 15:28.

2. George P. Shultz and Kenneth W. Dam, *Economic Policy Beyond the Headlines* (Stanford, CA: Stanford Alumni Association, 1977), 194.

3. Senators Trent Lott (R-MS), Tom Carper (D-DE), and Bryon Dorgan (D-ND) also helped shepherd the mileage efficiency bill through the Senate. Leadership on the broader energy bill came from Speaker Nancy Pelosi (D-CA) in the House and Energy Committee Chair Jeff Bingaman (D-NM) in the Senate.

4. *Keeping Faith,* 399–401 (see Chap. 2, n. 7).

Index